KALAMAZOO
PUBLIC LIBRARY

DEMCO

The Prince and I

The Prince and I

ROSEMARIE
BUSCHOW

DOUBLEDAY & COMPANY, INC.
GARDEN CITY, NEW YORK
1981

Library of Congress Cataloging in Publication Data

Buschow, Rosemarie.
The prince and I.

Includes index.
I.   Title.
PR6052.U764P7   1981   823′.914
ISBN: 0-385-17111-0
Library of Congress Catalog Card Number 80–938

Copyright © 1979 by Rosemarie Buschow

To Susu—
Prince Saud Bin Abdul Majeed Bin Saud Bin Abdul Aziz
—and his country

This is a true story: but for reasons the reader will come to understand the names of some persons and the location and time of some incidents have been changed.

The Prince and I

chapter 1

"Saudi Arabian Airlines announce the departure of their flight SV 107 to Riyadh via Rome. The flight is boarding now at gate 22."

Only when I stood in response to that summons did I realize that I was trembling. From other corners of the departure lounge, people were moving toward the big, glass exit doors. The announcement of my flight was repeated first in English, then in Arabic, a language that seemed to me designed to roll out over the hazardous, limitless desert that I was soon going to see for myself.

Unless I changed my mind.

"It isn't too late," I told myself as I walked dutifully toward the waiting plane. "Can they sue me for breaking my contract?" As I walked, I reached into my handbag and touched the contract. The terms, which I had drawn up myself, seemed reasonable at the time of signing, but then at the time of signing Saudi Arabia had been no more than a golden shape on the map and I was familiar with it only because I'd been good at geography when I was a child. Now it had become almost reality—my destination. What did a "self-contained flat," which my contract stipulated I would have, mean within the precincts of a prince's palace? Would it be furnished with low cushions and guarded by eunuchs, or would it be an air-conditioned replica of Heal's display windows? What if my future employer did not actually grant me the stipulated day off each working week? There was surely no trade union for nanny-governesses in Riyadh, nor did it seem likely I could take my employer to a court of law; she happened to be a member of the royal family.

"Is there any court of law, come to that, or does the patriarch himself pass judgment now as he used to do in days of old?" I asked myself, never dreaming that one day that question was going to be answered in a strange and tragic way.

Then, suddenly, it was too late for second thoughts. The seat belts were fastened, smokers put out their cigarettes, the plane moved forward, and I had no more power over it than a sardine over its tin. I gave into the melancholy comfort of being helpless. I had been in a condition of helplessness before, after the death of the man I had loved and lived with for nearly nine years. The dry, tearless pain of my loss had been so fierce then that I had let it carry me until it ran out and left me with nothing at all, empty, drifting, and numb. Feeling had stopped there, but thought would never stop, nor memories of words Stephen had said, words I had said, words I wished I had not said, and all the things we had done. We two who had come as foreigners to London from our far and separate homelands had discovered the city together and laid our claim to it. One of the reasons I would always love London was because it was there I had lived for Stephen, had felt for him, had shared his life. All I had never done was cry for the loss of him. In the eight months since he had died suddenly while visiting his own country and far from me, I sometimes felt the tears shimmering and close, but they would not come.

I looked down at the rows of suburban houses far below and the cars that, for all my years in England, still seemed to me to travel on the wrong side of the road.

The year was 1976—but I was on my way to live in a real palace in the Arabian Nights land of genies and talking fish. I was bound for this fantasy thanks to the efficient and hardly supernatural agency of International Nannies Limited. The woman who interviewed me had been kind and helpful though not precisely a fairy godmother. She had been pleased by my references—but not cheered to hear I was German by birth. "Actually, most of our clients prefer genuine English nannies," she said, not unkindly. "But let's see what we can do for you." Together we went through her file of vacancies. For me, since I have always had wanderlust, it was like opening a box of chocolates; there was a job in Washington in the home of a high-ranking diplomat, a companion house-keeper was needed by a rich widower in Teheran, and a Turkish princess wanted a nanny immediately.

"Tell me," the woman said, looking at me keenly, "why are you looking for a job abroad?"

For a moment I longed to explain to her as I could explain to no one who was at all close to me, that although I enjoyed my job with a shipping firm in London, I could no longer bear the inexorable arrival of five o'clock when it was time to return alone to my empty flat, haunted by the past. I wanted to tell her, tell someone, how I belonged in London and knew I would return to it one day, but how I needed a vacation from the stab of pain I felt when the parks spilled over with daffodils, or when I saw the barrows on Oxford Street full of the green apples Stephen had liked.

The need to talk to somebody about him was as great as my need to cry for him, but I could still do neither. "Frankly," I told her, being partially truthful, "I want to find a job where I can save enough money to buy myself a flat in London. I need the security of owning my own place. But I want to live away from London for a while, for personal reasons . . ."

"I understand perfectly," she said, and nodded; but there was a trace of speculation in her eyes.

At the bottom of the folder we came across a position she told me she was having a lot of trouble filling, although the salary was good and the working conditions were literally fabulous: private living quarters and personal servants as well as exclusive use of a car and driver.

"This must be a plum job!" I said.

"It's in Saudi Arabia . . ." she told me doubtfully, and immediately I was conjuring images of Bedouin horsemen and their tents silhouetted against the blazing sunset.

"You can't smoke or drink within the palace precincts . . ." she added as if to discourage me further. I explained eagerly that I had never smoked and drinking was of no importance to me. She then went on, with what I thought was a trace of reluctance, to tell me that the Princess Moudi Bint Mohammed Bin Abdul Aziz Al-Saud had lived in America with her first husband for six years and consequently wanted her baby, due to be born in about two months, raised in a way that would equip him to be at ease in his own country and in the West.

"What if 'he' is a girl?" I wondered, but said nothing.

"You must understand, Rosemarie," the agency woman said, "Saudi Arabia can be"—she shrugged—"difficult for a western woman."

For the next fortnight I did nothing more constructive toward the job I had applied for than to refresh my childhood memories of where Saudi Arabia *was* in an atlas at European Ferries, where I worked; and of course daydream about the story of Scheherazade. But the act of going to International Nannies and applying for a job seemed to have depleted my reserve of determination which had not been high since the telephone call from a mutual friend that had broken the news of Stephen's death to me. Therefore, I was confused for a moment when I received a summons from International Nannies to go to the office of a Mr. Yateem in the Haymarket. Mr. Yateem's wife, I was told, was a personal friend of Princess Moudi and was entrusted with the choice of a nanny.

We met in Mr. Yateem's office, and a very contrasting pair we made! I am tall and blond; Mrs. Yateem was rather short, pale-skinned but very dark-haired. I was dressed in beige and pastels; Mrs. Yateem wore a black trouser suit and a dramatic white turban, giving her eyes, outlined in kohl, an even more exotic cast, as if I were seeing them above a half-veil. Moreover, I was punctual; Mrs. Yateem was half an hour late. She told me, in her throaty voice with its exotic accent, that the nanny would be based in Jeddah but would travel frequently with the family to Riyadh and in the scorching summer months—here, she looked heavenward as if to seek celestial aid in her description of the Saudi heat wave—would accompany the family to Taif where every Saudi who could kept a villa. There were guaranteed trips to Europe and if either side was unhappy the contract could be terminated as long as sufficient notice was given for a replacement nanny to be found.

"The child cannot be without a nanny. Not for one day," Mrs. Yateem told me. "Now, have you any questions to ask?"

From the beehive my mind had suddenly become, I tried to snatch one sensible question that would establish me as a conscientious, serious nanny/governess type, but I could only recall what I had heard about the way women were shrouded and secluded in Saudi Arabia and combine that with the information I'd just received about the summer heat. "Will I be able to swim?" I asked, then blushed to think that Mrs. Yateem would report to Princess Moudi that the German candidate was light-minded and a possible exhibitionist. But Mrs. Yateem seemed unperturbed by the question.

"Naturally. Arrangements can easily be made for you to swim every day if you wish."

She asked me to leave my passport, a photograph, and a certificate of baptism so they could be sure I was not a German Jew; this last request produced a wry twinge when I recalled my family's flight from Berlin during the war with my eleven-year-old sister and me, only four. We were one of thousands of families to flee the encircling Russian tanks, but in our case the new fear was just an extension of what my parents had been feeling throughout that grim period when they, who showed so little charity toward each other, sheltered Jewish refugees in the basement of our home.

After a month of silence from the Yateems, I decided that Mrs. Yateem, as I had sensed at the time of our interview, had not liked me very much. I had already abandoned my dreams of sandstorms and towering palms when my telephone rang.

To my astonishment I was told by Mrs. Yateem that I had been accepted for the position. What was more, Princess Moudi was delighted that her child would have the opportunity to learn both English and German. Once I knew I was leaving, I started living on a cloud of surprise and romantic fantasies (a cloud made even hazier by a cholera injection, a smallpox vaccination, a typhoid injection, and malaria pills which, although they weren't strictly necessary for Saudi Arabia, made me feel more secure). Living on such a cloud may sound painless—but for me it was merely sleepless. I tossed through the nights, wondering if I should really pack up and go to an alien land, but at the same time aware that every day I allowed to pass made my departure more and more inevitable. Jennifer, my dearest friend and the only person to whom I had confided my plans, some of my pain, some of my secrets, showed saintly patience in this dithering period.

Even after the contract had been signed in Saudi Arabia by the princess and returned virtually the same day on an airplane by special messenger, I thought there was still time to change my mind. But a vestige of my German efficiency made me have the Arabic signature, just an odd squiggle to me, certified by Mr. Yateem and then have my own signature notarized by an official at the German Embassy. This last service cost me £1.95 and I thought, when I handed over the money, that symbolically I was sealing my bargain with the future.

Well, the future had arrived. I looked out and there was nothing between the plane and earth but clouds, real ones, that looked like the snow of my childhood. At Christmas I had gone back—I no longer thought of Germany as home—to Mölln, a town near Hamburg, to visit my mother and try once again to meet her as one adult meeting another. The town had changed a great deal since my childhood. From a quaint village Mölln had grown into an elegant spa. Near the new, expensive restaurants I used to hunt with my father in the forest, not for sport alone but also to fill our larder, bare as most were in Germany when I was a child. It would have been a happy place to grow up in except for my mother's bitter, angry frustration which only now, after her death, I am beginning to understand—although I still cannot accept the violence with which she expressed it. Like her, I myself will never be able to settle for bondage to sink and kitchen; I shall not even try. One lesson that was going to be reinforced by my life with the princesses of Saudi Arabia was that I, though a woman, will have life on my terms and will suffer the consequences of that choice too, when I must.

The most difficult thing I had to do before leaving London was to quit my job with European Ferries. Since I had been left alone, work had become the center of my existence. Except for my friendship with Jennifer, I seemed to have lost the knack of intimacy.

Looking back, I realize the people I worked with were enormously tolerant of my grief, which must have appeared to them as cold aloofness. It was not only the haste of the Saudis to secure my service but also, I have to admit, my own hesitancy that prevented me from giving in a courteous four weeks' notice. I felt awful about what I was afraid my employers would see as underhanded tactics but, in fact, they were so generous and understanding that I suspected that somehow they knew or intuited more about my private misfortunes than I had realized.

The very morning I gave in my notice, I was called to the Saudi Embassy to collect my visa, a formality that took only half an hour much to the perplexed annoyance of an English bystander who had been awaiting his visa for three months. I dare say the Embassy did not have a cable on his behalf, as they did on mine, signed by Prince Mohammed Bin Abdul Aziz, elder brother of King Khalid and father of Princess Moudi.

"I will not take a one-way ticket, Mrs. Yateem," I said. "I want a return ticket in my hand."

"But the baby has been born! You must leave! They are expecting you!"

"Return ticket!" I said sternly; inside I was marveling at my own firmness.

When the manager of the International Nannies supported my claim, Mrs. Yateem clearly felt put upon.

"Miss Buschow will discover after a while how very generous these people are," she said, sounding huffy. "Once Miss Buschow has proved her loyalty there is nothing they won't give her. If she should decide to stay until the boy has grown up, she will find she has been accepted as a member of the family."

"The return ticket, please . . ." we said, more or less in chorus. Sitting on the plane, I felt in my handbag. There it was, next to my contract, the return ticket: practical proof of my stubborn will.

The man in the seat next to mine began to fidget, evincing symptoms of mid-flight crisis: that moment when the book starts to be less gripping, the paperwork less absorbing, the legs are in danger of atrophy, and the person in the next seat, particularly if it hap-

pens to be a member of the opposite sex, begins to look like a suitable object for conversation. I made the back of my neck discourag-
ing as I peered intently out of my window. There had been times
when I spoke cheerfully to strangers, but I had learned the hard
way that halfway through a long flight with a long way left to go
should never be one of them—particularly when it was no ordinary
flight, but what I was starting to think of as a journey to destiny. I
wanted to savor every moment of that journey.

My neighbor cleared his throat softly and I stiffened my spine,
praying silently he would leave me to my memories and my fantasies, that he would leave me alone. With a spark of irritation I
wondered if he would have intruded so carelessly on the privacy of
another man. I knew exactly what was going to happen next: he
was going to twitch, he was going to clear his throat again, and
finally he was going to lean forward and say . . . "Do you smoke?"

He was an Englishman. He offered me a Silk Cut.

"Thank you, I don't smoke," I said, and I sighed because I knew
that now I either had to talk to him or spend the rest of my journey with an enemy smoldering at my side. He was a well-dressed
man in his thirties, possessing one of those English faces that glows
with boyish honesty. His accent was neither regional nor "BBC"; he
was in the comfortable middle. To me he looked married, perhaps
with one child. Before I had thought of anything to say, he was
telling me what he did and, to my surprise, I was interested. Can
there be any woman in the world who will not listen to a jeweler
with attention? He was a partner in his father's firm of wholesale
jewelers in Hatton Garden. His side of the business, he said, was to
build up trade with the rich Arab countries. "Ah! You sell them
gemstones," I said, glancing at the briefcase tucked behind his
knees, and picturing caravans swaying over the dunes and bearing
spices, silk, and sapphires for Arabian princesses.

"Sell? Oh, yes, I sell, of course. But in the Arab countries mostly
I buy. I have no direct contact with the royal women, actually, that
would be unthinkable. But there are ways. Yes, we have our ways,"
he said, attempting a James Bond imitation but looking more like a
well-fed sixth-form prefect. I smiled at him and sensed his auto-

matic flicker of sexual interest. After nine years of fidelity, I found
even the automatic response that brightened his blue eyes surprising
and a little alarming. I frowned.

"The royal ladies get fed up with their jewelry sometimes," he
went on quickly. "Quite often, actually, and then they arrange for
their most trusted servant to sell it to a middleman, a contact with
the outside world, you might say. Which is where I come in."

He smiled in a nice, open way and introduced himself as Winston Stuart. Feeling a little ashamed of myself for having suspected
him earlier, I smiled back.

"How can they trust these servants?" I asked. "Huge sums must
be involved."

"Trust their servants!" He looked surprised at my ignorance of
the country we were bound for. "Why, there's nobody a royal princess out there can trust like a good servant. You might even say
there's nobody she *ought* to trust but her servant. Anyway, the
clever servant who makes a shrewd sale is generously rewarded by
her mistress. I've carried on my transactions in the back rooms of
seedy shops after all sorts of complicated machinations; and once
late at night from the window of my car through the window of a
black limousine with drawn curtains! You should have seen us!
Passing rubies and rials back and forth on this pitch black road
. . ." While I tried to visualize the riches he carried in his dispatch
case, and the riches that might fill it when he returned, Winston
Stuart described to me the excitement he always felt on his jour-
neys to Arab lands at the possibility of finding a truly magnificent
jewel or a profitable new contract. It was only after we had chatted
for some time that he found courage to ask outright the question
that I had seen gathering in his eyes: "Are you going out to visit
your husband?"

"No. No, I'm not married."

It seemed inappropriate to explain to a stranger that I did not
intend ever to be married although that was a logical decision for
someone whose parents divorced each other twice, remarried three
times, and might have continued their mirthless game of musical
marriage had the death of my father not intervened.

"Please forgive me asking," he said, and did not continue until I had nodded, "but what is a pretty blonde like you going to do alone in Saudi Arabia?"

When I told him I was going to work there, he looked surprised, and when I told him my job was in one of the royal palaces, he looked downright incredulous.

"A palace! Forgive me saying so, but you're mad! You'll disappear into a harem!"

My heart gave an unpleasant thump when I saw in his eyes that he was not joking. Strangely, I had thought of many things about this journey and imagined even more, but the possibility of real physical danger had simply never entered my mind. Observing the jeweler's concern, I suddenly recalled an episode in my own life that I had completely forgotten. Years earlier, I had shared a flat briefly with a dancer, a French girl, and she had told me that when her troupe was in the Middle East, one of them, a long-legged blonde from Lyons, had vanished. "The show was over for the night," my flatmate had said. "We are all on the way back to our hotel. We turn around. We call 'Colette! Colette!' Pouf! She had disappeared. And we never see her again!"

Thinking logically—an ability I had always prided myself upon —were I to disappear, it would be a long time before anyone noticed. Jennifer knew I was not a good letter-writer, what's more she was the kind of person who looks at the calendar one morning and says "Good heavens! has a year gone by already since Rosemarie left?" My mother's only concern about my departure was that it made it even less likely I would settle down with "a nice German boy," presumably as she had done. We didn't communicate easily or often; she was ailing and self-absorbed and I did not fool myself she would notice if a silence from me extended into infinity. My colleagues at work, although they had been kind to me, could hardly be expected to keep track of my life, nor could the lady from International Nannies. I knew all this logically, but after my first stunned recognition of danger, I ceased to feel concerned; I put that kind of fear to one side but, as it turned out, only temporarily.

"After all," I told myself, "a French dancer might go off by choice. This is the twentieth century."

I was going to learn that the twentieth century was not so universal as I thought and that Saudi Arabia draws not only its faith and its bond of family from centuries long gone, but also the extremes of its justice and feudal divisions of its society which place women in life pretty much as they were placed in my copy of the Koran: between "The Cow" and "Divorce."

"You've been seeing too many B-movies," I told Winston. He shrugged and we talked about comforting things like the vagaries of airlines and the restorative powers of German beer until the plane made its stopover in Rome. There, the middle seat in our block of three was taken by a woman who had that fussy perfection of curls, silk scarves, and manicure that always turns out to be Middle American. She was talkative and very likable, with a fondness for minor expletives that first worried and then began to amuse the Englishman. She told us her name was Peggy.

"My God, honey!" she said, when I told her about my future job. "Do you realize that your Princess Moudi is the daughter of Prince Mohammed! Gee!" she said, and nudged the Englishman. "Hey, what would you say to a gal who was going to work in Buckingham Palace? Because, believe you me, this young lady is bound for the Saudi equivalent!"

Peggy turned back to me and sized me up with her shrewd, friendly gray eyes.

"Honey, if you're loyal to that royal house and do your job well, you are going to have a wonderful time! They'll wrap you in cotton wool and spoil you rotten. You'll have a ball!" She stopped, reconsidered, laughed in a self-mocking American way. "Hell, when I say 'a ball,' I don't mean 'a ball' exactly. Saudi is number one man's country and, believe you me, no woman has 'a ball' in Saudi Arabia. Not in the fullest sense of the word. Not so anybody notices. But I'll say this for them, they're generous to a fault."

It turned out that she was going to visit her husband who worked in Riyadh.

"My husband has a job down there and my kids are at school in America. I sort of commute. My husband and I meet three or four times a year in Saudi or he comes over Stateside. And let me tell you"—she winked at Winston—"it's the best way to make your marriage work."

For most of the journey we three chatted pleasantly about the comparative costs of living in England, America, and on the Continent.

After dinner Peggy and I tried to exchange addresses so we could meet again in Riyadh.

"Hey, this is really funny! I can't give you my address! We've got a house there but no address. The Saudis haven't got around to giving postal addresses to my neighborhood. Isn't that something? And if I drew you a map you'd end up in the Persian Gulf. There's another thing, I don't have my own phone number because the phone wasn't installed last time I was there."

I didn't know my phone number in Saudi either, nor did I know how a friend could go about contacting me. We both laughed but inside I felt chilled and a little isolated.

"Listen, honey," Peggy said, as if she had sensed my tremor of panic, "we'll meet up again, all right. *'Inshallah'* as they say in Saudi Arabia. 'Leave it to God!' Anyway," she added, laughing, "that's sure as hell what they said about installing my telephone!"

The lights dimmed on the plane. Peggy, who had traveled from Seattle, dozed off immediately, and Winston took out a pocket calculator and began doing important sums. I looked out my window and let the dark blue night of the Middle East soothe my nervousness and close in around the voices of Stephen and of my mother: the voices of my memory and of my childhood.

There are shades of night and beneath our plane at midnight the planet was visible only as a darker darkness than the space around it. Even after I felt the shift of pressure that meant we were descending, there was no sign on earth of any welcome for us. The landing gear was down before I saw lights at last. These weren't the bright white lights of verdant countries, or the blue lights of snowbound countries, or even the yellow lights that characterize dry, brown countries approached at night by air; the Saudi lights were like drops of liquid amber flung to earth by an imperious god. The lights of Riyadh seen from the air did not disappoint me, for with the darkness around them they had the human and defiant quality of campfires on the desert.

For one moment, as the plane's wheels touched the land that was to be my adoptive home, I felt a last flicker of fear; my hands grew damp, a knot settled into my stomach, and if it had been possible I would have turned around and flown on wings of my own back to the West, away from the unknown darkness ahead.

"Listen to me, Rosemarie," I could hear Stephen say. "Nothing in all time will ever end without something else beginning."

chapter 2

The plane door opened to let in a current of cool and odorless air that surprised an urban Westerner like me first with its primeval purity. Odd to think that the clean sweep of Saudi Arabia provides enormous quantities of the West's most valuable pollutant. When I saw the tarmac glistening with rain, I heard the distant "pop" of one tropical dream. I remembered Jennifer's laughter when she saw me about to pack my Wellingtons.

"Rosemarie, you're going to the desert, you dope! Not to the rain forests of the Amazon."

"The first surprise," I thought, drawing my light wool coat around me and regretting, not for the last time in that Arabian spring, my discarded Wellingtons. I kept my two traveling companions in view as long as I could, but they were hurrying to the familiar and the loved—she to her husband, he to pearls from the Persian Gulf, and diamonds that had begun to bore their owners. They had soon gone their own ways out of sight, leaving me in the crocodile of people moving toward the main terminal of the airport.

Although the airport itself was modern, featureless, and functional, the main reception area had some of the characteristics of a cattle market with soldiers herding human animals into designated channels. I noticed that the women were treated with special severity as if they really did need to be rounded up and corralled. In that hasty, frantic package of first impressions, I was also struck by the pristine whiteness of the men's robes; even the porters who were doing heavy manual work somehow remained spotless. The Saudi women were huddled in clusters and in their black robes—their

abayas—they looked like shy, frightened birds. Those shrouded
women, moving in groups and shrinking back from contact with
strangers, were the society I was about to join. I stared at them,
here and there meeting a bright eye that glanced at me, then
looked away quickly, retreating into the shadow of the thick veils.

After about half an hour, I was pushed and jostled along with
other passengers into the passport queue. While I waited, I studied
my Saudi visa and tried in vain to decipher something I could understand in the graceful, complex Arabic script. Jennifer, when I
had shown her my visa, had said it probably meant "Never Let
This One Out Again"; but when I finally arrived at the immigration desk and handed over my passport, the official did a classic
double-take, worthy of a silent film star, from passport to me, then
back to passport. Later, I learned that few—if any—European
blondes could have passed his way with their passports stamped:
"Visiting at the personal request of His Royal Highness Prince
Mohammed Bin Abdul Aziz." It was going to be a while before I
came to understand and appreciate the status of Prince Mohammed. He had renounced his claim to the throne on grounds of
ill-health, but he was a member of the "Inner Six," a council of
state composed of the chiefs from each of the huge family's six
principal branches. Neither King Khalid himself nor Crown Prince
Fahd enjoyed this distinction which fell upon Prince Mohammed
by primogeniture and, according to the patriarchal tradition of
Islam, gave him not only enormous prestige in his country but
power over his own branch of the family.

The luggage collection area was separated from the general public by a glass wall. I don't know what I expected to see out there;
maybe a sign with my name on it, maybe a chauffeur or messenger
standing apart, waiting for me. All I saw was a mass of men in
white robes, on their heads the red and white checked *dish-dashas*
that never stopped reminding me of tea towels. With no hint from
the cut of a suit or the stamp of a tie, I could not distinguish one
brown face from another and it crossed my mind how much we in
the West depend upon our wardrobes to indicate status and expec-
tations. What's more, as I looked in vain for someone sent to receive me from the palace, I was uncomfortably aware that bank

upon bank of dark eyes were, without exception, focused on me. With only the glass wall separating me from such passionate scrutiny, I felt like a star feature at the zoo, or a powerful magnet pulling all those eyes as if they were black, shining nails. Not only was I white and unveiled, but my hair is a true yellow and was that evening hanging loose around my shoulders. With those eyes watching, I pulled my biggest suitcase into a corner and sat down on it. Disappointment, panic, exhaustion, competed inside me and finally gave way to the familiar reaction of "what-the-hell!"

"What the hell," I thought. "I've got my return ticket. The very worst thing that can happen is I sit here until the next flight back to London."

What else could I have done? I didn't have Princess Moudi's address or any way to contact her. I might have gone to a hotel in Riyadh (if there were a hotel) but the thought of braving the people who were still watching me, then finding a taxi (if there were taxis) and making myself understood to the driver—all that was more unnerving than the thought of flying home again. I settled back on my suitcase and sat with my chin in my hands watching the crowd. At last, one figure detached itself from the mass of humanity and beckoned in my direction; I looked around to see if it really was me he was trying to attract. He beckoned again. I lifted up a lock of my hair and waved it, looking at him quizzically and, with absolutely no emotion or amusement on his face, he nodded. Picking up my suitcase, I pushed through the exit, trying hard to keep the man in sight and to distinguish him from all his compatriots who were similarly dressed. A group of men pushed between us and when they passed, my guide had vanished. Where he stood, there was only a space, empty for a moment, then filled with strangers.

"What now?" I thought. Even more puzzled were the men around me who stared at me openly, walking backward if they had to, to keep me in sight, but carefully not coming within an arm's length of touching me.

Suddenly, from among the milling men three small figures pounced on me. One of them pulled my arm, another tugged my dress, and the third grabbed my handbag. All the doubts I had been feeling exploded in a blaze of fear and anger. I yanked my handbag loose and with my free arm began to flail at the three creatures who stuck to me now like strange dry leeches. Violence creates a whirlpool, and I had the impression of being dragged into a dark sandstorm, when out of the flurry a small brown hand held up my own photograph; the very snapshot I had attached to my job application.

"Oh my goodness! I'm so sorry! I thought . . ."

From the crack between the folds of their shawl-like abayas three pairs of eyes looked at me, amused, I thought, but not comprehending my words. I covered my face with my hands to mime apology and embarrassment, whereupon one of the three began to giggle. As I smiled at my reception committee, I became aware of a perfume I had never encountered before; this exotic scent—sandalwood mixed with attar of roses—was to become a part of my life as, I fancy, it was once for the Queen of Sheba and for Scheherazade. To this day, on special occasions I burn sandalwood and its pungency never fails to remind me of Saudi's dark, velvet nights.

A cream and beige Cadillac was waiting outside the air terminal. When we had all sunk deep into its upholstery, my companions finally lifted their black drapery and I discovered they were young Africans. Having no language in common, we stared at each other for a moment in silence. Then one of the girls, who appeared to be youngest and barely sixteen, started to giggle. The other two joined her and, deep within myself, below the depths of uncertainty and fatigue, I felt a tickle that grew until I too began to laugh so hard it literally hurt my sides. Even the driver, although he struggled to maintain his masculine dignity, surrendered at last to the prevailing current and began to whoop with laughter.

When our laughter had at last subsided, it left a friendly, unstrained atmosphere and the women chatted among themselves, smiling at me whenever our eyes met. We were traveling at great speed through darkness sprinkled here and there with lights that could have been homes or offices. Looking out, I had the fantastic sensation that I was traveling not only through space but through time as well, back through thick, starry nights to some ancient morning. After a while, the car slowed down and the women stopped giggling; they became silent and thoughtful. The car stopped and the driver sounded his horn. I looked out of my window at a pair of huge, black gates, like the gates of a fortress, like gates that open only on command and only to admit the invited. A high wall slipped away into darkness on either side of the gates as they parted slowly. In front of us was a vast white stone palace illuminated as if to receive ambassadorial delegations, although it was already two o'clock in the morning and our car was alone. The gate clanged behind us. There was no way to go but forward, toward the building that was massive and imposing beyond my dreams. The women's palace of Riyadh had a grim majesty; its construction had employed every modern western technique, but its architecture maintained, nevertheless, the awesome dignity of a crenellated desert stronghold.

We did not pull up in front of the central staircase—the staircase of state was used only by visiting dignitaries, royal wedding parties, and Prince Mohammed himself when he came to visit; instead we drove around to a side entrance that opened into a large reception hall with floors of creamy marble. Two of the young servants led me up a steep staircase and then along a first-floor gallery where yellow curtains covering regularly spaced windows made a violent juxtaposition with the jade-green carpet that swallowed our footsteps. There was no sound at all, only an eerie stillness enclosed by stone walls. Reproduction antique furniture in pale wood and *petit point* upholstery was arranged in the corridor as it is in expensive western hotels: to be seen but rarely sat upon. I saw the central staircase which was like those I had seen before only in big West End cinemas; it was circular and enclosed by a half wall of clear perspex. A chandelier hung like a bunch of grapes grown for a giant, from the top of the three-story stairwell right down to the bottom. This gigantic fixture was reproduced in miniature, suspended from brackets along the wall.

At the far end of the first-floor corridor, one of the servants opened a door and I stepped into an enormous room decorated altogether in shades of purple with contrasting touches of white. The walls were white but painted with a bold pattern in purple, the curtains were purple, the furniture—and it took a great deal of it

to fill such a big room—was upholstered in purple suede, and the
carpet stretched out like a sea of purple, illuminated by lamps with
white or purple shades. On a smaller scale such a décor might have
been merely vulgar, but the sheer size of the room and its fittings
raised it past vulgarity to true eccentricity. The effect of all that
imperial color was overwhelming but what amazed me most, and
impressed me too, was the purple telephone.

Later I found out that the apartment had belonged to Princess
Moudi's niece, Princess Jawahir, and I was told what I had already
surmised: Her Royal Highness was partial to purple. When Princess Moudi had her baby, however, the two princesses exchanged
suites so Princess Moudi could have the larger one.

Blinded and breathless with purple, which seemed to add a
musky depth of its own to the ubiquitous scent of sandalwood and
roses, it was a moment before I realized that the room was crowded
with people seated on chairs, sofas, and purple cushions. It was another moment before I registered that all the people were women.
Like any Westerner coming from an unsegregated community I was
not accustomed to the exclusive society of my own sex or even to
simply entering a crowded room in which there were no men at all,
not even a token husband or two. It was the sound of female voices
en masse I noticed first, the higher pitch that permeated the air but
was not aggressive, although I did distinguish a whine of irritation
from one corner and a harsh laugh from another. For a flash, the
memory of the gates clanging behind me blended with those distaff
sounds to make me think of a giant aviary or a women's prison. In
the corner of the room a large television set was playing Arab
music.

The chatter stopped abruptly and thirty or forty pairs of eyes
turned in my direction and slowly, much more thoroughly than any
man would dare, all those long-lashed eyes examined every inch of
my five feet seven-and-a-half to rest at last on my hair. When the
chattering began again, I could be sure it was about me: about my
clothes, my height, my white skin, my hair. Now it was my turn,
and while the women compared notes I studied their faces and
picked out the pale women with fine bones who, I imagined, must
be the princesses. There were black women, ugly women, beauties,

hags, girls, women in Arab dress, and women in smart western clothes. All their faces were unveiled and most of them were wearing a lot of make-up, giving the lie to the theory that women only decorate themselves for men. Some of the women were servants, the descendants of slaves, and some of them might even once have been slaves themselves. Slavery was abolished in Saudi only in 1962 and will probably take a long time to disappear from the consciousness and subconscious of those who were slaves and those who were their mistresses. A few of the people in the room had come from Ethiopa but most of them were from the Sudan and their skin had the bloom of damson plums.

A servant took me gently by the arm and led me across the room to another door. She knocked. There was silence for a moment, then an answer from within. The door opened and I entered a brightly lit room. The woman who stood in front of me gave an immediate impression of glamour and of the lonely pride that so often goes along with it. She had shoulder-length hair that was titian red and her dark brown eyes expected admiration, yet begged for it at the same time.

"A beautiful woman," I thought, "who has always had more than she needs and still needs something she can't have."

We studied each other boldy, like Martian- and Earth-woman meeting, although we two strangers came from the same planet, I from its shady forests and she from the arid reaches of its deserts. She was slim, wearing an azure blue, sheer, chiffon negligee of the type more often seen on a movie screen than in life. Her mouth was too wide for perfect beauty but it was sensual, a little self-indulgent. When she smiled, the effect was dazzling. "Welcome to my home," she said, holding out her small, delicate hand. "I'm Princess Moudi."

When she closed her negligee over the nightgown, she did it with a grand gesture, as if it were a royal robe; then she led me back to the purple drawing room. I had been barely able to stutter a few words in response to her greeting, and now I followed like a sleepwalker and tried to show intelligence while the princess introduced me to her royal relatives. Since her English was not up to the intricate relationships that frequent marriage and divorce produce in such a household, she introduced everyone as "my sister." Finally she looked at me long and thoughtfully, smiled, and said, "I'm so glad you don't look nearly so bad as your picture!"

She spoke with such charm in her throaty, accented English, that I had to laugh—it was impossible to take offense—and then, when I looked at her smiling eyes, I was pleased to see that whatever happened, I was going to like this princess.

"Now," she said, taking my hand, "come along and meet my son Prince Saud. We call him 'Susu.'"

She put a finger to her lips and the room went suddenly very quiet as we opened a connecting door and entered the nursery. The nursery was dark but I sensed that it was a small room, and my German nose was outraged at its suffocating smell of stale air mixed with old cologne. I could just distinguish three or four heaped bundles and it was only when one of the bundles twitched and stirred that I recognized that each was a servant asleep on the floor. It felt strange to step over the sleeping forms, but they did not rise or seem to wake. In the corner of the room was a miniature grotto hung with an extravagance of white muslin falling from a golden circlet that gleamed in moonlight when the princess opened the curtains. She led me on tiptoe to the cot hidden under all the lavish froth, then she lifted a corner of the veil and smiled at me almost timidly, inviting me to see the baby.

As soon as I saw Susu sleeping in the bright Arabian moonlight, I felt a painful twist of my heart. He lay snuggled deep in a white mattress and fluffy blankets. His face was pale but he had a rich head of dark hair that I had to restrain myself from stroking softly. The sheet was bound around him like a bandage and I could see he was very small and vulnerable. His mattress was lumpy and not only bad for the health of a twenty-day-old baby but could even have suffocated him.

"First thing," I thought, trying to still the flutter I was feeling with practicality, "the very first thing, I'll get him a good, hard mattress!"

Next to me Princess Moudi had become more maternal than regal and I felt her questioning eyes on me and her need to hear that this was really the most wonderful, extraordinary, handsome baby ever born.

"He is lovely," I told her and it was with all my heart. "He is truly lovely. But he is far too small!"

She nodded and then beckoned for me to follow her out of the room, which was as hot as a greenhouse.

"Why didn't you come sooner?" she said to me with a trace of accusation. Before I could answer, a servant entered to announce that two of my suitcases had been accidentally left at the airport. Moudi's attitude changed immediately to genuine concern. "But aren't you too tired?" she said, when I volunteered to go back to the airport with the driver.

"No. No. Not at all," I told her. I was lying. I was so tired I almost felt as if the purple drawing room and its inhabitants, and Princess Moudi herself, were something I was reading on the top of a red double-decker bus and as if I would look up suddenly to find myself alone in London. Nevertheless I had already understood or intuited something about Saudi Arabia: if I wanted it done right away, if I wanted it done efficiently, if I wanted it done *at all*, then I'd better do it myself.

By the time I returned to the palace from the airport, this time with all my luggage ensconced in the Cadillac, I had passed beyond mere fatigue into the condition of a zombie. My feet floated over the green carpet and when I opened the door, the purple drawing room pulsated as if I had entered the heart of a colossal animal. Princess Moudi was sitting with some other women but as soon as she saw me, she rose and came toward me, closely followed by a small, dark woman who kept her eyes downcast as she moved on tiny, mouselike feet.

"Have you your passport and your return ticket?" Princess Moudi asked. Her eyes were expressionless but her voice commanded me to present the documents which I kept in my handbag. Reluctantly, I drew them out.

"Here . . ." I said, but before I could finish speaking the dark woman darted out her hand in an exaggerated, childlike way that set the pom-poms jiggling on her shawl. I pulled my papers out of her reach.

"This is Fauza. I have instructed her to look after your papers for you," the Princess said when I tried to brush the small woman away, and this time command was clear in her tone. I had no choice but to watch, miserable, as my precious documents, the only concrete proof of my existence in an alien country and my only way out of it, disappeared into the folds of the small woman's dress.

"*Al Hamdulillah*," I remembered the chauffeur saying to me at the airport when we returned to find my suitcases waiting untouched in one corner. He explained in broken English that the words meant, roughly, "thanks be to God!" I only hoped I would have reason to use them someday when my passport and ticket were returned to my own hands.

The princess said that my room was only a temporary arrangement and I would be moved next day to my own quarters, but I was too tired either to approve or to doubt. Clearly, the room I was shown had been a dressing room; its walls were lined with cupboards, but in the very center of the floor stood a camp cot covered with a red blanket; under normal circumstances it would have looked about as inviting as a bed of nails but in my state of fatigue it seemed as good as the finest goosedown.

"Would you like some servants to sleep in here with you?" Princess Moudi asked.

"Good Lord no!" I said. Her surprise at my vehemence was in itself surprising for someone who had spent years living in the United States. Dimly I realized it was probably this very quality of slipping totally and uncritically from one culture to another that the princess wanted to instill in her son and, somehow, in a fashion I was too exhausted to think about, I suspected there was a lesson too for me to learn.

"I just hope I'm not too tired to sleep!" I thought, slipping between the crisp sheets.

"There cannot be such a thing as 'too tired to sleep,'" I remembered Stephen saying to me once. "It isn't logical, Rosemarie. After all, have you ever heard of anyone being 'too wide awake' to keep his eyes open?"

I smiled, closed my eyes and fell immediately asleep.

chapter 3

I dreamed something deep and hidden, something I couldn't remember when I awoke beyond an impression of lightness and joy I had not known for months.

"I'm in Saudi Arabia!" I thought, opening my eyes to light filtering through purple curtains. I jumped out of bed and eagerly drew the curtains—to uncover opaque windows. I later discovered they were installed all over the palace to keep out the sun; but they had the added effect of increasing my sense of isolation by preventing any view of the outside. After considerable anxious searching I found a catch in the window frame, and when I pulled it the glass panel slid open. In the clear morning light I saw a vast courtyard and a number of low buildings set among palm trees that shot up high and thin, like lanky adolescents. The largest of the outbuildings I identified as the kitchen. A queue of servants and drivers holding plates in their hands moved through one of its doors and then emerged from another with bread and cooked food which they carried to smaller buildings. Around the courtyard, behind the buildings and the trees, was the palace wall, forbidding, unyielding, as bright in sunlight as it had been in floodlights.

"To keep in? To keep out?" I thought, pulling my dressing gown closer although there was no breeze. "One side of that wall isn't like the other."

A door from my room led directly into the drawing room, and I opened it gently and quietly. The room was full of sunlight and instead of the inky pools the glowing lamps had made the night before, I was confronted with a blaze of purple, as if every violet on

earth had been pillaged and brought to the desert. In the center of
this riotous color sat a servant as still as the sphinx; she wore a
blue-gray dress and her back was to me, but her head was tilted so
I could see where her oiled black hair had been pulled away from
her forehead. In her arms, straight out and motionless, she held the
baby prince. I made to step into the room, but then I stopped, for
as she sat gazing at Susu who was perfectly quiet and wrapped in
his swaddling, I felt a communion between them that I could not
interrupt. I would see to it he had his hard mattress, his regular
feeds, and all the benefits of hygiene any Westerner knows is for the
baby's best. Moreover, I knew already I would love this baby; and
for that very reason I could not deprive him of other kinds of love,
kinds of love I might not understand but that I knew were for his
benefit. I backed out of the room and closed the door softly.

I then had a good look at my room. Over the bed was a lamp
made of glass flowers, each with a small space for a bulb shaped
like a candle. The dressing table was imitation Louis XIV and the
etched, elaborate mirror over it had that quality of expensive
brashness which pretty much characterized the palace furnishings;
as if everything had been won at a carnival shooting gallery for the
very rich. The bathroom adjoining was tiled in a rosy color and
was the size of a typical western living room; the bath itself could
easily have held four normal-sized adults or maybe eight splashing
children.

I had already bathed and dressed when there was a sharp knock
at my door and I opened it to admit a slim woman in a long,
flowered skirt and a bright yellow pullover. Around her neck was a
tape measure and I remembered vaguely from the night before that
she was a Lebanese called Siam, one of the palace dressmakers and
also favorite servant to Princess Jawahir, niece of Princess Moudi.
Siam was older than she managed to look; her make-up was craftily
applied, her eyes big but not in the least pathetic, clever and quick
to fill with laughter as they did now when she told me in merry
sign language that it was time to eat. I followed her through the
corridor where I was surprised to see an African servant sweeping
the high-pile green carpet with a straw broom such as we normally
use in the garden. Whatever the comforts of their plumbing, the

palace caretakers had apparently not yet heard about vacuum
cleaners. The servant looked up at me as we passed with such curiosity I thought he must have been in the corridor for a long time,
transferring dust from one corner to another, waiting to catch a
glimpse of me. He was extremely thin, with very dark skin, black
eyes, and a small black mustache. He wore a white skullcap, bright
against his dark hair, but his white *thobe* was not very clean. As we
passed, he smiled at me with appealing impertinence.

"Sudani," my guide said, glancing in his direction. I didn't know
if she referred to his name or to his nationality and later I used the
word for both.

In the middle of the big dining room we entered was a big table
of pale wood and chairs upholstered in green velvet. One wall was
decorated with a mural of beech trees in an English garden, but the
artist, who had obviously never seen a real beech tree, had painted
the leaves brown. A chandelier hung like dangling grapes over the
table and bracket lamps on the walls were also shaped like grapes,
each bunch a different color. Adjoining the dining room was a pantry and there a counter was set with olives, goat's cheese, honey,
plum jam, clotted cream, and Arab bread shaped into small rolls.
Siam poured me some coffee but it was the bitter African variety
that holds a spoon upright in the cup. I tried to explain to Siam
that I wanted tea, but I could not get my point across and ended
up downing my first Arab meal with Evian water. It was months
later that I learned the coffee had been made specially for me since
it was what my employers thought I would prefer for breakfast. In
Saudi Arabia the men drink coffee throughout the day, but the
women normally take tea.

Through the most complex gestures, Siam introduced me to my
two servants; one of them to wash and clean, the other to help me
with the baby; the first, Esher, was an African and the other an
Egyptian but they both watched me with the same wary black eyes.

Princess Moudi had told me the night before that an English-
speaking nurse was going to come to show me where everything was
and to do some essential translating between me and the servants,
who spoke no English at all. The nurse, when she arrived, turned
out to be very beautiful, with skin the color of black olives. She

wore a long green dress over a long-sleeved white blouse; her hair was drawn back in two deep waves, then caught at the back of her neck in a bun. "Baby's nursery . . ." she said.

In daylight, the nursery resembled any nursery in a rich European household; the baby's dressing table came from Sweden, and the baby basket, equipped with every necessity, many of them untouched, had the look of Saks Fifth Avenue about it. On a smaller table of smoked glass there was a collection of bottles and I was astonished to see they carried the most sophisticated labels of western aftershave and toilet water.

"What on earth are these for?"

"In this family," the nurse said with noticeable pride, "baby must always smell nice. Whenever you change him, he wears cologne." She took a small brown bottle from among the elegant collection, unscrewed the top, and dabbed my wrist with the stopper; the whole room was flooded with the scent of sandalwood and roses that mixed with the sunlight to make a warm, perfumed cocoon around us.

"This is concentrated essence," the nurse told me. "It is the price of liquid pearls."

She cast a scornful look at the French imports on the table. "On special occasions you must always remember to put a dab of this behind baby's ear. And especially," she added, in a voice full of portent, "when he visits the King or his grandfather." Susu lay there looking at nothing, still too young to focus his huge, dark eyes, and I felt a wrench of compassion; he was too quiet. I walked over to his cot and looked down at him; he sighed like a toothless old man, and I knew I was going to have to fight for this baby, cajole him back to health and share with him my own stubborn, practical, bossy will to survive. Gently, I unwound the tight swaddling from his body.

"Aaaah!"

My involuntary cry attracted no attention; the nurse was busy rearranging bottles of scent. The baby had been literally bound in with his own excrement. His groin and upper thighs were fiery with rash and when I turned him over his bottom was blazing red. Oil and powder had been applied too generously and formed lumps, each one a center for inflammation. Despite the luxury of the Prince's surroundings, he had been ill-treated through ignorance. It was hard not to be enraged by the condition of my poor baby prince, but there was no time for anything so luxurious as a tantrum. Already, the nurse had ambled out of the room leaving me alone with my servants.

"Warm water! Warm water!" I said, but both servants looked at me with crafty stupidity. I picked up the baby, and he hadn't even the spirit for a good, lusty howl; he just whimpered a little as I carried him in my arms—he weighed little more than a kitten—to the bathroom.

"Warm water! Warm water!" I said again to the servants, who slouched in the doorway, and I pointed to the tap. Then I gestured to the one assigned to help with the baby and made her feel the temperature of the water I drew so next time she would know precisely how to fill the bowl. I sponged Susu down and he kicked his little legs, making a few throaty sounds I heard as gratitude.

"Warm water! Warm water!" I said, indicating that I wanted the bowl filled again. Esher, who had been watching me with a sullen expression, took the bowl to the basin and I heard the tap run, then she returned it to me full of ice-cold water. "This, Rosemarie, is going to be a bigger job than you bargained for!" I told myself; the thought produced a kind of angry courage. I took the bowl of icy water and held it out to my servant.

"You will be so kind," I said with deadly sweetness, "as to fill this bowl immediately with warm water or I shall be compelled to cut off your ears!"

Esher did not understand a word, but she heard and recognized the tone of my voice. With a mutinous expression she took the bowl and filled it again. This time the water was warm. I had won a skirmish—but the real battles lay ahead.

I reorganized the nursery, throwing the soft underquilt that threatened imminent suffocation into a heap in the corner, followed by the fluffy pillow. I was not rid of those dangerous bedclothes, however. Whenever I turned my back a servant, suddenly dutiful, replaced quilt and pillow. In the end, I had to do virtually everything in the nursery myself and I was never able to decide if the general intractability of servants assigned to me was simple laziness, whether it was stupidity, or whether it was fear of sharing blame should anything happen to the baby prince. Whatever the reason, my servants were never happy in their position; they showed energy, willingness to help and affection for Susu only when Princess Moudi or her mother were around to see it. Much later, after I had left Saudi Arabia, I began to think that within the palace social classes were distributed as they must have been ages ago in feudal Europe, with me representing the rise of the most mistrusted class: the middle class. In a true sense, I stood between the slave and her royal mistress. I was freer and more prosperous than the slave but that only made me open to envy because I had no right of birth, in their view, to give orders. A house servant could vent on me, as she would not dare on her royal mistress, vestiges of pride and rage.

The nurse returned to tell me that because Susu was so small the doctor had ordered that he be fed every two hours around the clock.

"That will have to stop," I told her. "It isn't good for him . . ."

"But he will cry!" she said.

"Babies do cry. Babies are supposed to cry."

"But he must not cry!"

I tried to explain that it was not wise to wake a baby every two hours for his feed and thus deprive him of sleep and of time to digest what he had eaten. Furthermore, I had noticed that whenever Susu whimpered someone thrust a bottle into his mouth and the more they did this, the more wretched he became. I was quite sure he was running a low temperature.

"No more food every two hours!"

"But he will cry, he will cry," the nurse kept saying, shaking her head.

While I tried to make the nurse understand and urged her to arrange for me to meet the doctor, I noticed the sounds of furniture being moved. Suddenly, the door to the nursery opened to admit four servants carrying my cot which they installed near Susu's bed.

"So much for my 'self-contained flat,' " I thought, wondering if it was worth a fight. But all my energy just then was needed to fight on behalf of Susu, so I shrugged and said the first word of

Arabic I had already learned: ". . . *Bukra. Bukra.*" It means
". . . Tomorrow. Tomorrow." It was a word I was to hear frequently.

I ate alone, sitting on a rug before a big tray of aluminum bowls
brought to me by Sudani who carried it on his head. There were
the breakfast rolls, a dish of rice, another of fried potatoes, and a
third of fried chicken; there were smaller bowls too, one of okra
and beans in a hot tomato sauce, so seasoned it could remove paint,
and another containing a salad of tomatoes, lettuce and cucumber.
A final bowl held a selection of apples, bananas, and oranges.

After lunch, I investigated three trunks full of baby clothes, all of
them with the Harrods labels still attached, and all far too big for
Susu. It seemed to me that someone in London, Mrs. Yateem perhaps, had telephoned Harrods and asked for a dozen of absolutely
everything to be sent to Saudi, including shoes, cuddly toys, packets
of safety pins, and special nappies. Maybe Susu was making me sen-
timental, but when I thought about the pleasure friends had taken
in choosing their nursery kit, the expensive but impersonal pile of
clothes in front of me seemed to represent another form of neglect.

In the middle of the first night, as I was giving Susu his feed, the
princess suddenly appeared at my side wearing a magnificent ivory
silk nightgown. She watched, bemused and smiling faintly as I fed
her son and she stood by me when I tucked him back into his cot.
Then she leaned over Susu for a moment and seemed about to
touch him, but changed her mind. She told me that the doctor
would come to talk to me in the morning. "You will have the final
say here," she told me, glancing around the nursery. "The only people you must on no account ever say 'no' to are my father and my
mother."

With a last shy, slightly puzzled look at the baby's cot, she left
the nursery.

Caring for an infant is the way I imagine painting a picture must
be: the sheer hard work of it sometimes disguises the creative process going on—the caring, the affection and the intelligence demanded—yet there is the satisfaction of seeing rapid changes take

place from one day to the next. "Yes indeed, Susu," I told him, "we're going to make a man of you yet!"

In just four days Susu had become a little plumper. His nappy rash was subsiding a little too, thanks to exposure to the nursery air which I had seen was kept cool and fresh. If I was already getting a reputation among the servants for being a tyrant, Susu knew me as gentle and loving, for I tried with my very touch to let him know he was already secure in my heart.

Princess Moudi's mother, Princess Sarah, was due to come from her own apartment below the nursery to visit her grandson and, I was sure, to give me the once-over too. Fortunately, I wasn't fully aware of the significance of that visit since I did not yet understand the matriarchal structure that existed within the walls of the women's palace, or the power of "Mama Sarah" as her family referred to her with noticeable awe. Mama Sarah was the divorced wife of Prince Mohammed and in her own sphere, among the women, she reflected his prestige.

At eight o'clock, when the matriarch was due, the servants seemed to melt away; the door opened and in came Princess Sarah. She was small, swathed in black robes and veils so the oval of her face with its sharp, hooked nose, her hands, and her shapely bare feet were the only skin visible. Mama Sarah was a contrast to Princess Moudi, her daughter, and yet she too had a kind of glamour; hers was the romance of the nomadic tribeswoman who had survived centuries from one campsite to the next. Now Mama Sarah's family was rich and still she could have been waiting in her chaste robes until the riches were gone, as all things must go, and it was time to move back to the desert. Clearly, Mama Sarah was custodian of the stern, old ways. On a less highflown note, I wondered if this noble figure was responsible for the life-size porcelain collie dogs lurking in various corners of the palace.

Mama Sarah ignored me and went directly to Susu's cot. The baby was sound asleep but she prodded him with her skinny finger until he woke up and then she lifted him out of his cot and held him at arm's length, much as I had seen the servants do, gazing intently into his eyes as if passing on to him a telepathic message.

After a moment she sat on the carpet and rocked Susu vigorously and rhythmically on her knee while her lips moved in a silent song or incantation. The entire procedure seemed ritualistic, almost religious, and very far from our western grandmotherly cuddles. There was even an unexpected ferocity in her movements. When Mama Sarah spoke to Susu in Arabic baby talk, he screamed louder than ever, and when she finally left the nursery it took a long time to settle him down again. During the next weeks Mama Sarah was several times to disrupt the calm of the nursery in precisely the same way and leave me with a red-faced, choking baby prince. Once, when I dared wag a finger at her, she began her violent rocking of Susu right after he had been fed, she paid no attention whatsoever, and then, when the baby yelled so hard his face turned crimson, she stormed out of the nursery shaking her head and grumbling. Finally, I had to complain to Princess Moudi and ask her if there was not some way we could restrain grandmotherly attentions.

"Rosemarie, look," Princess Moudi said kindly, "as you are well aware, I know absolutely nothing about babies, but if you say my mother is creating havoc in the nursery, I know you are right. The problem is, I cannot do a thing about it. I'll help you in any way I can. Would you like some new furniture for the nursery? Does the palace food agree with you? I can have you taken to the market to buy fruit, vegetables, anything you have a yen for. Anything, Rosemarie. But only one thing, I cannot say 'no' to my mother or my father."

I looked at the beautiful princess whose eyes beseeched me to understand and for an instant I envied her the steely, unquestioning respect for parental authority which parents in the West win only with bitter difficulty and often do not win at all. Nevertheless, when I then made a request for a teacher to give me lessons in Arabic, Princess Moudi drew away, looked petulant, and shook her head.

"No," she said. "I don't think so, Rosemarie. I want my son to learn German and English, sure, but if you learn Arabic you will speak to him in it, and that we can teach him ourselves."

Much later I could not help wondering if the real reason my employers preferred me not to speak their language was to prevent me understanding, and perhaps misinterpreting, conversations they had among themselves.

The following week Susu had some days when he was in evident discomfort and cried a lot. One evening I asked Princess Moudi if we could try another doctor, one who did not advocate two-hourly feeds or prescribe a powerful hormone cream for nappy rash. The princess said soon we would be leaving for Jeddah where there were much better pediatricians than in Riyadh. I had returned to the nursery after this conversation and was dozing a little, since Susu had calmed down at last, when suddenly the door flew open and in came an ancient man dressed in shabby robes, carrying a stick and leaning on one of the servants.

"Who are you? Who is he? What does he want?" I cried in English jumping up from my bed.

"Koran. Koran," the servant said. She found a chair and placed it where the old man could sit and lean over Susu who had awakened and was, understandably, screaming his head off at this bizarre apparition. Ignoring the child's frenzy, the old man made a few passes with his right hand over the cot and started chanting in a droning, singsong voice. I suppose I ought to have understood what was going on, but I had just been awakened from sleep, a rare enough privilege during those first weeks, and then to see Susu, who had been querulous all day, awakened in his turn screaming from his first real nap for hours, unhinged me, as anyone who has dealt with an ailing infant can understand. I fairly flew to Princess Moudi's room and actually pounded on her door.

"Who is that horrid old man, and what is he doing with my baby?" I cried as soon as she let me in. With Susu's screams resounding throughout the palace she explained that the interloper was a wise man of the faith who would "make Susu feel better" by lulling him with readings from the Koran. In time I gained great respect for many of the tenets of Islam and I wish I could report that Princess Moudi was right and that the power of the holy book soothed Susu into blissful sleep; but in fact it was literally hours after the sage had gone before I could calm the baby down again.

Princess Moudi had come to Riyadh so she could have her baby at the King Faisal Hospital, which is reputed to be one of the best-equipped in the world. A week after Susu's visit from the holy man we began preparing to move back to Jeddah where the princess usually lived with her husband, Prince Abdul Majeed Bin Saud Bin Abdul Aziz; and since the prince's new villa was not yet finished we were going to stay in the guesthouse at Prince Mohammed's palace.

In the afternoon before we were to leave there was noticeable tension in the corridors of the palace. Servants were suddenly animated by hectic energy—even my own two made an attempt to look industrious, and the languid princesses too were unusually restless. Eventually, someone was sent to tell me that Prince Mohammed himself was arriving that afternoon to see his grandson. I was instructed to dress the baby in his best clothes, a feat that entailed some emergency dressmaking since he had nothing presentable less than three sizes too big for him. I did remember to dab some sandalwood and rose scent on the cuff of his sleeve. The hygienic puritan deep inside me just could not bring herself to put perfume behind the baby's ears! Then I changed into a short, flowered cotton dress I had made for myself in London and with Susu in my arms I waited in the nursery, feeling suddenly, and illogically, very nervous.

"Come! Come! Come!" said the servant sent to fetch me, her face contorted with the manic self-importance seen backstage at amateur theatricals. Carrying Susu, I followed her down the central staircase carefully, because the steps were made of Plexiglas, and up to immense double doors I had never seen opened. There, I finally understood the servant's frantic signs and slipped off my sandals. Then the doors were opened and before me was a vast room carpeted in turquoise blue. Along the edges of the room sat thirty or forty women and a few little girls in deep armchairs; although it was afternoon, they were all dressed in evening gowns of such vivid hues—orange, coral, crimson, buttercup yellow—it seemed a dazzling flock of tropical butterflies had come to call. Only Mama Sarah wore her customary black and this time the veil was drawn in such a way it revealed part of her face to the women while hiding it entirely from the view of her former husband.

As I started on the long, long walk toward the far corner of the room where Prince Mohammed, dressed in a gleaming white robe and white dish-dasha, was seated, waiting for his grandson, the women, whose voices had been respectful and subdued, grew silent to watch our progress. Princess Moudi stepped forward a pace. She wore an evening dress of forest green that enhanced her flowing red hair; her face had been carefully made up, the lashes thick and fringed around her dark eyes that were now reflecting pride in her son as well as that puzzled affection with which she always viewed him. When I finally arrived in front of the prince I kept my eyes lowered and said, "Good afternoon, Your Royal Highness," to which he inclined his head. Then I placed the baby in his arms and the room became absolutely silent; even breathing seemed to stop, as if this moment were historical and potentially explosive. After a while, the prince smiled down at his grandson and the room sighed. I too relaxed and took the seat that Princess Moudi indicated next to the prince.

As Prince Mohammed fondled his grandson who, clever lad that he was, had not yet begun to cry, I looked at the patriarch discreetly. He had a wide, friendly smile that made comfortable-looking jowls on his face; as he played with the baby, his expression was so benevolent and loving I thought of a dark-eyed Father Christmas. I then glanced surreptitiously around the room. Some of the women there I had seen before in the purple drawing room or on one of my rare excursions out of the nursery into the corridors of the palace, but there was one stranger seated near Prince Mohammed whom I had never seen and whom I studied with admiration. She was in her late teens, obviously of the royal family; a princess, I learned later, called Mishaal. The bones of her face were exquisitely fine and her hands were unusually long for such a petite, slender frame. Jet black hair, slightly waved, fell to her shoulders and she was dressed with an elegance that showed real flair, a quality she shared with her Aunt Moudi and one a lot more precious than money in that gaudy palace. As I watched Princess Mishaal, she raised her head and for one moment our eyes met; hers were so dark they seemed to have no irises which gave them the inward look of a dreamer or of a blind woman.

In retrospect I still cannot believe no portent of Mishaal's awful fate was evident as she sat there, smiling a little at her baby nephew; or that the future did not cast its shadow over her beauty so that one of us might have recognized and understood, might have warned her: "Stop now, Mishaal, before it is too late!"

chapter 4

That very night we left on the last flight for Jeddah, a journey to the southwest and just over halfway across Saudi Arabia that was to bring us to the coast of the Red Sea. Jeddah was only a hundred miles or so from the holy city of Mecca, forever closed to me and all other Christians. As directed by Princess Moudi, I had packed everything for this journey except, literally, the nursery sink and some of the larger furniture which she said we would replace and install in Jeddah.

It was after Prince Mohammed's audience, while repacking my own bags, that I came across the paperback copy of the Koran Jennifer had bought for me the day before I left London. I slipped the book into my handbag and thereafter I often consulted it for enlightenment not only about the customs of Saudi Arabia but about its politics and its very soul.

Everyone on the airplane was spry, considering the hour, except for Susu and me. I would have wagered we were the only ones who had been up since five that morning; I had listened at dawn to the plaintive summons to prayer from the minarets of every mosque in Riyadh, a morning song that after only ten days was becoming as familiar to me as the bell of my old alarm clock, and as effective. I could even pick out a few words: Allah u Akbar . . . Mohammed rasoul-Allah." ("Allah is the greatest . . . Mohammed is His prophet . . .") I tried to doze in my first-class seat with Susu in my arms while next to me the princess laughed at what I assumed were a string of jokes being whispered by her favorite servant, Fauza, who still carried my passport and return ticket somewhere under her fringed shawl. Once in a while, Fauza darted a glance at me then whispered something to make the princess laugh harder than ever. The little servant was so comical with her twitching nose and her mouth pursed into an "o," I had to smile too because it seemed so incongruous: the tall blond foreigner who held a dark-eyed Arabian baby in her arms as if she were his mother.

I had left Susu's tissues in the baby-bag which was with Esher in the economy class, so I thrust the baby into Princess Moudi's arms —she held him as if he were a valuable and breakable doll—and walked through the curtains to economy class. There, taking up at least half the available seats, was virtually every member of our household. I recognized Esher and Nema, my own two servants, I thought I saw the three young Africans who had met me at the airport when I first arrived, and near the front was Sudani, the sweeper; he flashed his impudent grin at me and nodded his head.

"Well, of course they're all out there!" Princess Moudi said, when I expressed surprise. "Every last one of them except Ahmed, my driver. He was supposed to drive the Mercedes down for me but he said he wasn't feeling well, so I sent him ahead on another flight. Oh yes, Rosemarie," she said, laughing at the question in my eyes. "The car flew with him."

Fauza did not understand a word of English but when she saw her mistress was amused, she held her hand like a little paw in front of her mouth and giggled so hard the pom-poms quivered on her shawl.

At Jeddah, the princess preceded us all down the gangway, evidently delighted to be home, and I walked behind her, carrying Susu asleep in his basket. Before we had reached the ground a bright red Cadillac squealed along the tarmac and came to a halt alongside the plane.

"Irene! George!" the princess called to a couple in the front seat of the car. I slid in beside them with Susu in his basket on my lap. The princess sat behind us but leaned forward to gossip in Arabic, pausing only to signal to the soldiers who waved us through the airport gates as soon as they recognized her. I cast a sidelong look at the couple who had met us. They were a brother and sister the princess said in her rapid introduction, employed by the Al Saud

Establishment, which was a business Princess Moudi's husband was in the process of setting up. Irene and George were alike as two plump peas except that George was nearly bald and his sister had tinted her hair red.

It turned out that builders were still at work on Prince Abdul's offices as well as the flat destined for Irene, so she had to share Susu's living quarters with me, an enforced intimacy both of us resented. Irene, who knew everything about the household, had to be discreet out of honor and common sense, although I suspected she was by nature a gossip; as a result, she barely spoke at all, maintaining a resentful silence, and I never dared put to her any of my teeming questions. Gradually, however, I answered most of them for myself.

As soon as I saw Prince Mohammed's compound, I knew I was going to be happy in Jeddah. The gates were wide open and welcoming. After driving across the outer courtyard, built in a protective ring around the palace grounds, we passed through an archway that opened into the inner courtyard. This inner courtyard was in fact a magnificent park lit even at midnight by lanterns atop tall iron posts painted pale blue. When the car stopped, I stepped out of it into a night laden with the scent of jasmine. A curtain of eucalyptus trees and bougainvillea gave just a glimpse of Prince Mohammed's villa, which was of white stucco with a red-tiled Mediterranean-style roof. Our guesthouse, built of the same materials, was a few hundred yards from the main house. Although Prince Mohammed lived alone, he maintained several splendid residences; they lacked the fortresslike scale of the women's palace but they expressed a much more delicate and authentic Arabian taste. In Jeddah, I thought, the walls were there to shield us inside the scented bubble of a garden and not, as they were in the women's palace of Riyadh, to imprison us.

Although it was late, we behaved in the Saudi way, as if clocks had not yet been invented. As soon as I had settled Susu into his cot—my own bed had already been set up in the room next door—I tiptoed into the entry hall which was to serve us as a communal living area since Irene had taken the third room of our apartment;

there I sat on the floor and was served a meal which could have competed with any western restaurant on Michelin's roll of honor. There were plates of fish delicately fried in light batter, and a salad made of vegetables cleverly cut by a master's hand to look as good as they tasted. There was even a crème caramel adorned with glazed orange sections and, in the center of the table, a silver bowl of perfect grapes, plums, oranges, and bananas. Irene was with me; she said little, bolted a lot of food, and then left me alone to finish my peaceful meal.

Before that long night was over, Princess Moudi told me her husband was eager to see his son, whom he had seen only once before. As soon as Susu finished his bottle, I wrapped him in an embroidered blanket and took him to the prince's quarters, adjoining our own, where we were received in a typical Saudi drawing room, furnished with a royal blue carpet, chairs arranged all around the walls, and a music center with a television set dominating one corner of the room.

Prince Abdul was a slim young man who wore a sports jacket over his thobe and who folded the flaps of his dish-dasha stylishly on top of his head. He was an attractive example of the popular image of an Arab prince with long black eyes and pale skin; he had a prominent nose, which Arabs consider an attribute of male beauty, surmounting his fashionable drooping mustache. His English was excellent, more lightly accented than my own, and he had a soft voice in contrast to the voices of Arab women that rise to shrillness despite any efforts to modulate them.

"I am delighted you have joined our household," he said in a courtly fashion. He took the baby inexpertly in his arms but was clearly relieved to hand him back after a minute or two.

The next morning the pediatricians came to call. Unlike the doctor in Riyadh who was wedded to nineteenth-century nursery techniques, the Jeddan doctor was a Lebanese, more recently trained and much more in the western tradition. It was he I shall always think of as my savior; it was thanks to him that Susu went on four-hourly feeds and a normal sleeping pattern—which meant that it was thanks to him I was at long last able to claim some time of my own and to look around beyond the nursery. The doctor's heroic stature increased in my eyes when he even attempted, albeit with limited success, to persuade Princess Moudi that it really was normal for a healthy baby to cry once in a while.

Susu had settled down for his afternoon nap and I had Princess Moudi's permission to go to the *souk* and buy the heaps of things I needed for myself and for the baby. I was overjoyed at the free hours that lay ahead; the only plump fly in the ointment was the silent Irene who was asked to accompany me as guide and treasurer. It was in her role of treasurer that Irene paid me my first salary; as an adviser she was less efficient, as it was she who persuaded me to take the money in pounds sterling. Even Irene unbent a little, though, as our driver ran his hazardous course along paved streets wide enough to accommodate the cars that raced higgledy-piggledy and the throngs of people who believed that automobiles were like camels, subservient to humans and trained to move out of their way.

As all the buildings do in seaside cities, the buildings of Jeddah cast back extra light reflected from the water; the big white buildings of state and government were so dazzling against the bright sky it hurt to look at them. After the asphalt ran out, the roads became narrow, lined with older buildings of pinkish stone, their arched windows and overhanging balconies shielded by intricately carved jalousies and shutters; the balconies rose in layers, one above the other, looking deceptively fragile. As we approached the port and shopping center, the crowds in the street increased and became even more nonchalant about distinguishing pavement from road; several times our driver detoured around a fruit dealer sitting in the middle of the road and selling from his basket. The streets were noisy and dirty but they had the robust vitality I imagine nomadic merchants used to bring to their great bazaars.

Ahmed, our driver, maneuvered the big car into a space I would not have dared attempt. From our air-conditioned chariot Irene and I stepped into Jeddah's afternoon frenzy; the air was weighed down with moist heat and the harbor smells that lay around us mixed with the odor of strange foods and oils. Arab music was playing somewhere, accompanying the continuous squealing of brakes and blowing of car horns. I hurried behind Irene, terrified of losing her in the crowd around us that, I fancied, jostled me with a peculiar relish and amusement. The streets were lined with stalls and behind them were shops, a few of them similar to western department stores, built on two levels with balconies running the length of their display windows where, already in the late afternoon, lights were beginning to come on in readiness for the swift, flaming sunset.

Irene doled out cash from her pockets and handbag, for that was all we ever spent; no checks, no credit cards. On future expeditions she sometimes had to hurry back to the palace to replenish her stock of riyals. On that first shopping trip and others in the days to come we bought buckets, pots, pans, a baby bath, a refrigerator, bathroom scales, a television, a table, chairs, a radio, a vacuum cleaner, a carpet sweeper, and cassettes. At first I was very cautious, but in an alarmingly short time I stopped so much as glancing at prices as money became less significant for me and more an abstract means of getting the objects I needed or wanted. When we returned from our sprees, the princess asked to see what we had bought and she examined everything with girlish interest. She never once asked what anything had cost and I wondered whether that was discretion, or generosity, or her genuine ignorance of sums and equations that obsess most of the world.

Of all the purchases only my vacuum cleaner was a total failure, since my servant, Esher, eyed it with suspicion and managed to end up always shifting dust from one side of the room to the other with her old straw broom. Finally, I decided it was time to buy a washing machine so I could release Esher from my bath—and vice versa, since she seemed eternally to be crouching beside it using it as a convenient laundry tub. With Princess Moudi's approval I set off for the souk, but this time I went alone because Irene was busy and I was impatient. Leaving the Cadillac and driver waiting at the bottom of a narrow street, I took a deep breath and plunged into the melée of the bazaar. At first I did well and congratulated myself upon finding the correct shop for the kind of purchase I was going to make.

"Bukra, bukra . . ." the shop assistant assured me, smiling, when I asked about a washing machine.

"Bukra?" I asked suspiciously. "Bukra?"

"Bukra!" he replied emphatically. "Bukra!"

"Bukra," I sighed.

It is amazing how many nuances the word "bukra"—"tomorrow"—assumes in dealings with a Saudi merchant, especially since he and I were pretty sure that in this case tomorrow would never come.

Looking out of the window of the big shop where I had been promised "tomorrow," I saw in front of me an alley of stalls all offering bolts of beautifully colored fabrics. I glanced at my watch and was pleased to see there were more than two hours in hand before Susu awoke from his nap, wanting me. Dressmaking is my favorite hobby and I always loved to browse among fabrics as if among books or records. In London the bottom drawer of my big dresser was always full of material I had not been able to resist and then had not found time to cut or sew. Jennifer, who shared my hobby but was altogether more sensible about it, called the collection "Rosemarie's hopeless chest!" No doubt it is hard for someone who does not enjoy sewing to understand, but those bolts of fabric drew me irresistibly out of the shop into the warm, noisy streets.

"Just a quick look . . ." I told myself.

The twisting streets of this corner of the bazaar atracted groups of women in their abayas but, as the men seemed to take delight in jostling me, the women drew their veils closer when I came near. I caught no eye looking directly into my own eyes, but I noticed many people glancing at my blond hair and my short summer frock. Before me stretched a dressmaker's paradise, and I moved, like a bee among flowers, from Swiss cottons to Indian sari silk to printed man-made fibers. I picked up, put down, picked up again, and bought nothing simply because I couldn't make up my mind. Every time I settled on one pattern or weave, another tantalized me until, suddenly, I looked at my watch and saw that an hour had passed. Shadows were growing long. It was time to go back. I turned. The crowd pressed in around me but I was tall enough to see to the end of the street. I walked back to the corner. Before me was an intersection of three streets, each going a different way. Thinking I recognized a bolt of fabric on one of the stands, I

turned eagerly to the right but after a few paces I changed my
mind, and went back through the crowds toward the intersection.
But the intersection was no longer there. Instead, an unfamiliar
maze of streets lay in front of me.

"My God! Where am I?"

My heart started to beat faster. I looked up, vaguely planning to
orientate myself by the sun, but that was no good because I had not
the faintest notion whether I had walked north, south, east, or west
after leaving the car. Desperately, I looked around. Sometimes in
the market with Irene I had noticed other Europeans, pale or sun-
burned, among the white thobes and black abayas. This time I saw
no familiar face, no compatriot, no fellow European. My body was
moving of its own accord and around me now there were no longer
the bolts of fabric but stalls laden with cosmetics, children's clothes,
plastic toys, shoes, worry beads, and incense burners. My throat
ached. All I could think was that I did not have my passport. I did
not know my address. I could not even remember Princess Moudi's
grand and lengthy name.

"I don't exist!" I thought. "I'm lost!"

My eyes began to burn. Policemen in uniform moved in the
crowd, but even if I could make one of them understand me, what
would I ask him? All the loneliness I had ever felt gathered in a
knot around my heart and squeezed. I remembered a line from the
Koran: "Believers, take neither Jews nor Christians for your friends
. . ." What did I really know of the feelings of these people I had
come to live among with such bold innocence? Was it bad temper
or real hatred I surprised sometimes in Esher's eyes when I gave
her an order? If I disappeared, would Princess Moudi feel anything
but irritation at having to import another nanny? The crowd
pushed me and I pushed back in growing terror. Could they be my
friends? Would they help me? We did not even speak the same languages. Then came the thought to push me over the line from fear
into genuine panic.

"Susu will be waking soon, needing me, and I won't be there!
Someone will mix his feed too rich, too cold. He'll get colic. They'll
put him to sleep on his back on a soft pillow. Oh my God! Don't
let him suffocate!"

I shoved people out of my way and tried to run through the streets, thinking in panic that if I kept to a straight line one way or another I would have to come to the end of the maze. The street, however, seemed to twist back on itself under my feet. I had the impression that I was calling out, but in the noise of hooting horns and shouts and distant stringed instruments, I couldn't hear my own voice. I ran up to the door of a prosperous looking shop where I thought I might find someone to understand me. Suddenly, at that very moment, bedlam stopped as if a tap had been turned off. Shaking his head severely, a man bolted the glass doors in front of me from inside and in the hush I heard the call to evening prayer. Other gods must have been in attendance, for while Islam knelt in worship I raced heedlessly down a small, narrow street and there in front of me was the palace Cadillac, the driver beside it in prayer.

Later that night when Susu was tucked in bed, my panic subsided into a throbbing memory and into an even more throbbing need to have my passport back. If my terror in the souk did have its illogical elements, then that meant I needed my passport not only as proof of identity and nationality but also as a talisman. When Princess Moudi arrived for her usual nighttime visit to the nursery, I noticed a glint of laughter in her eyes as I confronted her with my request.

"It is the way you look whenever you're ready for a fight," she explained to me later, when we knew each other better. "All . . . all . . . you know . . . I haven't the English words . . . yes, just like one of my father's falcons!"

"I will have my passport back, Your Majesty," I told her on that occasion and then added, more like a sparrow than a falcon, "I am by law supposed to register with my Embassy. And my mother is seriously ill. And . . ."

"Of course, Rosemarie," she said. "I'll tell Fauza to give it to you."

The next day during my first free hour I had the car take me down Embassy Row where, after some confusion, I found my national flag half hidden behind a fence and a wall of cypress trees. When I registered my address in Riyadh care of Princess Moudi's family, the young man behind the desk took off his glasses, wiped them thoughtfully on a clean handkerchief, then put them back on his nose, as if he could believe neither his eyes nor his ears.

"And in Jeddah," I said, "we live on . . ." Like a child, I repeated verbatim the address as I had learned it that morning from Irene. "On Medina Road, Kilometer sixteen, opposite the Pepsi-Cola factory. It is the Palace of Prince Mohammed bin Abdul Aziz." "Lord almighty!" the young German said at last. "Are you ever the lucky one! Is it true their knives and forks are made of solid gold?"

The next weeks passed very pleasantly. Our apartments were comfortable and furnished adequately though without great style; the food remained delectable. Best of all, Susu started to flourish and gain weight. His eyes began to focus so he could recognize me by sight as well as by touch and smell. One morning when I bent over his cot to say "hello" he gave me the first smile of his life, an honor I accepted with full heart.

"Susu smiled this morning!" I told Princess Moudi when she came to the nursery that night.

"Oh?" she said in an absent-minded way. "That's nice, Rosemarie." Oblivious to the importance of her baby's smile—not even jealous that it had been addressed to me—Princess Moudi did however continue to summon the Lebanese doctor whenever she thought the baby cried too much. It was a practice that drove the doctor and me—and Susu—nearly wild, and one that she continued to pursue all the time I was in her employ. I am not sure what a psychiatrist would say (that was one kind of doctor we had no occasion to consult) but I think Susu's crying triggered Princess Moudi's maternal concern which she knew how to express only through the agency of hired help.

One evening I was feeding Susu in the entrance hall which we had done up into a comfortable sitting room, and singing to him, while a servant cleared the nursery of mosquitoes. This was done by spraying the room with insect repellent and then sealing it with the air conditioning turned down as low as it would go. After about twenty minutes, the room was free of insects; then the air was cleared and I put Susu to bed. I tiptoed back to the sitting room where I dozed and daydreamed to the accompaniment of Arab music from the television. Quite early, as usual, I retired to my small adjoining bedroom and switched on the light; beside my bed I saw—I still do not know what to call it—a lizard? An insect? It was about a foot long, shaped something like a salamander but colorless; its quality of nudity was what I found most revolting, that, and its eyes that, in my memory at least, were pinkish red. The horrid creature clung to the wall as if it had every right to be there. My scream rocked the house and brought running every servant within earshot; Princess Moudi herself, looking nearly disheveled, pushed her way through the door.

"Susu! Susu!" she cried. "What's happened to him? What did you do to him?"

Speechless, I pointed to the wall where the creature remained impervious to all the fuss. Princess Moudi first laughed with relief, then shuddered.

"Ugly isn't it? I'm afraid you'll see more of them. They come from the grapefruit trees. And do you want to know something, Rosemarie?" she added, an expression of distaste on her face. "It is said that if a Muslim woman kills one of those things with her bare hands, Allah Himself will greet her when she dies." Either my servants had already secured the greetings of Allah or they relinquished their opportunity for such distinction, because they killed the thing with a broom and from time to time thereafter I heard them thumping on walls in pursuit of others. Once I saw an entire family—a mama, a papa, and four baby "grapefruit monsters" walking across the ceiling while I had my dinner, but for the most part I stayed out of their way and prayed they would stay out of mine.

A paved terrace ran the length of the guesthouse, and beyond it manicured paths of sand led into a wall of vegetation. Grapefruit trees were bowed to the ground with fruit; lemons, still green, grew plentiful among glossy leaves and, especially in the cool after sunset, the smell of orange blossom was pervasive in the air. Towering

above the citrus trees were the loquats and figs, each planted in a
shallow depression to catch and hold precious water delivered daily
by the gardeners.

One day, while Susu slept, I strolled farther than usual into this
wonderland which, though hot and tropical, made me think of the
deciduous thickets of my childhood and of the slippery floors of
northern pine forests. Trees—pine, citrus, or oak—spread shade
and calm around their trunks. For me, forests and plantations and
orchards have always been healing places. Two gardeners I encountered on the path smiled at me without alarm or curiosity although
I was perhaps the first European woman they had ever seen up close.
As I approached the prince's villa, trees gave way to a riot of
flowers with emperor butterflies and swallow-tails reeling drunkenly
from golden herb lilies to the brink of scarlet hibiscus, then up into
the clematis growing in a profusion of color, from pure white to
deep wine red. Jasmine and roses grew everywhere, surrounding me
with texture and perfume. Among the trees, I found two tiled
swimming pools, both empty, although they had been swept and
cleaned. When I reminded myself that on the other side of the surrounding wall lay desert where life could still be claimed by thirst,
the vivid garden assumed a magical quality as if it were the gift of
an ancient brass lamp; an illusion that was solid but could disappear like smoke.

Suddenly the servant I called Sudani stepped from the foliage
near where I stood.

"You look . . . you look now," he said, gesturing toward the
prince's villa, which I could see, white under the fall of bougainvillea.

We walked on tiptoe, although there was no sign of life and a
path of thick sand swallowed our footsteps.

"You look . . . you look," Sudani said again when I hesitated in
front of French windows that stood ajar.

"Hush, Sudani!"

I listened. There was no sound at all, no breeze, no bird's cry. I
remembered how when I was a child I used to wander alone in the
forests of my homeland hoping to discover an enchanted palace
that slept under a witch's spell. It seemed I had found that palace

at last, half a world away from Europe. I followed Sudani over the threshold. The spell was not broken, for in front of us was another dreamland of glowing color and deep, soft fabrics. Both of us were nervous and we walked quickly. Even though I longed to stop and examine a picture, a vase, a piece of brocade, I was able only to receive an impression of grace and space and luxury as the villa's rooms unfolded in front of us like the panels of an imperial screen. Following Sudani over an intricate landscape of carpets and precious rugs, I recalled ruefully the garish colors of the woman's palace in Riyadh, its artificial flowers and porcelain collie dogs. He stopped at a door of pale wood and stood back, smiling, as if with pride of ownership, when I entered the prince's bedroom. The room was in light beige; at the far end there was a chaise longue, some chairs and small tables in gilded wood, upholstered in peacock colors. The bed itself was as big as the back bedroom in a London row house; its coverlet was beige to match the curtains and it was raised on a dais. Although Sudani was increasingly nervous with every illicit moment we spent in the villa—and so was I—I could not resist stepping up to the head of the bed and looking out at the view over a dazzling flower garden that greeted Prince Mohammed every morning he awoke in the splendor of his Jeddah villa.

On the way back to the guesthouse I plucked a spray of hibiscus, the first fresh flowers I had touched since leaving London. When I returned to my room I found there were no vases, so I put the hibiscus into a Pepsi-Cola bottle where it did not thrive for long.

After a struggle, I finally persuaded Princess Moudi that I could take my promised day off every week without Susu suffering unduly.

"What day off every week?" she asked with her wide-eyed ignorance of common practice.

"Princess Moudi," I explained patiently, "every nanny in the world has a day off."

"And what about my baby? Have you thought about him? How will he eat? What about his schedule? What about his comfort?"

After I promised to prepare all Susu's feeds, label and refrigerate them, and to rehearse my servant in every moment of his schedule, and to be within call if I should be needed, the princess agreed grudgingly to give me her car and driver for the next day. She advised me to go to the Al Atlas Hotel where I would find a swimming pool.

"It's near 'The Creek,' " she said, and I had to smile at the way she said "The Creek," making the word sound American and reminiscent of *Tom Sawyer*.

The next morning I woke feeling wonderful. I dressed in a long, flowing culotte with a backless halter neck made of pink and red silk, under which I wore my swimsuit; granted, this was unusual apparel for a nanny, even on her day off, but Princess Moudi had made no stipulations about my dress, so inside the palace or out I was able to please myself as long as I stayed within the confines of local taste and custom. The green Mercedes coupé was waiting for me and for a moment as I went down the steps toward it, the silk drifting around me, it was I who might have been a princess. "Oh Jennifer, if you could see me now!" I thought. But the only one there to admire was Ahmed, the driver. He was quite accustomed to seeing the princesses in their diaphanous nightgowns whenever he delivered papers or packages to the palace in Riyadh and he appeared unmoved by my fair skin.

The hotel pool was large, enclosed by high walls so that I could not see the terrain around it. Jeddah's springtime had become as hot as midsummer in London, and it was delicious to dive straight into the pool, then float there on my back looking up at a sky of electric blue. The single discomfort I felt was a prickle of longing to enjoy the sun, the cool water, the sensual luxury, with someone else: with someone I loved.

The only other person at the pool was an American woman. Her face was covered with cream, she wore a floppy straw hat, a plastic guard over her nose—"Freckles," she explained when she saw me looking at it—and her sunglasses covered an area from her eyebrows to below her cheek-bones. She was swathed in towels which she adjusted from time to time to cover or uncover a square inch of skin.

"I'm so damned bored!" she said. "My sister married a doctor, but I had to go and marry an engineer and he had to come to this Godforsaken place . . ."

When I began to tell her about my job and the palace, she leaned forward, fascinated, and even took off her sunglasses to see me better.

"Hey, is it true," she asked me after a while, "that their knives and forks are made of solid gold?"

I had no answer to that, so I switched the conversation.

"Tell *me* something," I said to her. "Why do they call this area 'The Creek'? Don't you think that's a funny word in a place like Jeddah? I would have expected, say, 'The Oasis' or 'The Wadi' . . . but 'The Creek'?"

She replaced her dark glasses and sat back, gesturing vaguely toward the high wall around us.

"There's a water hole or something out there someplace. So they call it 'The Creek.' How should I know why? I don't think it's particularly funny. I don't think it's funny at all." How right she was! For me at least "The Creek" was to become one of the least funny places in the world.

I returned to the guesthouse for lunch and to check on Susu, who was content, sleeping on his side with a tiny bubble of milk at the corner of his mouth. His forehead was cool and soft as a rose petal. Then I sat in the garden, thinking nothing, just basking in the sun and the sweet smell of flowers. Irene approached me once eagerly but seemed to change her mind before she reached me, turning on her heel and disappearing into the house.

Later, I sat as usual on the terrace outside the nursery. The night was as I imagined the very first night must have been in earth's first garden. Stars hung as heavy as fruit. Cicadas sang in the dark screen of the eucalyptus trees. My skin tingled from sun and water. I had not felt so good in more than half a year and I only needed someone to share the night with me. Alas, all I found were mosquitoes eager to share *me* with the night.

To my surprise when I made my usual check in the nursery, Princess Moudi was waiting for me. She wore a nightgown the color of tea roses that shimmered in the dim nursery night-light and I could see she was in her regal, imperious mood.

"Pack, Rosemarie," she said. "We leave tomorrow for Riyadh. I have divorced my husband."

chapter 5

"If a woman fears ill-treatment or desertion on the part of her husband, it shall be no offence for them to seek a mutual agreement, for agreement is best . . . If you separate, Allah will compensate you both out of His own abundance . . ."

That was the best I could find in the Koran to help me understand the surprising news of Princess Moudi's divorce; there was nothing to explain either the speed with which it had taken place or Princess Moudi's tight-lipped calm. My parents' divorces had been preceded by flaming battles, then followed by my mother's hysteria and bitter recriminations. I remembered how after these terrible scenes, I would awaken early with a metallic taste in my mouth and run barefoot to the hall cupboard where we kept our coats to make sure that my mother's coat was still there and that she had not followed my father out into the night, leaving my sister and me to fend for ourselves.

In the nursery, I looked down at Susu who was still sleeping, and I could not resist stroking his cheek with my finger. He stirred in his sleep and made a few babyish—but definitely masculine—sounds of annoyance. Dawn was just breaking and with its first gray light the call to prayer rang out, a command that was at the same time itself obedient to the laws of Islam. I slipped through the big nursery doors to watch the day being born. First rays of the blazing sun had awakened the birds who filled the garden with celebration; against the orange and fuschia sky of the Arabian dawn a nearby mosque was silhouetted, its minarets lofty and sharp enough, it seemed, to penetrate the floor of heaven and let the prayers in.

That morning, and other mornings too when I awoke to such magnificence, I felt totally at peace; even the deepest of my sorrows and my losses became as natural as petals that dropped from a full-blown rose. For during those moments in the garden of Jeddah I caught a glimpse of some pattern in which I was neither insignificant nor particularly significant: in which I simply was and would remain until I was no more. These were not only moments of consolation and repose, but perhaps as close as a Westerner could ever come to the center of the Arabian soul.

The furnishings of the guesthouse had to be dismantled before our departure and everything packed except for the largest pieces which were stored, I saw with a leap of hope, against our possible return to this place I had come to love. Princess Moudi had dark circles under her eyes and she was unusually quiet, but I kept marveling at her control, especially since my observations, and the attitude of my servants when the princess came to the nursery, told me she was a woman of considerable temperament. By the time we finally left for Riyadh, Princess Moudi seemed her old self; even Fauza, who had walked silently behind her royal mistress since the divorce had been announced, started again to tell her jokes and sing merry snatches of songs. As usual, we traveled during the night, arriving at Riyadh in a downpour that marked the last gasp of the rainy season, but did little to cheer me about the move; nor did my first sight, through car windows streaked with rain, of the familiar black gates of the women's palace.

We had been moved from the purple apartment into the apartment of Princess Hessa, Moudi's sister who had moved downstairs. The promising sound of hammering and sawing came from a room being furnished for me with a king-size bed and fitted wardrobes, but for the time being (time being a very loose concept in Saudi Arabia!) my camp bed was back in the nursery. The nursery had two doors, one giving out into the corridor and the other to Princess Moudi's dressing room. Aware this time of well-meaning threats to Susu's health and harmony in Riyadh, I kept the corridor door locked, and pushed my bed next to the other. These isolationist tactics did not add to my popularity around the palace, but they did at least help me control Princess Moudi's disruptive late-night visits and prevent the more distantly related members of the family who came to call from bouncing the baby into hysteria, or from kissing him on his mouth.

"Princess Moudi, you hired a western nanny and now you must put up with it," I said, half joking. "My baby is to be kissed by Mama and Papa only!"

"Yes, yes, Rosemarie. You're the boss," she said in mock fear of my firmness. "Nobody kisses my child! But don't forget my mother and father. They too must kiss Susu."

Susu was growing up. He had begun to respond to stimuli. He followed motion with his eyes and I sensed curiosity awakening in him. At the souk I bought him the most beautiful blue pram in all of Saudi Arabia. (To be strictly honest, there were only three prams in the souk and a few more—one of them ours—in the ware-house. Poor Arab babies, from what I noticed in the streets, did not go out until they could manage on their own. Rich Arab babies went out in Cadillacs.) Our first stroll was on the balcony that ran the length of the building; we went up and back in the morning sun and the warm air that was much less humid than the atmos-phere of Jeddah. My biggest problem during those easygoing morn-ings was Mama Sarah, who had started coming to the nursery every morning at precisely ten o'clock to jiggle her grandson, poke him with her finger, and dislodge his breakfast. Since she paid not the least attention to my frowns, I developed the subterfuge of feeding Susu early and then taking him in his pram to the most distant corner of the balcony. I could hear Mama Sarah looking for us everywhere in the palace but it never occurred to her to look outside.

"Rosemarie, Rosemarie, Rosemarie! This cannot go on," Princess Moudi said one night during her nursery visit. I blushed because I knew what she meant. That very morning Susu and I had hidden in our favorite spot behind the air-conditioning vent on the bal-cony, and while I jiggled the pram up and down to keep the baby quiet, I heard Mama Sarah screaming in rage because she couldn't find us!

"Mama Sarah is his grandmother, Rosemarie. She is supposed to see the baby. Besides, when she can't find you in the mornings she gets cross with me. And that I cannot have. You understand, Rosemarie?"

Princess Moudi's tone had grown harder. My servant Esher looked up in alarm from some linen she had been pretending to sort. Another servant, fat and slovenly, who had accompanied Princess Moudi to the nursery gave me a look of inexplicable triumph, as if the small display of royal temper were her own doing.

"I understand, Princess Moudi," I said. "You know, I have only ever acted for Susu's well-being."

"I do know that, Rosemarie. In America I saw how everyone runs to do things for the baby, you know what I mean? Here, it is not like that. Here, the babies must please the grown-ups. Do you understand what I mean?"

I told the princess that I understood, but inside I promised Susu silently that just as he was born into the best of his own culture, so I would deliver to him as much as I could of the best of my own culture; and among those best things I did count the small, loving sacrifices we make eagerly to the happiness of our offspring.

Before she left, Princess Moudi asked if there was anything I needed; as usual, when the moment came, my mind went blank of all the urgent requests I really did have to make and the only thing I could think of was to ask her if I might be able to pursue my hobby of dressmaking. I knew there were sewing rooms on the floor above our own for sometimes in the still of the afternoon I had heard the whirring of machines. To my surprise and embarrassment, Princess Moudi did not grant me permission to use the sewing room but instead promised me a brand-new electric sewing machine of my own.

"Zuchia will get it for you tomorrow," she said. The fat servant cast me a look so full of malevolence, it made me gasp. When they had left, Esher, who had learned a few words of English and grudgingly given me a few of Arabic, made a face of disgust and all but spat on the floor where the fat Zuchia had been standing.

"Zuchia, bad! Bad!" she said. She rubbed her fingers in the universal sign for money. "Zuchia big thief!"

Be that as it may, it was a long time before I forgot the real hatred I had surprised in Zuchia's eyes.

The next day, Susu and I were going to visit Prince Mohammed for the first time in his own palace. This was a debut for Susu and a very special occasion, so I dressed him as well as I could from his Harrods wardrobe, though most of the clothes were still much too big. Even the blue babygrow I found that nearly fitted him had to have its cuffs turned up several times. I dabbed rose and sandalwood essence on his hair and stood by biting my tongue, while a servant held him over a small brazier where the rose-scented sandalwood was burning so the smoke impregnated his clothes, his skin, and, I dare say, his growing consciousness and his memory. To do Susu proud, I wore one of my long dresses. Princess Moudi had told me it did not matter if I wore sleeveless clothes inside the palaces or the cars.

"Only when you go to the souk, Rosemarie, don't forget to cover your arms or they will kill you," she told me, laughing. Although Prince Mohammed's palace was virtually across the palm-lined boulevard from ours, the prince and I had to go there in the cream-colored Cadillac. In Saudi Arabia, as I believe is the case in southern California, walking is unseemly for the rich. We passed a mosque and then in moments we were at the high, imposing walls of Prince Mohammed's palace. Just outside the gates stood a crowd of people; the women, in black, crouched against the wall like patient stones, the men milled around a pushcart where Pepsi-Cola was being sold. These were the people who wanted to be admitted to the prince's presence so they could air grievances and receive judgments; they gathered in the road every day and, as I heard later, nobody bothered to tell them whether or not Prince Mohammed was in residence. They often sat all day with no reward but hope itself.

Our car swept past them through the first set of gates. We were stopped twice inside by guards before we finally passed through the inner gates. Here, Susu and I were transported again to the magical atmosphere of Jeddah. The garden was awakening in the spring, buds were heavy on the trees and vines; early flowers were

already blooming. On one lawn, an arrogant peacock spread his
feathers and his crown for a harem of peahens. Near the main door
was a huge cage filled with gazelles who watched us pass, their eyes
swollen as if with homesickness.

"Oh, Susu," I whispered to the baby who lay placidly in my
arms, "when you are a big boy, how you are going to love to visit
your grandpa!"

Just inside the entrance hall were three glass cases, in each of
them a bird of prey, ignobly stuffed but sitting proudly; they must
have been favorite hunters of the prince. Opposite them was a traditional incense burner, a *mabkhara,* that stood almost six feet tall;
it was covered with brass sheeting and mirrored discs. The atmosphere was masculine, as if we had just entered the most exclusive
men's club in Saudi Arabia. The man who had greeted us and led
us into the palace, signaled me to wait while he informed the
prince of our arrival. Watched by the falcons' wild glass eyes, Susu
and I waited patiently for only a minute before the servant returned to usher me, with the baby in my arms, into the prince's reception room.

This was the world of men. I entered it for the first time since
my arrival in Saudi Arabia. I was struck immediately by the
difference in sound. Sometimes in the women's palace when the res-
idents were all gathered together, I heard their voices, high-pitched
and rising swiftly to shrillness, as if their words were pointed arrows
the women would hurl over the walls around us into the free air.
Here among the men, voices were low and made a murmur less
volatile, more confident and serene.

The air was hazy with smoke from incense burners that gave me
the feeling of important things taking place, as if I had entered a
boardroom thick with cigar smoke. The usual armchairs circled the
carpet, leaving a big empty space in the middle of the room which
a nudge from our guide indicated I was now expected to cross with
Susu, walking past ten or twelve men in rich robes toward Prince
Mohammed, who sat in pure white on a chair slightly elevated
above the others. After my weeks of isolation among the women,
the presence of so many men filled me with a nervousness not far

from awe. Prince Mohammed seemed more reserved and stern than
he had been in the women's palace until I put Susu into his arms;
then his face became radiant, tender, and loving. He looked at the
baby for a long time and then raised his head to look slowly around
the room with touching pride. When Prince Mohammed handed
the baby back to me I had to smile. Those who loved Susu auto-
matically found a friend in me, and I think Prince Mohammed understood my feelings because he gave me a friendly nod and as
close as dignity could come to a royal wink. Even Susu was happy
and had not so much as whimpered during the ten minutes he
spent in audience with his noble grandfather.

Although the princess did not speak of our visit, I heard her on
the telephone in her room talking to Prince Mohammed soon after
we had returned. Thanks to Esher I knew that *yupa* meant "father." Princess Moudi's voice when she spoke to Prince Mohammed was as I had never heard it before; it was young, respectful
yet cajoling. Without understanding precisely what she was saying,
I knew she was charming her father, flattering him, slipping in a
request for a favor and then surprising him with a little joke; in
other words, the princess was behaving as pretty, favorite daughters
do everywhere in the world when they are accustomed to getting
their own way and intend to continue doing so.

That night, Princess Moudi arrived in the nursery accompanied
by a girl whom I remembered from my first meeting with Prince
Mohammed.

"This is Princess Mishaal," Princess Moudi said, putting her arm
around the younger girl. "Mishaal is my little sister. No, no, not my
sister!"

She said something in Arabic and the young girl laughed; she
had the uninhibited giggle of a child. She was wearing one of Princess Moudi's nightgowns, a bright yellow creation that was so big
for her she had to keep it hitched up under her arm so as not to
stumble.

"Not my sister, no," Princess Moudi said. "I mean she is the
sister of my brother. No, no, no! Not the sister of my brother!" She
threw her arms into the air.

"Can you understand, Rosemarie?"

"I think Princess Mishaal must be your niece, Princess Moudi."
Princess Moudi spoke in Arabic. The younger girl made a face,
rolled her eyes to parody horror, and they both laughed at their
own jokes again.

"Mishaal loves to dance!" Princess Moudi said, and as if she had
understood the little princess clapped her hands and laughed.

For a moment she looked like an adorable child: innocent,
effervescent, and delightful.

"But at a loss in the world of grownups," I thought.

Princess Mishaal twirled around her aunt suddenly in a silly little
dance so the nightgown wrapped itself around her slender body;
then she stopped, breathless and laughing. As Princess Moudi
watched the girl I was surprised to see pass over her face the same
look of bewildered concern she wore when looking at her own son.
Princess Mishaal darted to the cot where her baby cousin slept and
leaned over him; she was still for a moment and I heard her sigh.
When she looked up, her big, dark eyes were puzzled, as if she had
just felt pain for the first time and didn't know what it was; but in
a flash she was back at her aunt's side, laughing again, and
prattling in Arabic. Princess Moudi put her arm around Mishaal
again, protectively it seemed to me.

"She had a baby inside her, you know, Rosemarie," Princess
Moudi said. "But she lost it after three months. You understand?
She danced too much." I nodded and mumbled something about
first pregnancies being problematical. The little princess watched
my mouth as if wonderstruck that it could make words; then she
looked at Princess Moudi with deep respect that her aunt could understand my gibberish.

"Her husband is in America," Princess Moudi said.

The young girl shook her head up and down. "America!" she
half-sang, as if it were a jingle. "America! America!" I heard her
laughing as the two princesses went down the corridor; it was like
the laugh of a child who had just been told that when she grows up
she will really, really, *really* be allowed to eat as many chocolates as
she wishes. "Susu," I whispered to the baby who slept, his thumb
tucked neatly into his mouth despite his mother's strictures against

it. "You have an adorable cousin! And when you're big enough, she will teach you how to dance."

Princess Moudi had said that Ahmed would bring me the English papers next time he brought her own papers to the palace. The evening after Princess Mishaal's visit to the nursery, I was handed a carrier bag with what must have been every newspaper printed in English for the past week anywhere in the world. Because Ahmed could not read English, I had twenty or thirty duplicates as well. There, in the women's palace of Riyadh behind high walls, to read of western heads of state, of strife, of strikes, of treachery, of Broadway flops, and West End hits it was as if I were reading the first piece of fiction to arrive from outer space. Fantastic stuff to be sure, but nothing that could affect the peculiar kind of chaos that made it so hard for a conscientious nanny to establish order and hygiene in her Saudi nursery. Let East and West shake fists at each other, but how on earth was I ever going to make Esher understand the use of a vacuum cleaner? Or the subtleties of water temperatures? Or the dangers of feather pillows in a baby's cot? Purdah has its own priorities, I was discovering. Nevertheless, I did feel a twinge of nostalgia when I looked at my favorite paper, the *Financial Times,* and saw that European Ferries were doing well. Admittedly, I was also wickedly satisfied to read about storms and cold weather in London. There was one piece of news that struck me to the quick and made me very annoyed indeed: pound sterling had been devalued. No more was I a well-paid nanny but, thanks to the vagaries of the British economy and the bad advice of Irene, I was suddenly a pauper. That was another grievance to add to my list which I filed mentally under "B" for "Bukra."

The next day Princess Moudi, wearing a peach silk negligee, arrived in the nursery late in the afternoon. She studied Susu, who was asleep, seriously for a while without making a move to touch him.

"Princess Moudi," I said without any preamble. "I have so far had precisely twenty-four hours off-duty. I am tired and overworked. I have not got anything like a self-contained flat . . ."

"We have not got 'self-contained flats,' " she said quickly. She drew herself up and narrowed her eyes. "This is not what Americans call a condominium or a block of flats. This is a royal palace!"

"Princess, I was promised a day off. And what about my weekends? I was to have one free every month . . ."

"Weekends? Weekends? Does *his* week end?" she said, gesturing toward the cot. "What is this about weekends?"

For reasons no doubt due to paranoia, ever since I had lost my way in the souk and Fauza had returned my passport, I had taken to hiding all my important documents in out-of-the-way places. Now I stood at my wardrobe with my back to Princess Moudi and, embarrassed, I fished inside the brim of a straw sunhat that I never wore.

It was there I kept my contract. In my own defense I can only say there was something in the air of the women's palace, in its very strangeness, and in the sulky faces of the palace servants, that made me uncharacteristically cautious.

"There!" I said, thrusting the document under her very nose.

"What is that?" she said, drawing back as if I had offered her a very old kipper.

"That," I said, "is my contract. You have a copy of it. It promises one weekend every month, it promises me a self-contained flat. It promises me a day off every week. It promises me the moon, Princess Moudi! And, so help me, you have signed it!"

She pushed the document away with the back of her hand. "I have never seen this . . . this . . . this paper in my whole, entire life!"

"Well, Princess Moudi," I said, "you signed it!"

Her eyes narrowed to slits that were orangeish in the light of the setting sun and her voice went shrill, like Mama Sarah's voice when she hunted fruitlessly for Susu and me.

"This is not my signature," she said. "That is no contract. That is a piece of paper, only a piece of paper. Now, I told you I would do anything for you. Pots, pans, baths, television, carpet sweepers! But you must do everything for Saud, my son. Everything. Do you understand? You must. You *must*. For no other reason are you here!"

My knees began to shake as they always do when I'm angry, and my own voice rose enough to entertain the servants who, I had no doubt were crouched, listening, on the other side of the door.

"I will do everything for Susu, but I'll do it because he is a baby, because he needs me and because I love him. You, in exchange, must give me my private room, give me my day off, give me my weekend monthly. You must. Because you hired me. I am employed by you. I am not a slave, Princess Moudi, nor will I ever be!"

She looked at me, her eyes suddenly wide in surprise.

"I have a choice," I said in a softer voice, having sensed that Susu was stirring in his sleep. "In my world, we have choices!" Head high, she swept from the room and left me trembling with anger and with fear that I would be torn from my dear baby and sent away before I had even heard his first word or seen him walk.

I sat on the edge of my bed, my head in my hands and burning tears banked behind my eyes. I was all by myself in that desert country. The only person who responded to me as a human being was a baby not yet two months old.

"For no other reason am I here," I whispered, remembering Princess Moudi's words. It was a reason that moved me and one I loved, but even my baby Susu could not stop me having rights of my own, among them a right apparently denied most palace servants and in a sense denied the princesses themselves: the right to call a piece of time all my own, to use it in a way for which I need account to nobody. I had other rights too; the right, for instance, to close a door and stand by myself in a space that was mine.

For me a piece of space and piece of time was freedom. Misery became righteous indignation that set me pacing back and forth in the gathering night. Susu awoke, screaming, as if he knew what had taken place. I changed him, fed him, and then rocked him in my arms and tried to explain why I might be leaving in the morning; why we would not take our walks along the balcony anymore or listen together to the morning call for prayer.

"It's a principle, Susu, even beyond the need I have for a little rest sometimes. I don't want to drift into slavery, Susu, do you understand?"

Susu blinked very seriously and I nuzzled him on my shoulder, his soft hair against my cheek, I rubbed his back and a little bubble of milky wind whispered near my ear.

"You see, Susu, as a slave I'd be no good to you at all."

I stroked his back and weighed his solid little body in my arms. It grew dark. For a little while Susu and I played with finger-puppets which he could follow with his eyes. I had wanted to hang a mobile over his cot to amuse him but the palace ceilings were too high. Then, I lay Susu down and sang him a lullaby in German until he was asleep.

"Oh Susu, Susu, how I'll miss you!"

A knock sounded at the door, I went to open it, expecting and hoping to find Princess Moudi. Instead, there stood a woman in a pink dress; she had long dark hair, she was short and although she looked to be in her early or mid-thirties, her figure was already becoming matronly. The most unusual thing in that palace where I saw no book but the ubiquitous Koran was that she wore glasses.

"I am Dr. Nabia," she said. "We met the first night when you arrived but I think you were too tired to remember me."

I did vaguely remember being introduced to Princess Moudi's gynecologist.

When she smiled, Dr. Nabia was as attractive as any woman in the palace.

"This is not a medical visit," she said in her excellent English. "Just a friendly one."

"At the moment, Dr. Nabia, I need a friend more than a doctor!" So as not to disturb Susu, we went into the adjoining room which was supposed to have been my own. Dr. Nabia looked around at the half-constructed bed, the sawdust on the floor.

"Bukra! Bukra . . ." I said, and she laughed softly.

"Look, I've had a long talk with Princess Moudi and I think I've helped her understand your position. I've tried to explain to her that you are in a way like me; that you are doing a skilled job and from what I've heard, Miss Buschow . . ."

"Rosemarie, please," I said.

She nodded but she did not suggest I use her own first-name and in fact during all our subsequent meetings I always used her title. Moreover, I used it with pleasure because I had the impression that

"Doctor" was a very noble title for a middle-eastern woman to obtain.

"Rosemarie . . ." she said shyly. "Well, Rosemarie, from what I can gather you are doing your job very well. Susu is thriving, I think?"

I nodded.

"So the princess has asked me if you would consider this proposition: instead of leaving the baby for a day at a time, would you be willing to take off every day from eleven in the morning until three in the afternoon? One other thing, Rosemarie," Dr. Nabia said, as I was considering, "I speak now as a friend and, maybe a little, as a doctor too. You are a western woman and you may find life in the women's palace unbearably claustrophobic. In the long run I think a daily break will refresh you more than a weekly one."

She had put her point very well in dignified, slightly stilted English, and I agreed to her proposal. Then we chatted pleasantly for a little while about London, a city she knew well.

"Dr. Nabia, will you tell me something. Why has Princess Moudi divorced her husband?" I asked at last.

"You know, Rosemarie, I am in a position of confidence," she said. "I must continue to earn that confidence with my discretion."

She smiled at me.

"I am rather an old-fashioned person," she added. In all our talks to come, Dr. Nabia never once gave me a piece of gossip or even showed a temptation to. I admired her reticence—but sometimes I regretted it!

Just as Dr. Nabia promised before leaving me that night to talk to the princess, Fauza was sent to fetch me the very next morning at eleven o'clock. Ahmed drove us both to the Al Yamama Hotel where there was a swimming pool. I stood by while Fauza, acting as my treasurer, paid the membership fee of £150 and I was delighted to see when I filled in my application form that I was number one for 1976! I had worn my swimsuit under my long dress, and when Fauza, accompanied by Ahmed took me to inspect the pool, I could not resist peeling off my dress and diving straight in. I'm a strong swimmer, and I had swum practically the length of the pool underwater when I surfaced to look back at Fauza and

Ahmed crouching by the pool where I had dived in, searching wildly for me. It may have been my imagination, but I fancied they both regarded me with a little more respect after that exploit. Arab men are sometimes champion swimmers on the international scene, but the women are severely landbound.

Once again, as it became clear we were going to stay in Riyadh for some time, I had to re-equip our living quarters, even installing a small kitchen. I had begun to develop aches where I'd never even known there were supposed to be muscles; this was the result of taking all my meals from the floor. I decided I had to have a table and one or two chairs for my own room which had been finished at last, soon after Dr. Nabia's visit. Oddly enough, a simple chair and table turned out to be the most difficult purchase to make in the fashionable Riyadh furniture shops where the customers were too rich to be bothered with paltry purchases and bought everything by the roomful!

"Okay, good, good," said the young Arab salesman in his smattering of English. Fauza had finally persuaded him to break up a dining-room suite. "Okay. Good. Six hundred riyals, for you." The price, around £100 at the exchange rate then, was grossly inflated, but that wasn't unusual in the shops of Riyadh, so I turned to Fauza, my treasurer on these expeditions, for the money. To my surprise her comical face was drawn into a frown. She shook her head firmly, turned, and started to the door.

"Fauza! Fauza!" I called, but she paid no attention. Even the folds of her black abaya looked immovable. I shrugged at the young man and, feeling rather silly, I trotted behind Fauza.

"Fauza, what is it? What's wrong?" I asked but she hissed at me through her teeth. Just as her small, dark hand reached out for the door handle, the salesman appeared suddenly behind us.

"Five hundred and fifty riyals," he said to me. "Sure and final!"

"Well, I don't know . . ." I replied.

Fauza's severity had relaxed a mere fraction. She turned from the door and spoke a few words; the gist, I understood, was an offer of three hundred riyals. The young man's jaw dropped. Now it was his turn to walk away, purposefully, toward the back of the shop.

"But, Fauza, I really need . . ." I began, but again she replied with a little hiss.

This time Fauza actually had the door open before the salesman reappeared. There was no longer any pretense that I was a contributing party to the transaction. He spoke rapidly to Fauza in a moving tone, possibly about the amount of bread it took to feed his children; then he quoted another price in a way that told us this was absolutely his final offer.

"Five hundred riyals. Sure. Final. For you," he said in English. Fauza closed the door and half-turned from it toward the salesman; somehow she let her posture hint at the slightest possibility of interest. Then she quoted a price a lot lower than the one suggested by the young man; I could be sure of that, because from under his mustache emerged a strange moan like one that might be made by a coward catching sight of the dentist's drill. Then he spun on his heel and walked away from us.

"Oh, Fauza . . . don't you think . . ."

Fauza was magnificent. Her eyes flashed, she drew herself up so she nearly reached my shoulder, and she gave her robe a regal snap that Princess Moudi herself could have envied as she turned, intending this time, I was convinced, to walk out without making the purchase I so badly needed. I looked beseechingly at the young man who had stopped his march to the rear of the shop, and was facing us. He too held his head high, but there was a wilt to his mustache, a nearly imperceptible tightening of his mouth, that had not been there before.

"It's Fauza's game!" I thought.

"For you," the young man said. His head dropped, he sighed. "For you, four hundred riyals. Sure. Final."

Fauza turned from the door and gave him a sparkling smile. The sale was concluded. She smiled all the way home and once or twice laughed aloud under her veil, rehearsing, I guessed, the story she was going to tell Princess Moudi.

The princess continued to summon doctors to the palace whenever she heard Susu hiccup, a practice that ended at least temporarily one afternoon when one of the doctors exploded in anger.

"I have not got time to come all the way out here to examine a perfectly healthy baby. My surgery is full of patients who are really sick!"

"The princess asked if you would wait until she is dressed. She wants to talk to you . . ." I said, but the doctor exploded.

"Certainly not! What does she think I am? This child is fit and well, which is a lot more than I can say for a hundred other children in my care!"

At last, after the doctor had stormed out, I was able to persuade a nearly contrite Princess Moudi that we should register Susu as an outpatient at the King Faisal Hospital. To my surprise, Princess Moudi had no idea how such an undertaking was accomplished, nor did anyone else in that palace full of divorced and single women have any more practical knowledge about the workings of a big hospital than they would have done about a blown fuse or a leaky drainpipe. It was only when Princess Moudi had consulted her married half sister, Noave, who lived in a palatial home of her own, but with a husband and children, that we found out how to register Susu and also discovered that even for the grandson of Prince Mohammed, there would be a long waiting period. When Susu and I did begin to avail ourselves of the hospital facilities we never once saw the same pediatrician twice or were given any sort of preferential treatment. In medicine, at least, equality prevails in Saudi Arabia. Maybe that's why rich Saudis choose to come West for medical consultation.

The princess made some innovations in our nursery. She finally permitted me to give Susu a pacifier and she stopped complaining whenever she saw him with his thumb in his mouth.

"When I was a baby," she said, watching her son make a meal of his new pacifier, "the slaves used to tie my arms down so I couldn't suck my finger."

Once more I was struck by how much poverty of understanding can accompany masses of wealth.

Having given in on the battle of the pacifier, the princess reasserted her authority by sending the servants to the nursery to turn Susu's bed so his head would always be toward Mecca. She gave instructions too that a Koran should be placed in his bed and there, as everywhere else, nothing must ever lie on top of the Holy Book.

In fact, this superstition was so rigorously upheld in the palace that I still get very nervous if one of my guests inadvertently rests anything at all, even an elbow, on top of my own Koran!

"There is a small line between superstition and faith," Dr. Nabia said on one of her visits to my quarters. "Unfortunately, the confusion is particularly prevalent among the uneducated and in this country at least that means among women."

I asked Dr. Nabia if she thought Princess Moudi would like Susu to say prayers at night when he was big enough. I was recalling how grown-up and important it used to make me feel when I was little to enter into my nightly dealings with God and present to Him my list of loved ones for his blessing.

"Susu will not begin to learn the faith until he is seven," Dr. Nabia said. "What would be the point? Allah does not want prayers without true understanding. When Susu is seven, the men will teach him the Koran and how to pray. That isn't your job, Rosemarie. After all, you're a Christian and this is a Muslim household. He must learn about Allah from his own people as you learned from yours. Never try to instruct him. You know, Mohammed tells us that Allah wants each person to worship in his own way. You must respect our way as we do yours. But we will never share your way because we do not think it is the right way. Fortunately, Rosemarie, people can disagree and still respect each other. Isn't that so?"

I thought about my nightly prayers and our family Sunday mornings at church; those and holidays were the spiritual high spots of a typical Christian family in the West; but the faith of Islam, I was beginning to see, like the scent of sandalwood, and like a code of justice I did not yet understand, permeated the very fiber of Arabian life.

One evening, for the first time since my arrival, Princess Moudi invited me to dine with her in the room where I had taken my first meal. I dressed for this occasion in my favorite long dress which I had made myself in London. My hostess, however, was in a silk nightgown and peignoir that glowed like mother-of-pearl. Jawahir wore a purple nightgown and matching peignoir; the color suited her aristocratic beauty although I found her fixation for it peculiar, especially in one so young. Jawahir had keen, intelligent eyes and it was apparent even to me that she found life among her divorced and single female relatives excruciatingly boring and it was the pain of that boredom that made her seem aloof and even a trifle arrogant. The eldest of the unmarried royal princesses, Princess Hessa, was of Mama Sarah's temperament and preferred to live in the traditional way. She ate in her own apartment next to Mama Sarah's, appearing infrequently among her frivolous kinswomen and always, when she did appear, modestly dressed with arms covered from shoulder to wrist. Princess Mishaal had joined us again and apparently had the permission of her mother, with whom she lived in a neighboring palace, to spend the night for she too was wearing a nightgown, an orange one of her Aunt Moudi's that made her look charming and fragile. As well as the royal women, favorite servants were at the table; some I did not know, but I recognized Fauza, the hard bargainer, and fat Zuchia who eyed me balefully and made a slight gesture toward me with her head that managed in a subtle way to be offensive. We sat around a table set in the western style with exquisite china. I nearly laughed out loud when I saw that the cutlery was of gold.

"Next time somebody asks me about the knives and forks," I thought, "I won't be at loss for words!"

Despite the splendid settings, when the food arrived on big trays the servants carried on their heads, it was the usual Riyadh fare: greasy, highly spiced, and gone stone cold because of the distance between the kitchen, in the courtyard, and the dining room. Nobody ate much, but Princess Moudi ate barely anything, merely pushing a morsel of chicken from one side of her plate to the other. She seemed detached from the lively chatter at the table and even Mishaal could not draw her into conversation. For the first time I saw her as one woman does another, and I realized that it was deeply humiliating for her to return, divorced and with a young child, to her mother's palace where she became a subject for pity or gossip. I wanted to make an overture of friendship toward her because I sensed it was as a friend and ally she had invited me to dinner, but it was she who spoke first.

"Are you happy, Rosemarie? You have everything you need?"

"Yes, Princess Moudi," I said. "Thank you."

"Tell me, Rosemarie, are you enjoying your new sewing machine?"

I was surprised that she had remembered my request.

"I'm sure I will enjoy it, Princess Moudi," I said, "when it arrives. I haven't received it yet."

Across from me, Zuchia was listening intently as if she could by sheer force of will understand English.

"Not arrived? I don't understand," Princess Moudi said. She turned to Zuchia and I didn't need to understand Arabic to know the servant was being roundly ticked off for not having bought me the sewing machine, as ordered. While her mistress railed at her, Zuchia's fat fingers closed on the handle of her knife and the expression in her eyes told me that she longed to plunge it into my heart.

I did not join the princesses after dinner in the drawing room where they sat on low Arabian chairs listening to music and watching television. Instead, I went back to the nursery to tidy up and to tuck Susu's blanket back around him from the heap he made of it at the bottom of his cot. Then, as I almost always did before retiring, I stepped from the women's palace into the vast night. During the day, from my balcony I could see over the wall out to an expanse of hot, tan sand, past the neighboring compound and a few greenish trees, until there was not more to see but the desert. At night, however, the very nature of Arabia changes from sand to velvet, oddly cool; from brass to silver. The midnight sky was thrown to the horizon where I could distinguish heavens from earth only because there the spray of stars stopped. Were I to have walked into the desert and to the end of night, that horizon would remain unchanging in front of me so I could not know I was moving at all or that time was passing; only the stars would tumble slowly in space over my head, dancing to a music that we do not hear in western cities. I still close my eyes and think how small all other nights on earth must seem to me after the Arabian night-sky that centuries ago inspired the creation of astronomy, and centuries from now will still dance, after science, art, and love are gone.

chapter 6

I was starting to see everything with an added dimension: that palm tree, this orange, that Koran bound in dark blue velvet, were objects I held or looked at but they were also objects Susu would see one day and I wondered what he would make of them. Susu's world was growing around him and quite soon it would burst free of the nursery to include his family, the servants, even the big black tomcat who paraded his harem through the palace and its grounds. Frequently, out of loneliness and out of love, I talked to Susu as if he were already grown-up and able to understand . . .

"Look! Susu, look!" I said, holding him up in my arms as we stood on the balcony at dusk. "The feathered fireworks have begun!"

As always, the birds who had taken shelter from the heat of the day in chinks, drainpipes, knotholes, and other shady corners, flew out to feed on insects in the cool time when the sun had just set and night had not quite descended. Taken singly, any one of those small brown birds was no more to the sky than a beetle is to the earth. But en masse, in the delirium of freedom and hunger, they put on a show that never stopped delighting me, as one day I knew it would delight Susu. As if the pearly sky were an unmarked scroll, the birds wrote huge circles on it in a script that swooped and dived and made a pattern to be read by anyone who understood their language. Suddenly, a group of them would mass and drive a wedge straight across my field of vision, then turn and come so close to the ground I was sure they must drive themselves, beak first, into the earth; but instead they rose straight up, broke ranks to scatter like drops of ink, before meeting in a new formation. Sometimes one bird would cry out in excitement—a thin, distant sound—but usually they were silent in pursuit of their evening meal.

"Oh, Susu, Susu, what a wonderful country you come from! And how good it is to look around again and see so much beauty. Sometimes, Susu, sorrow makes grown-ups turn to stone; it makes them blind. May you never know that, Susu!"

I held him up so his face was in front of mine. In his big eyes were stars of reflected light from lamps being lit in the palace behind us, and he made baby sounds that, like the skywriting of the birds, seemed to be a language just beyond the edge of my comprehension.

Dr. Nabia had been right. In the long run, a few hours off every day was worth more to me than one full day a week would have been. If the princesses were isolated in the women's palace, I was doubly isolated; not only was I enclosed behind walls but I was also isolated by my ignorance of the language. It was like being deaf and dumb except that I could hear the laughter, not the joke.

As spring drew on, I began to understand the nature of heat as Westerners never know it; it was as if Riyadh sat on a plate in the middle of a big oven and the oven was in the middle of a bigger oven so whenever the door was opened, the wind that entered was even hotter than the air within. The palace was fully air-conditioned of course, but despite its sophisticated design, the machinery brought in sand that sifted into corners of the marble stairs where it would be collected by the servants only to reappear as a constant reminder of the patient desert. From one window in my room I could look out over Riyadh and watch it baking in the sun, its houses dust-colored as if they had grown like rock formations out of the desert itself. When I ran down to the car to take me to the Al Yamama swimming pool, my sandals raised puffs of dust and sand. As my driver threaded through the eternal traffic jams, people pushed and shouted, in a hurry to get their business done before the midday heat drove them to take shelter in a long siesta. Where there were no buildings or people, there were bulldozers creating new buildings for yet more people. In those moments from the back seat of the palace car I felt I was in a frontier town that was pushing its boundaries forward into the desert.

The swimming pool was salvation. It quenched my skin's thirst for relief from the heat and dust, while appeasing my hunger for a little western conversation. The pool was big, the water was not too highly chlorinated and it was kept very clean thanks to the offices of an Egyptian attendant who cleaned the dead flies from the surface and did his best to spray the air clear of their living relatives. I have never been water-shy, not since the day a neighbor's son in Germany pushed me into the deep water of a lake and I learned I could swim; but, as everyone is, I am sometimes a little shy of strangers. On my early trips to the pool I was trapped in the paradox of wanting to talk to Europeans yet feeling too detached because of my palace experience to enter into easy conversation. A touch of purdah had crept into my personality. I selected a palm tree in a corner to give me necessary shade and to protect me from unsolicited company. In other lands I had been asked by strangers if they could share my beach umbrella. There were umbrellas around the pool, but it was unlikely I would be asked to share a palm tree.

Although I am a good swimmer, on my first visits to the pool I waited until the attention I attracted from a hard core of foreigners subsided and then, against my own inclination to dive straight into the water, I slipped in gently, feet first, and joined the few women, mainly Americans in rubber swimming caps decorated with plastic flowers, who were paddling doggedly from one side of the pool to the other. Only when I was sure nobody was any longer interested in me, did I strike out in an over-arm crawl. Then it was back to my palm tree to bask in the sun as long as I could stand it before moving to the shade or back into the pool. The attendant, having probably checked my credentials on the registration card, was soon careful to see that a chaise longue always awaited me under the palm. There I lay on my stomach and through half-closed eyes I watched life in that luxurious oasis.

A few Arab men came to the pool with their children and then sat, heavily robed, watching their little ones splash. For the most

part, only European adults swam and a few Lebanese women.
Therefore, I was surprised one day to see a young Arab appear in
his robes and enter one of the changing rooms. He emerged in a
swimsuit, dived into the pool, and swam its length several times
with a quick, strong stroke.

"Educated in the West," I thought, as the young man pulled
himself out of the pool and stood with his head back, drying off in
the sun. I closed my eyes and when I opened them again I saw two
women, shrouded in their abayas, standing inside the entrance to
the pool. The entrance had been ingeniously designed so it was impossible for anyone to see into the pool or the area around it, without actually passing through the gate and past the scrutiny of the
attendant. The women stood like timid forest animals, ready to run
at the first snap of a twig. My palace experience told me that the
woman standing a few paces in front was the mistress and the
other, stooping a little in her drapery, was the servant. The young
Arab, who had been seated at a table between me and the entrance,
saw the two women and rose immediately to his feet; as he did, the
taller woman started toward him a few paces, then stopped suddenly and spoke to her servant, who sat awkwardly in a chair near
the entrance—it was apparent to me she would have preferred to
crouch on the ground—where she could watch the gate for any intruders who might recognize her mistress or the man she was meeting. Her mistress walked to the young man's table and sat in the
chair across from him, facing me. She was wearing a sheer veil and
from my vantage point I could see that she was exquisitely beautiful. I didn't need to understand a word to know the couple were
having the intense kind of conversation that takes place between
lovers who cannot meet easily or often. The young woman turned
her head away and to one side while the man spoke; then she
raised her eyes to his and a current passed between the two as hot
as any breeze from the desert. She looked away quickly, but let her
hand rest on the tabletop where he covered it for a moment with
his hand. They talked some more, the woman glancing frequently
behind to the gate where her watchdog sat. After a short while the
young couple rose; I fancied her almond-shaped eyes above the veil

were filled with tears as her servant got up to follow her out. The young man returned to the changing room, emerged in his robes, and left the pool. I never saw them again. I knew I had seen something rare, but I did not know how very dangerous such a meeting could have been.

Among the foreigners whose faces became familiar to me was an elderly woman with blue-rinsed hair who used to go into the pool twice between eleven and two, swim once each time from shallow to deep end, then back again, carefully holding her head straight up out of the water so she resembled a large tortoise. When she was not making this ritualistic crossing of the Al Yamama pool, she sat in a corner of the enclosure with a group who were there almost every day, speaking English in loud tones and mostly complaining about the heat. One day instead of rejoining this group after her dip, the blue-haired woman detoured past my palm; she stopped and stood at the foot of my chaise longue.

"Hot, isn't it?"

"Rather," I replied.

"Rather, yes. Rather hot," she said, and walked away, thus ending the first exchange I had made with a foreigner in English since my arrival in Saudi. The next day she stopped again.

"I think it's hotter today than yesterday."

"Yes, I think you're right," I told her.

"In the summer it will be hotter still," she said. "Quite unbearably hot, actually."

"I suppose so," I told her.

"Terribly hot place, Riyadh."

"Where do you come from?" I asked, noticing a hint of an accent. She drew herself up.

"England, of course," she said, and walked away, leaving me feeling that I had committed a *faux pas*. The following morning she was accompanied by a man of about her own age, sixty or so. He was plump, sleek, and perfectly bald but with a drooping white mustache. He swam the length of the pool underwater and when he surfaced near me at the deep end, he snorted, for all the world like a walrus, as his wife paddled slowly behind him, her head stiff and high. This time both of them stopped at the foot of my chaise longue.

"My husband," she said to me. "Trevor Smythe."

Somewhat taken aback, I sat up and put out my hand.

"Rosemarie Buschow."

Close up, Mr. Smythe still looked like an amiable walrus.

"Can I get you a drink, Miss Buschow?" he asked me in a very proper English accent. "A gin and tonic? A whisky and soda? A nice glass of chilled champagne?"

If a walrus could laugh, it would laugh just the way Mr. Smythe did. I was to learn that he had made a favorite joke of the poolside community, since it was well-known that the little outdoor bar served only Evian water, Pepsi-Cola, and orange juice.

"A pleasure to have met you, Miss Buschow," he said, as if we had just taken tea together, and ambled off to rejoin the others in their corner. His wife stayed behind and pulled a deckchair into the shade of my tree.

"Insufferably hot today," she said.

"Indeed."

"A little less than yesterday, I think."

"Perhaps."

"My husband teaches English," Mrs. Smythe said, "at the university of Riyadh. They all teach there"—nodding toward the group in the corner. "They're English, most of them. Of course."

"Of course," I said.

There was a pause. A fly landed on the end of Mrs. Smythe's nose and she brushed it off.

"Well, what are you doing in Saudi Arabia?" she asked, sounding annoyed that I hadn't volunteered the information. I told her that I was a nanny in the household of Prince Mohammed's daughter, Princess Moudi. As I spoke, I noticed all the foreign teachers were watching us expectantly.

"And they let you out!" Mrs. Smythe said. "There are other foreign nannies in Riyadh of course, but you'll never see *them* outside. Certainly not at a swimming pool."

"Nobody is going to lock *me* up, Mrs. Smythe!"

"Tell me, is it true that . . ."

"Yes," I said quickly. "Real gold."

"Fancy that!" She shook her head and three flies were dislodged from her blue hair; they circled and landed again in different spots.

"I've heard that Prince Mohammed is absolutely ferocious. A tyrant! I've heard he has an ungovernable temper and that's why he couldn't be King."

I thought of the kindly grandfather and of the love he so patently felt for Susu.

"He has always been kind to me," I said.

Mrs. Smythe pulled her deckchair closer.

"I've heard there's been another divorce in the royal household. I've heard Princess Moudi has left that playboy she married: one of the dead King Saud's sons, I believe. Her own first cousin. She left him once before, when she was pregnant."

I remembered Dr. Nabia's dignity and emulated it with difficulty.

"Princess Moudi is living in the women's palace," I said. "Prince Abdul is traveling abroad, I believe."

Normally, I wouldn't have been patient with Mrs. Smythe's avid curiosity, but something about her blue hair and her proud tortoise head when she swam made me take stock of how terribly difficult life must be for the wives of the foreign community in Saudi Arabia where women are not even permitted to drive cars. The foreign women too lived behind a veil, dependent upon their menfolk to take them shopping, take them to the pool, and take them to the Lebanese hairdressers for their blue rinses.

"Where do you come from, Mrs. Smythe?" I asked, eager to dislodge her interest from the royal family.

"We come from Surrey."

She squinted at the water, bright as melted silver in the sun. She brushed another fly from her nose.

"Surrey," she said again softly.

"It's lovely there in the spring," I said, remembering a field of daffodils where Stephen and I had once taken a picnic; was it in Surrey?

"The daffs must be finished now," she said, as if she had read my mind. "But the lilacs will be coming out soon. Lilac is so heavy on the branch after the rain. They like a little acid in the soil, you know." She sighed. "A little mulch."

"Do they? I'm afraid I lived in London. I did have a window box, though. I used to grow nasturtiums."

"Ah yes, London!" Mrs. Smythe said. She clasped her hands under her chin. "Did you have any trouble with aphids, Miss Buschow? I always found London rather bad for aphids."

As the great waves of eastern heat beat down on me, my throat ached suddenly for England's cold, wet spring.

"But you aren't English, are you Mrs. Smythe?"

"No, no," she said. "I'm a Swede."

Thereafter, I often stopped to chat with the Smythes. I could tell from the curious glances the others gave me that Mrs. Smythe had reported to them about my job and I knew they wanted me to join their group, but I wasn't tempted. They had their chairs, their corner by the pool, their twelve o'clock orange juice, their one o'clock dip; they were the Riyadh foreign establishment, or part of it, and I preferred to maintain my privacy and to keep my air of mystery.

Admittedly, my heavy-lidded air of mystery was due in part to sheer fatigue. Despite the riches of my employers, life in the women's palace was chaos. Meals arrived cold and at odd times, cars turned up an hour after they had been ordered—or sometimes not at all—servants were sluggish and surly during the day, and the princesses never appeared until nightfall; visits to the nursery were impromptu and usually very late when eager aunties thought nothing of waking the sleepy baby, despite his roars of anger. The image of my servant, Esher, sweeping the dust from one corner of the nursery to the other while the vacuum cleaner lay unused in a corner, became for me an image of the disorganization in which I found myself. It often seemed to me that of all the inhabitants of the palace, I was the only one burdened with a sense of responsibility. I, and Mama Sarah.

Although she was not always visible, Mama Sarah's presence was everywhere. Her responsibility was to the traditions of Islam, to

Allah, and to the world of men; it was her responsibility to see that
the old ways, that Allah, that men, were always honored by the behavior of the women in her charge. So strong was the aura of
Mama Sarah in the palace that once when I heard an unearthly
voice from the corridor below ours calling "Maa-Maa," I had the
whimsical thought that, in the ancient magical way, she had summoned up a flying creature to take her into the desert. In more
ways than one, I was right. When I went out and peered down,
there on the precious marble before Mama Sarah's door, calling
"Maa-Maa," was a goat who had stumbled into the air-conditioned
palace. As for soaring magically to the dunes and oases, I learned
that sometimes Mama Sarah was seized by a desire as strong and as
basic as the sensual desires she feared in her daughters; when that
call came, she rose before dawn and retreated far beyond the
boundaries of Riyadh, out of sight of the city, to spend a day or
two with only a few servants under a tent on her beloved desert.
Mama Sarah went, I must add, in an air-conditioned limousine.
Even so, her pilgrimages had more authenticity than those of the
Arabian princes who amuse and entertain guests sometimes not so
much by going to meet the desert as by going to defeat it with
every urban comfort that can be transported in a fleet of vans and
cars.

It had been a difficult morning. Breakfast had come two hours late
and inedible, Esher had misplaced all the nappy pins, Susu had
tried to eat his Koran, Ahmed had forgotten to pick me up for my
free hours at the Al Yamama, and, not for the first time, I'd had to
travel to the hotel in the palace delivery van. Ahmed was mar-
ginally more reliable about picking me up at the pool, probably because then he had a chance to stand at the entrance and ogle female flesh while I gathered up my possessions. Still, he was often
late and that was worrying because it meant Susu could awake and
not find me: his one anchor in a sea of disorder. The air was heavy
and hot. I was in a bad temper.

    "Why, hi there!" a woman's voice said. "You look absolutely fan-
tastic! Could this suntanned glamourpuss be the same pale flower I
met on the plane?"

I opened my eyes and leaning over me I saw the friendly, clever face of the American woman, Peggy, from Seattle. Had it been my oldest friend, had it been Jennifer herself, I couldn't have responded with more delighted surprise.

"I can't believe it! I can't believe it! What are you doing here?"

"Hey, honey, cool it!" she said, but she was obviously pleased at my excitement. "Hell, there are only about one and a half places in Riyadh to go, and the How's-Your-Mama Pool is one of them!"

She sat down and looked at me with her head to one side. She took off her sunglasses; the lenses were blue and there were tiny daisies at each corner of the frame; in the sun I saw the laugh wrinkles at the corners of her gray eyes and pure white streaks growing into her dark blond hair.

"Lonely, huh?" Peggy asked.

I considered my own feelings carefully.

"No, not lonely exactly; sort of bottled up."

"So, unbottle. Talk to me," Peggy said.

I took her at her word and for perhaps half an hour solid I talked; I told her about the palace, about Princess Moudi's sudden divorce, about Dr. Nabia. I told her about Prince Mohammed and his stuffed falcons. I told her about the birds swarming at dusk, the goat on the landing, the black tomcat, Mama Sarah, and the beautiful garden of Jeddah. I told her about Susu, about his first smile, about the way he was growing and beginning to fit some of his elegant clothes, about how he stopped crying when he saw me and then, when I picked him up, about the sigh of sheer contentment he breathed into my ear. Peggy was the perfect audience; she listened with silent enthusiasm, asking enough questions to let me know that she was paying attention. Only when she saw I had talked myself out for the moment, did she tell me how her husband had recently been occupied making arrangements for the flying visit of one of his company's top executives to Saudi Arabia. These VIP visits were nightmares for the resident company men who had to create some semblance of smooth-running efficiency out of the turmoil and procrastination that marked Saudi's day-to-day business affairs.

"I call it bringing Musak to the desert. Americans seem to need

it, but who knows? Maybe the natives are better off without it." Be
that as it may, Peggy's husband accomplished the feat with the help
of other old Saudi hands. The VIPs' plane arrived on time at
Riyadh Airport.

"Miracle number one," Peggy said. "Because you do know what
we call the national airline, don't you? 'Inshallah Airline.' God
willing you get there on time, God willing you get there at all; God
willing your luggage gets there too!"

The red carpet unrolled without a wrinkle. The VIP and his luggage passed through immigration with no trouble, the hired limousine was actually where it was supposed to be—and when; the VIP
got to all his meetings on time and thanks to Peggy's husband he
also got out of his meetings on time, a much more unusual accomplishment, demanding great tact.

"Walter—that's my husband—was a gibbering idiot at the end of
it, but the visit went like butter. There weren't any power failures,
the bigwig didn't get stuck even once in the hotel elevator. That, as
you know, was another miracle. He didn't get caught in one gigantic traffic jam, either. And that's more than a miracle! That's a
whole new chapter of Genesis!"

After the VIP left, Peggy's husband congratulated himself on his
accomplishment and waited for accolades from the home office. Six
weeks later, the letter arrived from America.

"It would have come much sooner," Peggy said, "but the post-
man mislaid it for a while and then he couldn't find Walter."

The VIP thanked his resident for a really productive visit, but he
added that he never again wanted to hear any of his American resi-
dents in Arabia utter one word of complaint about slow deliveries,
lost deliveries, incomplete deliveries, traffic jams, power failures, or
any other petty annoyances, since he had seen for himself the admirable Saudi efficiency.

"Efficiency-wise," he actually wrote, "we Americans might have
something to learn from the Saudis!"

"Anyhow," Peggy said, when we had stopped chuckling,
"that's all finished now. Walter's been posted back home. I'm
over here to help him pack up. We're leaving tomorrow. I only
hope living together doesn't ruin our marriage!"

I felt a stab of regret that this happy meeting was to be so brief, and to be our last.

"Peggy, I wish I'd seen you before," I complained. "Where have you been keeping yourself?"

Peggy looked puzzled.

"Keeping myself? Honey, I just got here a few days ago. I've been back to the States since we met. In case you don't know, Rosemarie, you've been in Saudi Arabia damn near three months!" She smiled at the expression on my face. "They are treating you well, aren't they?" she said. I surprised a flicker of concern in her eyes. I nodded. "Good," she said. "You see, I told you you'd have a wonderful time. Well, not actually wonderful-wonderful, if you know what I mean. Wonderful in a manner of speaking."

"They treat me well," I said. "And yet . . ."

I stopped, unable to explain how dense my isolation within the palace felt to me sometimes, and how inexplicable I found so much that went on around me, how even my own behavior confused me: why, for example, had I taken to hiding my papers with such paranoid caution? Why had I shouted at Esher that very morning in a rage such as I had rarely, if ever, expressed before in my life? And why did I still feel that I was being tested and judged, that only Susu really accepted me?

"Let me tell you something, honey," Peggy said. "Remember this, Rosemarie, an Arab tourist in Harrods is one person, but an Arab at home is an altogether other can of oil. A prince, a pauper, and the women too, whatever an Arab is, he lives at home by a code I'm not sure any of us Westerners has ever completely understood. At home, the Arab plays his cards real close to his chest. His most powerful principles, his plans, and his emotions are a secret from outsiders. Don't even try to understand everything about life here. Don't ever try to change anything, for God's sake; and do your best not to criticize. Accept. Just accept, Rosemarie, if you want to stay sane. Okay?"

It was high noon. Peggy and I watched the pool attendant. As he did every day at this hour, the young man switched off his blaring transistor radio, then, having covered his bare shoulders and head with a fresh white towel, he went to the corner of the enclosure facing Mecca; there, he knelt and he prayed.

"I've learned about myself, Peggy," I said. "I'm pretty stubborn. If I come up against something I'm sure is wrong, I cannot accept it. Try as I might, I simply can't. So far, nothing here has offended me deeply although I'm busy every day struggling to make some order out of chaos. And I do respect their faith a lot, Peggy. I admire it."

"Yes, me too," she said. "But I've got to warn you, Rosemarie, where you find faith you also find judgment and where faith is strong, judgment can be pretty damned harsh. Every coin has two sides, like my wise old mama used to say. The other side of piety has been known to be cruelty. Or, at least what those of us who are less pious would call cruel. Hey!" she said suddenly. She pointed to a fly that had landed on her arm and was marching from freckle to freckle. "You know what that is? That, Rosemarie, is the national bird of Saudi Arabia!"

I laughed so hard the English teachers stopped talking to turn in my direction, and while I laughed I was remembering how good it felt to laugh with a friend.

Peggy and I said our farewells and I left the pool with her address in my bag—"in case you're ever passing Seattle!" she had said. She looked thoughtful, then smiled, "most people do pass Seattle eventually; they usually pass by it, or over it."

Ahmed was in a surly mood and that meant a rough ride home with many "shortcuts" off the main roads, across rutted, sandy fields where it was hard to imagine any cream-colored Cadillac had ever been seen before. To increase the hazards of Ahmed's temper, just as I entered the back seat of the car the sky split like an overripe melon and down came a sheet of warm rain that turned the hotel parking lot immediately into a yellow lake set in the center of the yellow sea that Riyadh had become within seconds of the deluge. As swiftly as the rain had begun it ended and the sun came out, making the road in front of us virtually steam in its heat. Because of the inefficiency of the sewer system, it was a long time after these flash downpours before the puddles dried—first, into traps of mud and then into familiar dusty sand. In the meantime, Ahmed could indulge in a favorite national sport, as dangerous as bullfighting, as competitive as football, as essentially silly as golf. In front of us was a red Mercedes that, I knew, Ahmed would find an irresistible opponent. Not only was it a car of our own class but it was so new I thought I could see the sales sticker still on its rear window. I knew what was coming, but before I could object or do more than brace myself and close my eyes, Ahmed had stepped on the accelerator, zoomed past the Mercedes and managed in so doing to send up a wall of muddy water that coated the other car and slid down its polished walls. Ahmed was very good at this game but the driver of the Mercedes was apparently no amateur! He speeded up behind us and feinted to the inside—in the heat of competition whatever vestigial road-code is respected in Saudi can be suspended; and then he roared past us on the outside so that in one split second our windscreen was a gritty, yellow curtain of mud.

"Ahmed! Ahmed, stop immediately!"

It was too late. Ahmed had tasted mud and my cries were as effective against him as they would have been against an angry hippopotamus. For a while we were side by side with the Mercedes, tearing down a narrow street, parting puddles, oncoming traffic, and pedestrians before us! Ahmed's windscreen was already so plastered he had to lean against his door and crouch down so his chin was on the steering-wheel to see out of the few square inches of clean glass that remained. Suddenly, he braked so I was thrown backward, then forward, and the Mercedes, caught off guard, was forced to pull into the space in front of us. With a cry of triumph Ahmed gunned forward and we overtook the Mercedes again, this time covering it in a drapery of mud so thick it hid the color of the car entirely.

"Ahmed! Ahmed, you will stop right away. I'll tell Princess Moudi, so help me I will!" I cried, pounding on the back of the driver's seat. Ahmed appeared to think I was praising him and he turned his eyes away from the road, which was the last thing I wanted, to look back at me and laugh. Fortunately, the Mercedes departed from our road and Ahmed had to be satisfied with less spirited competitors: a few bulldozers, women, children, some lorries, and an ancient bus, all of which he covered dutifully with mud but in the offhand way of a champion who knows the available competition isn't worthy of his skill.

Saudi driving is amusing only in retrospect; it's hair-raising for foreign passengers and very hard on the vehicles. Princess Moudi had two cars but one or the other of them was always in the garage being repaired; therefore, even after the princess hired Susu and me our own driver whom I christened Ahmed-Two, transport remained uncomfortably hit or miss.

Late that afternoon I bathed Susu, dressed and fed him, then took him into my room where I lay back on the pillows and cradled him in my arms. Susu's little hands played like butterflies around my eyes and my face; he tugged a lock of my hair, then laughed when I nuzzled him under his chin where he was milky, soft, and smelled like sunshine. My room was quite comfortable; the wallpaper was an inoffensive geometric pattern and the big bed was covered with a utilitarian spread that I intended to replace with something more glamorous as soon as I had a chance to use my new sewing machine. The machine had appeared while I was at the pool and it sat on my table, looking just a little menacing, as if some of Zuchia's malevolence had rubbed off on it. There was my chair, a wardrobe, a rug beside the bed; it was in effect a western room except for the view out over Riyadh.

There was one puzzling feature to the decor. In a corner of my room stood a very large, old-fashioned safe. Nobody knew who had installed it or how long it had been there. Nobody knew the combination that opened it, and neither servants nor princesses knew where the combination could be found. Did it hold rubies? Gold? Ancient manuscripts? Or only sand? Nobody knew the answer and nobody cared. Even I, after initial curiosity, began to think of the safe as merely a convenient surface for mementos and photographs. Cradling Susu, whose thick lashes were weighing him down irresistibly into sleep, I remembered what Peggy had said at the pool, and the safe became a convenient symbol of the locked door between me and the Arabian soul. What riches were behind that door? What words? Or was there nothing there but space? Whatever it was, I could not open it, I could not change it; but I never stopped thinking about it.

Susu had fallen asleep on my breast with a trust that was more important and valuable to me then than any secret behind locked doors. Holding the sleeping baby in the gathering dark, I felt perfect peace, perfectly uncomplicated. I kissed his fine hair and sang to him softly in English. Suddenly, I became aware that Princess Moudi was standing in my doorway; I didn't know how long she had been there, watching us. Her face was in shadow and I wondered if she was jealous, as western mothers often are of their babies' intimacy with another woman. However, when she stepped forward into the light I saw that she was smiling. Her smile was ambiguous; it was not at all unfriendly, yet it seemed oddly triumphant.

"I was raised by slaves," she said. Her voice revealed nothing but the bare words; it could have been a complaint, a boast, a subtle insult, or merely a statement of fact.

"Princess," I said, "as long as I am here, Susu is being raised by a friend."

This time, she looked surprised. I thought she was going to say something, but she just smiled again and left the room.

Later, as I put Susu to bed, I wondered if his mother had clung to the slaves who raised her, and loved them.

chapter 7

Something was strange about the morning. Ever since sunrise, when Susu and I had awakened with the call to prayer, time seemed to have slowed down, as if only the hour hand on my watch was functioning and moving at a snail's pace across the dial. Susu was irritable, complaining even after he had been changed and fed. I wondered if he and I were coming down with something.

I carried him out on to the balcony. The sky was cloudless but heavy and close. Where rubbish was being burned in the courtyard, a thin column of smoke rose so straight into the air it could have been a taut gray cable fastened to the upper branches of a palm tree. Then I realized that around us the morning was growing dark by almost imperceptible degrees; and suddenly the birds stopped singing. I heard the blood pounding in my ears, and I held Susu so tight he pushed with both his hands against my shoulders. On the desert—on its darkening and misty horizon—I saw a gray wave made small by distance approaching our hushed and expectant compound in slow motion. From moment to moment the darkness that reached from earth to sky grew larger in my view and the air around us grew misty. The atmosphere had become an unfamiliar element in which I could move only with difficulty. I knew I must turn and run with Susu into the safety of the palace, but I stood as if mesmerized, watching the approaching maelstrom, until I heard my servant, Esher, calling me with unusual urgency. She pulled Susu and me into the nursery and then together she and I ran from window to window, locking them and pulling the yellow curtains over them. Throughout the palace I could hear other windows being pulled to and doors slamming. The room was nearly as dark as night. From my own window before I drew the curtain I saw that lights were being switched on in the city. Esher turned off the air-conditioning, and it was only then I understood we were about to be hit by a severe sandstorm. Mrs. Smythe, for whom the weather was always an enthralling topic of conversation, had mentioned that when a sandstorm came it defeated the very best air-conditioning units. If Esher had not switched our unit off, it would have worked like a vast vacuum cleaner with us inside the disposable bag! We lit our lamp. Esher sat huddled on the floor; I sat on the bed with Susu in my arms. Sand was blowing in through any small opening, even between the closed panels of our windows. Although the walls were thick I heard the wind howling around us at that moment, menacing us, as if we were sailors on a dry, desolate sea. As darkness had come, so it lifted slowly until our thick curtains were sheer against the strength of the sunlight behind them. Over everything was a thin layer of sand.

I found it for weeks afterward, even between the pages of books that had been closed on their shelves during the storm. Later that morning, I took Susu for his usual stroll on the balcony. Except for the omnipresent sand, it was as if nothing had happened. The palm trees were still upright in the courtyard, Princess Moudi was presumably still asleep, and the smell of frying food arose from the kitchen. It was uncanny that there were people just a few miles away who had endured the fury of that storm out on the open desert with no shelter against the driven sand but puny tents and rugs. Once upon a time, the ancestors of Susu himself had survived such trials and seen them as the expression of a just but unyielding god. Such storms were among the powers that had shaped the Arabian peninsula and its people.

One morning in April I awoke early and went as usual directly to Susu's room next door, where I was surprised to find a stranger leaning over his cot, watching him. She was a child, no more than twelve or thirteen; she wore a long bright blue dress and silver necklaces but she was barefoot, and this, combined with her unruly hair and a quick glance from eyes that were too bold and too wise for one so young, reminded me of street urchins whom I had seen in the big cities of Germany when I was about their own age, not very long after the war.

"Now who on earth are you?" I asked, rhetorically I thought, never expecting to have been understood.

"I am called Nedula," the girl said. Her voice was husky and it broke in the middle of her name, like the voice of an adolescent boy. The smile she gave me was the impish grin of a child who knows she can outrun any angry grown-up. "We call you 'Mama Saud,'" she told me.

"And who are 'we,' Nedula?" I asked. I knew the Arabs had difficulty pronouncing my name but it was the first I had heard of my sobriquet.

"We . . ." She gestured toward the balcony and the courtyard below. "We . . ."

Nedula watched me take Susu up from his cot and feed him. Once, she ran to get me a box of tissues, intuiting what I needed without my having asked; I heard a faint jingle when she moved, an ankle bell perhaps, or the clink of bangles on her skinny arms. Then, sitting on the floor, Nedula watched me entertain Susu with the finger puppets; she shouted out loud and clapped her hands at my incomparable impersonation of Little Red Riding Hood. "What is Riding Hood?" she asked and soon we were both in fits of laughter over the difficulty of communicating such a simple concept while we had already communicated easily, and without words, our spontaneous liking for each other.

Suddenly, a terrific commotion sounded throughout the palace, normally still and sleepy until late afternoon. This early hubbub happened twice every week on the morning of Prince Mohammed's regular visit to his women's palace, and it was created by a press-gang of Mama Sarah's servants, rounding up the rest of the household staff to help them prepare for the prince's visit. Servants of the easygoing princesses were not at all eager to have their lethargy disturbed and they tried, ineffectually for the most part, to hide from Mama Sarah's agents. Nedula, holding a finger to her lips, squeezed into a small space behind Susu's wardrobe and crouched there while the commotion drew closer, until my door burst open to admit a large, fierce-looking woman from Mama Sarah's contingent. I shrugged and indicated that I was alone with the baby. The woman, a dark-skinned Egyptian, glanced around swiftly and left.

The moment she had gone, Nedula came out of her hiding place, doubled over with laughter she couldn't control. Then we stood out on the balcony and watched the less elusive servants dashing around the courtyard, raising dust with their brooms, beating carpets strung on ropes between the palm trees, and altogether displaying unusual industry, while from the balcony directly under mine Mama Sarah's voice, as keen as any lash, screamed threats and orders. Little Nedula, who had not stopped laughing, began to mime Mama Sarah's rage, cavorting like a lunatic monkey on our balcony in full view of the servants below who were soon hooting with laughter that puzzled Mama Sarah, as she could not see Nedula's performance, and only increased her fury. I don't know what would have happened, had I not bundled the child quickly back into the nursery where we both laughed until we were crying.

"Nedula, you little clown," I said after a while, "what are you going to be when you grow up?"

A moment after I had asked the question, I thought how few choices could be open to the daughter of a servant in the Saudi royal household, which is what Nedula clearly was. Her eyebrows, unruly as her hair, shot up in surprise.

"I'm going to be a woman," she said in her odd, hoarse voice. "That is what I must be."

Nedula became my friend. Her English, learned at day school in Riyadh, was excellent and she obviously had a gift for languages as well as one for impudent mimicry. She was the daughter of Fauza, Princess Moudi's favorite, and she had inherited her mother's tiny frame and quick, bright movements. It was thanks to Nedula I began to learn more about the functioning of the palace. Often, during her school holiday she came in the morning to collect me and Susu; then she helped me down the stairs with the big blue pram that we had to drag back upstairs every day so it wouldn't be flooded in a flash rain, buffeted by a sandstorm, or laid claim to by the black tomcat and his harem. It was Nedula who introduced me to the servants' quarters, composed of one-story simple brick houses clustered inside the walls around the palace as, indeed, similar huts once were built in the shelter of the great castles of Europe. Here, sitting in the morning sun and sipping tiny glasses of sugary tea, was a society I had known nothing about, one that was dependent upon the rich women in the palace—and ultimately upon Prince Mohammed—yet remained totally apart. The members of this community were more natural and more relaxed than the princesses' favorite servants who worked within the palace itself; although, as Nedula explained, many of them were the parents of the privileged household staff and a number of them had been descended from slaves, born themselves into slavery.

"Where do new servants come from?" I asked the girl.

"From the holy places," she said, and she told me how after the great annual pilgrimages of Moslems from all over the world to Mecca and Medina, both located in Saudi Arabia, many of the faithful from poorer countries managed to stay behind illegally and attach themselves to rich Arabian households like ours, where at the very least they were assured of meals and shelter.

Some of the women in our compound were wives of men who served Prince Mohammed; these servants were responsible for the day-to-day functioning of the vast palace and they reflected the chaos and carelessness that triumphed over Mama Sarah's attempts to keep the house in order. Thus, a lot of the women seemed to have nothing pressing to do. A blue-tiled swimming pool was in the center of the servants' court; for whatever purpose it had originally been built, the pool was dry and serving as a convenient, if insanitary, rubbish dump. Because by Islamic law the household had to eat freshly slaughtered meat every day, there were pens inside the palace grounds for animals. There was also a slaughterhouse that I never had the stomach to visit. Nevertheless, goats, sheep, and chickens found breaks in their fences and wandered pretty much as they pleased around the grounds.

Certainly these servants were not employed by the most efficient house in Riyadh to do the most demanding work, but they had a lot of charm and good humor. When they gathered around Susu's pram I didn't need much more than my basic Arabic to know they were admiring him and even blessing him with quotations from the Koran, just as women everywhere in the world bless and admire the beauty of a healthy baby. Nedula stood back from these clucking sessions looking rather like the manager of a very successful sideshow. Once in a while, she translated a question I had not understood; generally it was precisely the sort of question women ask in the West about babies.

"Does he eat well? Does he sleep well? Has he gained much weight?" Frequently, the question asked was of a personal nature. "Was 'Mama Saud' married? Divorced? Was it true western women drove cars and ate with the men, as they had seen on television?" Sometimes, I could tell, Nedula censored a question which in her opinion was too near the bone. In just such a way, despite her good knowledge of English, Nedula would not give me certain information about her own life, as if she knew I could not understand her reply. Or would not accept it.

I entered my own room one afternoon, having returned early from the pool, and found Nedula sitting on the floor in front of my bed. The child jumped up when I came in, and for the first time she appeared furtive and embarrassed. She hung her head, looked down at her bare feet. In her hand she held a book with her fingers between the pages she had been reading when I interrupted her.

"What are you doing, Nedula?"

I thought she would cry. She raised her hand and held out my own copy of Hans Christian Andersen's *Fairy Tales*. I told her, of course, that whenever she wanted to read any of my books, she was welcome to do so and she need never ask my permission. Thereafter, I rarely saw Nedula without a book in her pocket or under her arm.

"Why don't you go to England someday?" I asked her once.

"My mother would never let me do that," she said. "And I cannot go without her allowing it. So I will never go anywhere but here." If there was any bitterness in Nedula's tone, it was so quickly suppressed I could not be sure it was there.

"I'm going crazy in this place!" she cried out suddenly, pulling her hair with both hands; but then immediately she turned her lapse into a joke by doing a silly imitation of a mad child trying to catch a butterfly.

Late that very afternoon, I heard a hair-raising racket in the long corridor where Mama Sarah was apparently marching up and down, screaming in rage.

"What is going on now, Nedula?" I asked my little mentor. She concentrated on Mama Sarah's voice that rose and fell in volume as she passed from the nearer end of the hall to the further one.

"Aaah! She is very angry. She sees everything. She knows everything. She smells everything. She has discovered that late last night Princess Mishaal smoked a cigarette!"

No doubt Mama Sarah had her informer among the princesses' staffs, but on a more mundane level I had noticed that the air-conditioning vents telegraphed snatches of conversation from one end of the palace to another. Privacy has never been a privilege of royalty, it is true, but in the women's palace of Riyadh it seemed to me the royal princesses had no privileges at all, save money.

During one of our early morning rambles, Nedula took Susu and me to a house that lay apart from the others and had a more prosperous appearance, with a small yard of its own in the process of being swept by a servant. From the doorway of this small, comfortable building stepped a woman of unusual appearance; she was dark-skinned, but fairer than the Sudanese and Egyptian servants, more the coloring of a Neapolitan or Spaniard. Although she was plump, nearly fat, she moved with a grace rarely seen in the West and her posture was the kind that Swiss finishing schools charge a fortune to instill in young debutantes: proud, yet totally feminine and supple. She wore her abaya but it was open over her face, which I could see had once been of astonishing beauty and still reflected that rare serenity that comes only to a woman confident of her allure. The abaya she wore was of fine stuff, not the thick quality most of the servants wore, and when she leaned over the pram to examine Susu I noticed the glint of jewelry under her robes. Even my impudent little Nedula was subdued, answering respectfully in her hoarse whisper when the woman asked her some questions, then making a kind of introduction between me and the

stranger who drew her head back a little to look at me as if she
were more accustomed to seeing distant objects.

"She is a Bedu," Nedula told me as we walked back to the palace. "She comes from a desert tribe. Once she was very, very, very
beautiful. Maybe the most beautiful woman ever, anywhere.
Moudi's brother 'took' her when she was very young."

"Do you mean he married her?"

Nedula looked puzzled. "He took her," she repeated.

We walked on in silence for a while, then Nedula said, "She is
the mother of Princess Jawahir."

So the proud Princess Jawahir with her fixation for the imperial
color had been raised to her title in tribute to the beauty of the
tribeswoman who bore her. I felt that I understood much more
about Jawahir, and I suspected too that I had a deeper understanding of the words that echoed through the palace corridor from
time to time when Princess Moudi quarreled with her niece,
Jawahir, and screamed at her in anger.

I had started to look forward to Prince Mohammed's visits; they
gave a reassuring pattern to life for they rarely varied in their routine. The prince arrived at four and was received in the big drawing room; he always left his slippers at the door, and the princesses
always wore their most magnificent evening clothes. Susu and I
waited upstairs until summoned to present ourselves, then we drank
small cups of Arabian coffee, black tea, or tea flavored with pep-
permint, until a subtle nod from Princess Moudi told me it was
time to leave; or until Susu began to yell, a sound that has never
been known to please any grandfather in the world.

When Princess Moudi announced during one of her visits to the
nursery that Susu and I were to visit her uncle the next day, it was
a moment before I realized she meant we were going to visit King
Khalid, the ruler of Saudi Arabia. Every Arabian princeling was
presented to the King at the age of six weeks and then again after a
year; given the numerous branches of the royal family this duty
alone kept Princess Moudi's uncle quite busy. Susu, however, was
of the immediate family and his presence had been specially
requested. I had never before met a king. The prospect filled me

with eagerness and alarm for although I told myself he "was just like any other man," uncontrollable awe lay at the bottom of my royalist heart. The next morning, I dressed Susu in his most magnificent outfit—just a little too big—and I put on a long dress I had made in London and had been saving for a special occasion. Fauza and Zuchia were to accompany me with Ahmed and a second driver. The solemnity of the event affected even Zuchia and instead of her thinly veiled insolence, she chose to ignore me, engaging Fauza in rapid conversation. Since Princess Moudi had told me that royal children, and most Saudis of high birth, were raised entirely by slaves, I had been wondering if Zuchia had wanted my job in the nursery. The claustrophobic atmosphere of the women's palace made small disappointments inside loom larger than any war or disaster outside; nothing would be more natural than for Zuchia's grievance against me to dominate her, the way a weed, unchecked, will take over a hothouse.

At the gates of the King's palace were soldiers in khaki uniforms and there was a military atmosphere about the place. This, I suspected, was one establishment in Saudi where meals arrived hot, cars were on time, and all the machinery worked. I was concentrating hard on Susu, trying by the force of my own will to keep him from crying, so I could not look around as much as I would have liked. The drawing room was stately and opened on to a splendid garden; in the center of the floor was a huge, circular carpet, woven in a traditional pattern. I was surprised that not only Fauza and Zuchia but also the two drivers followed me into the room.

We had barely entered through our door when the King himself, dressed completely in white, entered through another door and walked slowly to an upholstered easy chair placed at the very end of the carpet. When he sat down and looked at us, I could see how much he resembled his older brother, Prince Mohammed, but the King's face was thinner and he looked very tired. I knew that in 1972 he had undergone open-heart surgery, and gossip at the Al Yamama pool had it that his health was chronically bad. Certainly he could not conceal his weariness that day, or did not try to.

To my astonishment both our drivers greeted the King by kissing

him on his forehead. He then addressed Fauza, who told him in
Arabic that the baby was the son of Moudi Bint Mohammed Bin
Abdul Aziz. The King beckoned to me; I stepped forward and put
Susu in his arms, then I stepped back to the edge of the carpet.
After he had looked at the baby very solemnly, the King asked
Fauza another question I could not quite understand. Fauza shook
her head and mumbled.

"No, not English, sir."

"French?" the King asked.

"No, not French, sir. She is German."

He raised his eyes from the baby and looked at me for a moment.
I wondered if he was recalling that once his country had been at
war with mine; but there was no expression in his eyes at all; I
seemed to stand before a camera that registered me and filed me
away. In a few minutes, the audience was over. The King rose first
and left the room.

"But I told you the King was my uncle! You knew that!" Princess
Moudi said later. She was amused by my excitement at the visit.
"Aren't kings ever uncles too in the West?" she asked. The princess
was in a cheerful mood so, remembering the gossip I had heard at
the pool about Prince Mohammed's choleric temper which had
caused him twice to be passed over for the kingship, I dared ask
Princess Moudi outright why her father was not King.

"For many reasons," she said. "But there is one big reason,
Rosemarie."

"Is there, Princess Moudi?" I asked, trying to contain my curiosity.

"Oh yes, Rosemarie. The big reason is my father does not like to
wear shoes and a king must wear shoes!"

Her eyes were wide and innocent, but I thought a spark of
laughter lay behind them.

Princess Lulu, who was Mishaal's older sister, lived with her
three children in a palace near our compound. When I had seen
Lulu at Prince Mohammed's weekly audiences, she had been increasingly pregnant so it was no surprise when Princess Moudi said
we were going to visit her and her new baby.

"It's another girl. Her name is Anud," Princess Moudi said. "Her fourth daughter," she added, unable to disguise her satisfaction at having borne a son like Susu. Lulu's palace and the courtyard around it was a maze of walls, constructed so men and women, servants and masters, could move on parallel lines without ever meeting each other. Had I not stayed close to Princess Moudi, I would have lost my way long before we entered the big reception room. There, Lulu lay on a bed surrounded by women. Standing just inside the door, was a lovely woman in her mid-forties whom I had noticed during Prince Mohammed's audiences, but whom I had never met. Princess Moudi introduced us, and the woman put out her hand to shake mine in the western fashion, although she wore a traditional Arab dress that had clearly, to my dressmaker's eye, been custom-made.

"Mama Mishaal," Princess Moudi said and I recognized that this woman did, indeed, have the same high cheekbones as the young princess; however, in Mama Mishaal the promise of her daughter's beauty had ripened and glowed as the ropes of perfect pearls around her throat. Later, I learned that her older daughter's name, Lulu, meant "pearl" in Arabic.

"How are you?" Mama Mishaal said, obviously proud of her smattering of English. She smiled the way her daughter did, without shyness, but Mama Mishaal was much more reserved than the young princess and her eye more penetrating. Next to her stood her son who, I learned, still spent a lot of time with his mother although he was already receiving the segregated education due to a young prince. With a few English words of her own and Princess Moudi's help, Mama Mishaal asked if I would consider giving her children English lessons, an offer I had to sidestep as gracefully as I could, since I had barely enough time in my day to keep the nursery in order.

We paid our respects to Princess Lulu who was obviously exhausted; her eyes kept closing and she spoke in a thin, toneless voice. To my intense disapproval, the new baby lay in a cot just next to the entrance hall, subject to every noise, every draft of dusty air, and every intrusion.

"This is our way, Rosemarie," Princess Moudi said, recognizing

the look in my eye. "This baby will be raised in our way. This baby
will not be like Susu, awake with the birds, no kissing. This baby
will go to bed late and will know all the noise, all the people."

She shrugged. "It is her mother's wish, just as I wished Susu to
know your ways." I could not help but wonder silently if the baby
would have been treated the same way had it been a boy like Susu.

"And where was the baby born?" I asked Lulu through Moudi.

"Henna. Henna," Lulu said, which I knew meant "here."

I looked around for a doctor or a midwife in attendance.

"Who delivered the baby?"

"Anna. Anna," Lulu said.

I thought I couldn't have understood properly, for I knew that
"anna" meant "myself." I looked at Princess Moudi, but she did
not seem in the least surprised at her kinswoman's fortitude although she herself had given birth in the hospital—possibly because by
any reckoning she had been past the ideal time to have her first
baby.

In the hall, Princess Moudi showed me a poster about five feet
high that hung on the door to the reception room. It depicted a
family tree of the royal house, Moudi said. She showed me in the
very center of the poster an apple that represented the late King
Abdul Aziz; one of history's angriest and most powerful warrior
kings who carved the kingdom of Saudi Arabia out of desert sand
and ruled it for more than half a century, until his death in 1953,
in strict accordance with the laws of Islam. From this apple,
branches extended for each of his marriages. Hanging on these
branches were small red apples where sons had been born, and
small yellow pears to represent daughters. The names were written
in Arabic script which Princess Moudi read out for me, explaining
that *bin* meant "son of" and *bint* meant "daughter of," a key that
became a great help in trying to decode some of the more complex
relationships in the veritable orchard of royal births before us. Here
and there, much less frequently as the chart approached modern
times, there were white apples and pears without names; these,
Princess Moudi explained, were stillborn babies. It would have
taken hours to sort out the marriages and offspring; at a glance,

however, it was evident that Mrs. Smythe at the pool had been correct and first-cousin marriages were commonplace.

"Where are you?" I asked Princess Moudi, and she stood on tiptoe to show me a pear right near the top of the tree.

As much as I was learning about Saudi life, at the heart of the palace remained one unsolved mystery. How did the princesses spend their time? I knew so little about them. I did not often dine with them because they rarely ate before midnight and I had to rise just after dawn. Except for the days of Prince Mohammed's visit, the corridors were usually quiet most of the day, and Princess Moudi's door firmly shut. Her visits to the nursery were always during the late afternoon or at night and as far as I could tell days went by when she wore nothing more conventional than one magnificent nightgown after another.

There was an afternoon that I returned from the pool in time to catch sight of Princess Moudi just leaving the palace; she was dressed in a long, clinging gown designed of harlequin panels in black and white. Before she drew her silk abaya closed, I saw the glitter of diamonds, and her face was carefully made up. Although it was not yet four o'clock on a hot afternoon in Riyadh, she was dressed as if for a banquet in Paris or Rome or London. I told Nedula what I had seen and how splendidly the princess had been dressed.

"Of course," Nedula said. "Princess Moudi was going to the hairdresser in Riyadh."

I had met women in the West who would not be seen at the supermarket without their false eyelashes, but never before had I met anyone who wore a formal gown to the hairdressers.

"All dressed up and no place to go," I told Nedula, but she did not understand me, which was perhaps as well. Royal employers are like any other: they pay for efficiency and they deserve discretion from their staff. But royalty might be more outraged than other bosses to find they are receiving pity too from their underlings.

chapter 8

The nursery was functioning fairly smoothly. Princess Moudi tried hard to keep to her word and for the most part I really was completely in charge of Susu's routine. Princes and princesses who wanted to see Susu made formal application for appointments that required my approval. It was only Princess Moudi herself who would often bring a party into the nursery late at night, turn on all the lights, make a lot of noise, and then depart to leave me with a very angry prince. The Holy Man too had constant access to the nursery and would appear at odd times, led by a servant who arranged him by the side of the cot and put a chair under him. Then he droned his incantations, without fail waking Susu who needed only one look at the half-blind old man to begin screaming his distress. Mama Sarah, at least, had given up trying to find me and Susu during the mornings, and in exchange for this courtesy I took the baby down to visit her most afternoons. Her reception room was furnished with low tables and cushions, as spare and functional as the decor of a desert tent; a huge television set was the only anachronism. Even the women of Mama Sarah's entourage were always dressed in long skirts and sleeves that covered their arms. Once, the servants were cleaning Mama Sarah's bedroom when we paid our call and I caught a glimpse of a simple camp cot, much like the one that had been mine when I first came.

Mama Sarah and her staff rejoiced in Susu, bounced him, tickled him, pinched his cheeks; but they treated me with a nervous courtesy that told me more plainly than words that it was not *their* idea I should be Susu's nanny, nor were they really sure I did not present a threat to the moral caliber that Mama Sarah upheld in her house of women. Although Mama Sarah's nose, her eyes, her ears, and her spies had reported nothing reprehensible about my deportment, her suspicious eye made it clear I was on uneasy probation.

When Susu began to want solid food, new problems arose. Sometimes Fauza or Esher and I would spend hours going from chemists to supermarkets, trying to find some staples other than puréed peas. The very next day, there would be no more puréed peas on the shelves but a glut of carrots, and sometimes there were no vegetables at all, only puréed apples or pears. No matter how large a stock I tried to lay in, Susu's appetite raced ahead of my selection. There was no question of puréeing our own food for the baby, not after it had been carried atop Sudani's head on an open tray from cookhouse to palace with a cloud of flies paying their compliments *en route*. Susu's diet presented a constant difficulty to be solved from day to day; I knew he had to accustom himself to the native cuisine but in my first months in Saudi I had suffered several attacks of what was known delicately at the pool as "the national disease," and I didn't think Susu was ready to be put through such a terrible test.

Just about the time Susu started eating solids, began the saga of the Saudi washing machine. Ever since my arrival at the palace, as other women might desire gold or rubies, I had longed for a washing machine. One evening, while Ahmed Two was driving me back from our baby-food safari, I saw in the window of a big shop near the supermarket, a real European washing machine—gleaming, white, new, and utterly magnificent. My heart ached for it on the spot.

"This evening, Princess Moudi," I told my employer, "I met my washing machine, at last."

The very next day a palace estate car was sent to fetch my dream machine and Ahmed Two with another sweating manservant delivered it to my own bathroom.

"And where is the man from the shop?" I asked. "The man to install my wonderful washing machine?"

Ahmed looked puzzled at first, then his face brightened; he

reached into a pocket inside his robe and handed me a brochure: "How to Install Your New Washing Machine." Although the instructions were in English, they might just as well have been Arabic as far as I was concerned and, as it turned out, they might just as well remain in English as far as any of the Arab servants were concerned. Ahmed himself examined the washing machine with some interest but I had no confidence in his ability to install it. We used to have to wait until most of our light bulbs were blown in the palace and then ask Prince Mohammed's staff to send us a maintenance man to change the lot, because Ahmed didn't know how and they were too high for me to reach. True, there was a maintenance man of our very own someplace in the women's compound, but when he was finally found he turned out to be very old and in need of some small repairs himself. He circled my washing machine, which was standing in the center of the bathroom floor, and he made some wise-sounding comments in Arabic reminiscent of the Holy Man's incantations over Susu's cot. Then he disappeared and I never saw him again.

"Princess Moudi," I said, after several days had passed. "We need a plumber."

The princess looked at me and blinked.

"A . . . what?"

"A plumber. A plumber. You know, Princess, a man who fits pipes and basins and baths . . . and washing machines."

"Oh," she said, "that kind of man!"

She then called Ahmed Two and asked him to find "someone for Mama Saud's machine."

In the next fortnight I saw three different plumbers. Each came once, sagely nodded his head, got down on his hands and knees to look behind the machine; then each rapped its side and listened to the sound appreciatively, like a doctor thumping a healthy chest. Finally, each departed forever. A fourth plumber stayed long enough to remove my bidet, for it was in the space the bidet occupied that I planned to fit the washing machine. Then he too left forever, abandoning the bidet outside on the balcony, where it remained for months, a monument to the bravery of Saudi plumbers. At last, a young workman arrived who seemed to have some idea of how to install a washing machine. For two days he worked in my bathroom while I tiptoed around outside, afraid to disturb him, until he emerged, smiling and exhausted, to say the job was done. Esher and I couldn't wait to put the first load into our new machine.

"No more soaking nappies in my bath, Esher! No more scrubbing our fingers to the bone! Let the twentieth century begin in the women's palace of Riyadh, Saudi Arabia!"

Feeling like the lady of the manor opening a fête combined with an afternoon television commercial for soap powder, I set the program and watched the machine jump into action.

Half an hour later I was sitting in my room sewing when I heard a racket from the bathroom.

"It could be just an earthquake," I told myself, but I knew that it was something much more dreadful. Sure enough, I found my machine shuddering across the floor from one side to the other as far as its pipe would let it, like a wild, albino animal tethered to a slender stem. I switched the machine off immediately and called for help.

In the next few days, every man in the palace had a look at that washing machine and offered a solution. Nobody actually did anything, of course, although it was apparent that the problem was a result of the machine being unevenly balanced on the stone floor. Finally, the man who had originally installed the machine came back to have a look. Unfortunately, he arrived while I was at the pool and I returned to a *fait accompli*. He had carefully unscrewed the four rubber feet from my beautiful machine and then he had nailed the entire chassis to an empty orange crate. Not only did the washing machine now stand eight inches higher than its designer had intended, but it was far too top-heavy and when it began to spin, it hopped as far as its pipe would let it, then threatened to pull out pipe, palace wall and all in its frenzy to escape.

In the end, the washing machine did not represent one of my great successes. We continued to use it but as a glorified laundry tub, since we never dared let it finish its cycle. There, in the middle of one of the richest palaces in one of the richest countries on earth, my servants and I spent hours wringing out all the clothes by hand!

The washing machine, lamps that wouldn't light, a wobbly leg on my sewing table, the doorknob hanging by a single screw; under an accumulation of small collapses, I finally decided I would have to go into the souk and buy myself a hammer, a screwdriver, some nails, maybe even a pair of pliers and a small wrench. When I finally made Princess Moudi believe what I wanted, she laughed so hard that Fauza, who had not understood my request, looked distinctly nervous; afraid, no doubt, that I planned to take over her role as court jester. Then Princess Moudi summoned Ahmed One and told him in Arabic what I needed his help to buy. He looked at me, wide-eyed, then he too began to laugh, joined this time by Fauza. Suddenly, both of them must have been struck simultaneously by the memory of my plunge into the Al Yamama swimming pool, for they stopped in mid-laugh and stared at me with amazement verging on horror.

Once upon a time where the old souk of Riyadh now stands desert traders must have congregated and pitched their tents to display goods to the nomad tribesmen; there, tribesmen and traders met, paused, bargained, then moved on their separate ways. Each time I visited the old market, its endless sprawl of luxury and necessity made me feel illogically that this was my last chance to stock up on food, spices, pots and pans, on gold too, and jewelry, before spending a year—or a lifetime—in the wilderness. Although it was a permanent fixture in Riyadh, the souk had the atmosphere of a gigantic fair or a carnival, miles long, that parked for a while, then moved on. How else could all those traders in identical goods survive? What profit could they make standing shoulder to shoulder in their small shops selling the same things to an unchanging populace? In the gold souk, for example, there were feet, yards, miles of gold chains, all of them attached to the ubiquitous medallion imprinted with the Saudi seal, a palm tree surmounting crossed swords. How many of these medallions, these cuff-links, these watch fobs, could each customer buy in his lifetime? Here, the precious

metal was sold by weight with no reference to quality of workman-
ship or design. And in the spice souk, the atmosphere was vivid
with aromas that seemed to color the air red and dark gold, rising
from mountains of spices I would not have believed an entire nation could consume in a decade. Yet, despite this multiplicity of
goods, there was a feeling of busyness, business, and prosperity in
all the bustle. No doubt many dramas had been enacted in the
noisy confusion of the souk; dramas of commerce and dramas of
the heart.

However, I was soon convinced that one phenomenon never before seen by the hagglers in all their long history of trade was a
western blonde trying to buy a hammer! I had become accustomed
to stares in Saudi Arabia; after all, the men there rarely enough
saw the face of any strange woman, let alone a face as strange to
them as mine! But after that expedition with Ahmed One into the
hardware souk I knew how it would feel to be a bright green
Venusian, the first of my kind ever seen on the whole of the planet
Earth. At least by the time we returned to the palace I was an alien
equipped with mankind's basic tools: hammer, nails, and a very,
very thick skin.

"What do the princesses do all day, Nedula?"

The girl was seated on the floor, reading, Susu was having his afternoon nap, and I was sorting out his wardrobe.

"They sleep," Nedula said.

I knew most of Saudi slept in the afternoon through the heat of
the day, but the morning was a time for business.

"They can't sleep all day! Not all day long!"

"What would you do all day, Mama Saud, if you had nothing to
do all day?"

"I'd sew. In my own country, I'd walk in the park, window-shop,
I'd have lunch with a friend, tea with a friend, dinner with a
friend. I might go out to the theater or to a movie. What about
you, little monkey?"

"I'd read," she said.

We both sighed, then laughed.

A few days later my question was answered. I was in my room,

THE PRINCE AND I

sewing, and Nedula was, as always, reading, when there was a
knock at the door. There stood one of Moudi's servants. "Telephone! Telephone!" she said.

I looked around.

"For me? But who . . . ? Are you sure? For me?"

"Telephone! Telephone!" she said again, and she tugged at my
skirt.

"She says there is a telephone call for you," Nedula told me.

"Telephone" and "taxi" are two words the Saudis have taken
whole into their language; I had understood the servant perfectly
but I found her words hard to believe. I started out into the hall
that led to the drawing room where the telephone in general use
was kept, but the servant shook her head and pointed to the door
of Princess Moudi's dressing room which adjoined the nursery,
opening on the other side into the princess's bedroom: an inner
sanctum I had never entered although it was a short-cut to the
drawing room. "Princess Moudi! Princess Moudi!" I said, shaking
my head to show my reluctance to enter the private room. The servant laid her cheek on her folded hands to mime sleeping.

"She says the princess is sleeping," Nedula said, eager to show off
her English in front of the servant.

I walked behind the servant through the dressing room and then
into Moudi's bedroom. Before me was darkness that stretched the
width of a ballroom to its far end where I could just see light shining under another door. The servant who had come to fetch me
stepped confidently into the night-dark space. I took a deep breath
and followed her. And fell flat on my face over a heap on the floor.
I rose, rubbing my bruised knee, and the heap sat up, complaining
in Arabic. My eyes had accustomed themselves to darkness, and I
saw all around me on the floor similar heaps, most of them silent,
one or two snoring softly. At one end of the room I could just make
out the silhouette of a bed, as round and big as a duck pond. With
out approaching it, I knew that Princess Moudi lay there, asleep on
that vast, circular mattress surrounded by her servants just as her
ancestors used to sleep in their desert tents, encircled by sleeping
slaves to protect them from evil spirits, nightmares, and assassins.

By the time I got to the phone, whoever was ringing me had either given up or had been accidentally cut off. For a few moments I felt sick with disappointment.

"Never mind," I told Nedula when I returned to the nursery, actually talking to myself, trying to cheer myself up, "if it's anything important they'll ring back."

"Zuchia has a man-friend," the child said. She raised her eyes from the book and I was struck once again by an understanding in them rare and not really desirable in one so young.

"Zuchia's man works for the telephone company in Riyadh," she said.

"Are you telling me someone might be playing a joke on me?" I asked her. I felt disproportionately afraid, disproportionately angry. Nedula let a familiar shutter fall behind her eyes as implacable as the shutters that fell over shop windows during the hours of prayer, and I knew from experience that no coaxing, no pleading, or scolding would make her say more on the topic.

"Was Moudi asleep?" she asked after a while, mischievously.

"Yes. And there were many servants too asleep on her floor."

My involuntary grimace must have showed how repugnant I found such a practice.

"Princesses do not sleep with servants in the West?" the girl asked.

"Certainly not!"

I folded clothes and Nedula watched me quietly.

"My mother often goes with Princess Moudi to the bath," she said after a few moments.

I nodded. I imagined such a job kept Fauza busy. Due to an eccentricity of palace plumbing, whenever Moudi bathed or showered the pipes in my own bathroom gurgled; thus, I knew that Moudi bathed two, even three times as long as necessary.

"Also and as well," Nedula said very softly, "mother goes with Moudi to the water closet."

I looked at her quickly, but she appeared to be engrossed in her book and her eyes would not meet mine.

In my childhood I used to like a fairy tale about twelve royal princesses whose father was concerned because his daughters slept all day long and because their little satin slippers were always worn through. A prince, eager for a reward the king had offered, spied on the princesses and found that every night when normal people slept, they went to an enchanted grotto where they danced until dawn. Well, give or take a "happily ever after," that fairy-tale prince's experience was pretty much my own. One night I awoke long after midnight from a troubling dream. I switched on my bedside lamp and because I didn't want to risk returning to the dream that had awakened me, I thought I would make myself a cup of tea.

My own small kitchen was subject to Esher's whimsical house-keeping and apparently she had decided that day to dispose of all cups and spoons. I had made up my mind I would have some tea, and I was not going back to sleep without it. I put on a dressing gown and slipped out of the nursery into the long corridor, intending to go through the drawing room and dining room into the pantry where I expected I could find a teaspoon and a cup. The hall was brightly lit but silent, the carpet was thick under my bare feet; there was nobody in sight and the very walls seemed surprised at my intrusion, for it was that deep part of the night when I felt I was the only person in the palace, in Riyadh, in the world, awake and walking around. The door to the drawing room was stuck so I put my shoulder to it. There was a cry in Arabic. The door gave suddenly, and I entered the room; the first thing I saw was Sidney Poitier, handsome, smiling, and speaking in English.

"Yella! Yella!" a woman screamed, meaning, I knew, "let's go!"

"Close the door, Rosemarie!" shouted Moudi's voice.

"He is beautiful! Oh, he is beautiful!" someone cried in heavily accented English, as Poitier turned his elegant head toward the camera. In the flickering, bluish light I saw that the big room was full of women, sitting on sofas, on cushions, on straight-backed chairs, and all watching what I recognized as the film *Guess Who's Coming to Dinner* on a video cassette that was run through the big television set. This, then, was how Moudi and her entourage spent almost every night until dawn, waltzing in a Hollywood fairyland.

The next day I crept into the drawing room while Moudi slept and there I found shelves under the television set full of videotapes running the gamut of entertainment from cartoons to films that audiences in London and New York and Paris were seeing on their first runs. A quick survey suggested that Mickey Mouse, Charlie Chaplin, Michael Caine, and World Cup football were among the favorites. As far as I could interpret their typical day in Riyadh, the Princesses Moudi, Jawahir, and Mishaal, when she stayed with us, rose in the late afternoon, ate whatever their perpetual slimming diets advised, had their hair done in Riyadh or visited a neighbor, or went for fittings with the palace dressmakers, then took their main meal around midnight, and finally watched video cassettes until morning when it was time to go back to bed and sleep through the day.

"Of course we stay up all night," Moudi said later, when I knew her well enough to express my surprise. "And we sleep all day. What else can we do?"

I had no answer for her. There is no work for a princess in Saudi Arabia; she is not even supposed to appear alone or unveiled in public; she has no challenge in life but romance and the only safe romance for her is depicted on the shallow, flickering image of film.

So far as I ever knew, Mama Sarah and her entourage did not participate in these pre-dawn film orgies. Once, however, I heard Moudi raging in anger late one night, storming up and down the long hall. The next day Nedula told me the princess had been furious because Mama Sarah had sent a servant up during the day while the princesses slept to take their brand new videotape of the film *The Prophet,* so she could view it in her own apartment.

Princess Moudi asked me if I would take Susu one morning to visit her sister, Anud. I had seen Princess Anud with Ahud, her daughter, who was about two years older than Susu, at Prince Mohammed's receptions but I had not realized before they lived in our compound.

"Anud's husband has left her," Nedula explained as she led me and Susu toward Anud's house. "Her husband is the brother of Moudi's husband."

She paused to let me decipher the relationship.

"But Anud waits and waits and waits. Every day she says, 'Maybe today he is coming back to me!' "

"That's very sad for her, Nedula," I said. The girl shrugged. I reminded myself she was only twelve and her sorrows were not yet those of a woman, but the sorrows of a girl becoming a woman in a society that, I suspected, would never make her altogether happy.

Anud's residence was large, half-hidden by a small grove of palm trees at the far end of our estate. When we reached the front door I was surprised that Nedula hung back, clearly intending to wait for me outside.

"But surely you can come in with us, Nedula?"

"No, no," she said. She sat down under a palm tree and from someplace under her long dress she drew out a book. "I'll wait here for you."

A servant took Susu and me directly into a fairly large room, unfurnished except for a fine, thick carpet that covered most of the floor. Sitting cross-legged on the floor was Anud in Arab dress and wearing many gold and silver chains. She resembled Moudi but her face lacked her sister's high spirits and glamour; it was a pleasant face, but a little sad. The toddler, Ahud, sat next to her mother and next to her was an older woman, the servant called "Mama Hessa," who—Nedula told me later—had raised the Princess Anud and was now rearing her baby, Ahud. I was motioned to sit down and I did, as gracefully as I could, joining the circle next to a child of about Nedula's age. This was Mama Hessa's daughter, Hessa; and I called her "Little Hessa" to distinguish her from the Princess Hessa. Little Hessa wore a lot of silver necklaces; she was slim, her dark eyes were heavy-lidded and moved slowly, assessing the value of everything they saw; their calculating expression gave Little Hessa's face a sly and unpleasant cast. I knew instinctively that Little Hessa was the reason Nedula had chosen to remain outside. As the daughter of a surrogate mother to two generations of princesses, Little Hessa was surrogate sister to royalty and thus had everything she wanted and many special treats—even a trip to Europe once in a while—that Nedula would have sold a piece of her very soul to have. Although Nedula's mother, Fauza, was Moudi's favorite, it was the servant-nannies and their offspring who received the most munificent benefits; and it amused me sometimes to think that it was this sorority to which, in a sense, I was an initiate.

When we were all seated in a circle, a steward threw a plastic tablecloth down on the splendid carpet; he was followed by another servant with bowls of food. No sooner had he placed these bowls on the tablecloth than little Ahud grabbed one and began to gobble its contents greedily. I was surprised to see a little black and white rabbit hop out from behind the child and dip its pink nose into the bowl which she offered it. Mama Hessa asked one of the servants in attendance to remove the rabbit, but the moment he started to reach for the animal Ahud set up an awful screeching. Immediately, the servant drew back and Mama Hessa murmured comforting words to Ahud while the rabbit hopped from bowl to bowl helping itself. It was as fine an example of how not to rear a child —or a rabbit—as I had ever seen.

The rich have always given their children to others to rear. There is nothing especially Arabian about paying to avoid the dirty work of nappies and running noses and, later, of multiplication tables and endless nursery puddings. When those responsible for the rearing of children have been trained and apprenticed, as western nannies are, the children in their care can be as fortunate as any other children and more fortunate than some, for there are a lot more inept parents in the world than there are inept nannies. However, among the Saudis babies are assigned to servants who are upstanding and well-meaning, but who as a rule have a better grounding in old wives' tales than in common sense. Moreover, a nanny-servant who gives offense and is dismissed from her desirable position in the nursery cannot go off to find a similar post; she falls to the bottom of the household hierarchy. In the opinion of Saudi parents, the less a baby cries, the more successful its nursemaid; a great confusion exists there between the happiness of a child and the unbroken sleep of its adults. There is no trick to keeping a child from tears: just give it everything it wants except, of course, those things such as its thumb which superstition says will do it untold harm. Under such a system, babies are quiet, toddlers are tyrants, and the tears come later, after the child has outgrown the nursery and has joined the world of adults.

With disbelief—and anger on the child's behalf—I witnessed the spoiling of Ahud. When the little girl was about a year older, I was to watch with similar emotions as she made her usual demands— demands she could not know were unreasonable because nobody had ever dared tell her—only this time Ahud had the misfortune to make them not of her servants but of her mother who was in a bad temper and slapped the child so hard, she almost bounced.

Princess Moudi developed a passion for photography. More specifically, for photographs of Susu, and most specifically, for me to take those photographs of Susu. Most of her nursery visits were accompanied by the popping of flashbulbs which leant to them an extra theatrical quality. One evening, Moudi brought her new Polaroid camera for me to take pictures of Susu in the bath. I darted around the room, trying different angles, and doing a pretty fair imitation, I thought, of a professional photographer, while Moudi made helpful comments and asked questions about her son's well-being.

"Rosemarie, is it normal that when Susu cries his eyes stay dry?"

I was standing on tiptoe, aiming my camera lens directly down on the top of Susu's head while he, with total indifference to my contortions, splashed his family of yellow ducks and his mother who was holding him steady. I had noticed that Moudi seemed to need a worry of some kind about Susu and now that he no longer cried, now that he had gained weight and was patently a normal, healthy child, she was going to worry about his dry eyes. Beyond the usual maternal affection, her concern reflected a political motive. It took no great imagination to realize that in Saudi society, a woman without a husband staked much of her future on her son. Putting down the camera, I fetched a reference book I had brought from London and read aloud to Moudi the passage in which worried parents are assured that it is perfectly normal for an infant's tear ducts not to function.

"Mmmm," Moudi said vaguely, after I'd finished. She motioned me to hold the baby while she took a photograph and the flash popped over a masterful study of the top of Susu's head and his left earlobe.

"Still . . ." Moudi said from the door, "I wonder if it is normal that his eyes stay dry when he cries . . ."

"It is normal, I promise you Princess Moudi," I said. She paused with her hand on the doorknob.

"Oh yes, Rosemarie," she said, "Susu's daddy and I are married again."

Although I was no longer absolutely confident of the permanence of Saudi marriage bonds, and I had no idea how or when or where the princess had seen her former husband, made it up with him, and remarried him, I was delighted for her. For her, and for Susu who would become a prince in his own establishment.

"Everything is so nice with my husband now," Princess Moudi told me the next afternoon. "It's going to be good for us, I'm sure. I'm very happy."

She looked radiant, almost as young as Mishaal who was with her and stood watching her aunt with shining eyes. Moudi laughed and the two princesses clasped hands, smiling at each other. Then Moudi released her niece and held her hand out to me; I took Moudi's hand in mine—her grip was warm and surprisingly strong —and for a moment we three stood in a communion of joy for we knew that to be restored to her husband's house was not only a triumph of romance, but it was also Moudi's only escape route from her idle life among the women overseen by Mama Sarah. Prince Abdul was coming the next day, Moudi told me, to see his son.

"And then . . ." she said, "Jeddah! Jeddah! Jeddah!"

She clapped her hands in rhythm to the words and Mishaal did a pretty dance around her aunt. Then Mishaal stopped and said something that must have been naughty because Moudi pretended to be angry and chased her little niece up and down the corridor, shouting with laughter until Mama Sarah roared for silence and dignity.

Early the next evening Prince Abdul Majeed arrived, and it wasn't very long before I was summoned to join him in the drawing room for a drink: chilled orange juice, to be sure. He was alone with two menservants whom I took to be his favorites and the male equivalents of Fauza and Zuchia. The prince rose when I came into the room, receiving me courteously in the western fashion.

"May I say I am very pleased, Prince Abdul, that your family is to be reunited and little Saud to have a real home again."

"Thank you, Rosemarie," he said in excellent English. "It is very kind of you to say so."

His words were perfect but there was an expression in his eyes that disconcerted me because it was so like the look in Moudi's eyes when she was being imperious and difficult. Prince Abdul came with me to the nursery and watched his sleeping baby with exactly the same puzzled surprise I was accustomed to see on his wife's face when she leaned silently over Susu's cot.

"If you come to the nursery tomorrow morning, Prince Abdul," I said, feeling defensive of Susu who slept on as peacefully as a beautiful doll, "you can see your son in action. That's when he's at his best."

After a final exchange of courtesies, the young prince left. It was my turn then to look down at the sleeping baby, my heart swollen with unpleasant foreboding.

Prince Abdul did not come to the nursery the next morning, nor was there any trace of him at all except a trail of his distinctive scent caught in the halls as if he had snagged it there in his haste to be gone. Princess Moudi did not appear in the nursery either for several days, and then I was sent word that she was going to Jeddah with Fauza for a little while. The morning after I had received this message, I was changing Susu and talking to him, when the door to the nursery was flung open and in came the princess. Her eyes were blazing with rage and as she walked she tore off her abaya and hurled it into a corner of the room.

"It's done! It's finished! It's all over! This time it is truly all, all over!"

Without a glance at Susu, she strode into her dressing room, slamming the door behind her so hard the room seemed to vibrate and Susu began to cry.

About a week later, late one afternoon, I heard such a terrific banging from the princess's bedroom that I went out on to the balcony to see what was happening. Through the big french windows of Moudi's room, the servants were bringing out pieces of what at first sight looked like a dismantled spaceship; then I recognized it as

Princess Moudi's huge round bed. That very day, with rare efficiency, a brand-new bed was delivered for Princess Moudi even larger than the old one and equipped with a canopy as billowing and spacious as a circus tent.

"I've heard your Princess Moudi is having her problems," Mrs. Smythe said to me at the pool after her usual preface about the weather. I lay back on the chaise longue, closed my eyes, and brushed away a fly.

"I've heard she's finally broken with that husband of hers. I've heard he's been unfaithful. Again. He married her for her money. Of course. He's quite a bit younger than she is, you know."

I said nothing. Mrs. Smythe shifted in her chair.

"What do you think?" she said at last.

I opened one eye. Her blue-rinsed hair was lank and the skin on her back, even after all her time in Riyadh, was still peeling. Unwillingly, I felt sorry for her.

"Mrs. Smythe," I said, "I honestly think it's hotter today than it was yesterday."

My routine had claimed me and time was passing quickly. Nedula still managed to visit me sneaking away from her schoolwork and whatever mysterious activities filled her days. Although she chattered merrily and wasn't reluctant to gossip, Nedula never spoke to me about her own life and avoided answering my direct questions. Sometimes Dr. Nabia stopped in for a cup of tea and a chat. Like me, she read the English newspapers and we spent some time weighing the moves and countermoves of western politicians who, from our vantage point, seemed to be playing an abstruse chess game. From time to time, it happened that Ahmed did not deliver my newspapers to me. I mentioned these lapses to Dr. Nabia, and I suggested that Ahmed probably preferred on those days to enjoy a snooze with his cronies, the gatekeepers, who had a lodge in front of the palace. I had noticed that the drivers and male retainers liked to gather there to drink tea from cracked cups, watch television, and sit on broken deck chairs chatting in the shade. Often I took Susu on our morning stroll as far as the gatekeeper's lodge, eager to expose him—and myself—to its distinctly masculine and relaxed untidiness.

"Maybe I should speak to Princess Moudi about it," I said.

"Today again, for instance I received no newspapers." Dr. Nabia's face assumed a look I was beginning to recognize; she lifted her chin high and pursed her lips. I knew then she was going to give me a piece of information about Saudi Arabia she feared I would misconstrue.

"Sometimes there are no papers in Riyadh," she said in her most precise diction, "because it is deemed best the public should not be subjected to certain problems that are a concern more suited to heads of state."

"I see," I said. "Censorship?"

She unbent and smiled at me.

"Rosemarie, we are a nation moving into the twentieth century. If we move too fast, can you—can anyone—promise our brakes will hold?"

That night, after Dr. Nabia had gone, I stepped out on to my balcony. For both the preceding days at just the hour of my departure to the pool spring rain had descended in such torrents there was no way to take the car out into roads suddenly more suitable to a rowboat. Instead of going to the Al Yamama I had spent the afternoon at my window looking down at a few lone figures in the back court scurrying under the torrent, lifting their soaking abayas high up out of the mud. The rain, however, was not without its benefits; it washed the days clean of dust, of perspiration, even of heat itself, and for a few hours after each downpour we lived in a sparkling new world.

I looked up. The freshness of the day after rain had carried on into night and the stars had added luster. Those very stars had seen Susu's great-grandfather create the nation of Saudi Arabia fewer than fifty years earlier, out of disparate tribes; and they had watched the introduction of firearms, airplanes, telephones, and telegraphy to peoples still not altogether certain these were not diabolical inventions contrary to the tenets of Islam. Most wonderful and terrible, however, tribesmen of Saudi born to faith and poverty suddenly discovered that the unyielding earth beneath them held a great treasure, but one they could not tap without the expertise of the infidels. It had only been since the end of World War II that Arabian oil was drawn up out of the earth with the help of an influx of foreigners. The most serious problem still facing the Saudis was what price they would have to pay for their great wealth. The stern, immovable laws of Islam had prevailed in isolation, but now the alien with his greater tolerance of neglected vows and his greater tolerance of alternative moralities, was inside the bastion. Would the old ways continue to be respected? Would those desert stars I watched continue to shine down on a nation of true believers?

chapter 9

I was living in looking-glass land: what I had always considered untouchable was close at hand, and what I had always taken for granted was out of reach. We, the inmates of the women's palace, were surrounded by rubies, diamonds, silks, and the trappings of incalculable wealth, but at the same time we were forbidden to walk outside the walls, we were cut off from men, and we had no outlet for ambition or creative energy but quarrels and small vanities. What was truly big—the achievement and the struggle of mankind —seemed insignificant to us, while what was insignificant loomed large. When Princess Mishaal had her long hair cut, for example, Moudi reacted with a horrified excitement I would have thought only due to a palace revolution.

For all the fuss over minor events like Mishaal's haircut, however, Princess Moudi's final parting from her husband seemed barely to ripple the surface of our routine. I suspect her strength derived from her pride, but after Moudi's first explosive rage, Prince Abdul was not mentioned again, although sometimes when she looked at Susu she became very quiet and I knew she was noting his resemblance to his father. Prince Mohammed's affection for his grandson was so apparent at our weekly conclaves that I began to console myself that even if Susu lacked a father he would always have an interested and powerful benefactor in his maternal grandfather.

One morning, I was sitting in my room sewing; the sun streamed in through the window, Susu was asleep in the nursery and I became aware of a contentment which only a few months before I expected never to feel again in my life. I was overworked, it was true, my promised weekends off had dwindled to barely one full day a week, and there was still much around me disturbing and strange. However, a great flower had blossomed in the center of my life and a great cause for contentment: Susu. Even when I was not thinking of him consciously, my dear Susu was blended inextricably with my every thought. He was bringing love back to me.

A servant knocked timidly on the nursery door and I put my sewing to one side. She was very young and very full of the importance of bearing a message to the nursery. Unfortunately, she had not one word of English and my Arabic, although it was increasing daily, wasn't up to the speed of her delivery. She twisted some imaginary something under her nose, lifted her hand to show height while continuing with her rapid-fire chatter. When I failed to understand her pantomime, she stamped her foot in impatience and finally took me by my wrist and led me out to the balcony. There, far in the distance, standing at the massive gate was the small figure of a man; he must have seen me, because when I stepped out on to the balcony he began to wave furiously.

"But who is he? But he's a European. Who on earth is he and how did he find me?"

It was the servant's turn to look at me in perplexity, for she did not understand a word of the questions that I had asked aloud. A wild hope blazed in my heart: a hope so totally irrational I could not speak it, even to myself. A sudden tide of pain and memory took my breath away.

"Stephen is dead," I told myself as I ran down the staircase. At the bottom, I stopped, counted my breaths and gained control of myself.

"It cannot be Stephen. Stephen is dead," I said to myself again; and then, feeling calmer, I walked in a ladylike way to the gates.

The man who stood at the gates was someone I had known only slightly but because our acquaintanceship had been in London, I felt he was an old friend.

"Gordon . . . it is Gordon, isn't it?"

I put out my hand and he shook it with grave courtesy, as if we were just meeting in the lift of the office building where we had both worked, as if this were not, literally, the middle of a great desert. Gordon was an international lawyer and his office had been just below mine. Although we had often nodded and exchanged a few words, we had only once had anything like a conversation. After I had applied for the job in Riyadh I mentioned my application in passing to Gordon and he had given me his copy of the *Kuwaiti Times* which, he said, would enlighten me a little about the part of the world I might be visiting. Then, after I got the job, Gordon told me he often went to Saudi Arabia. Vaguely, half-joking, we agreed to meet there one day. I had forgotten all about him until that moment.

I greeted him with genuine delight. He was a big, solid man, into his middle years and tending to overweight; he had kind, thoughtful hazel eyes behind the official-looking spectacles many lawyers choose to wear, and there was a comforting slowness to his speech as each word emerged, considered and trustworthy. As I grew to know Gordon better and to count him as a friend, I realized that under his sometimes ponderous delivery was the imagination of a shy and nimble poet.

"You cannot think how much trouble I had finding you!" he said. "Do you know how many Abdul-Aziz's there are in this city?"

"I'm not awfully sure how many there are in this palace," I said, and we both laughed.

The only place to sit was on the stone steps leading to the palace entrance. Gordon looked around slowly, registering every detail: the gatekeeper's lodge, the heavy gates, the fountain that never had water in it. Then he turned the same contemplative, gentle gaze upon my suntan, my hair, sunbleached and loose to my shoulders, and the floating long dress of cream and cornflower blue that had replaced my London office suits.

"You look splendid," he said at last.

"That's odd," I told him. "I hadn't really thought about how I looked until now. Princess Moudi teases me and says I'm getting 'black,' but of course she spends all day avoiding the sun. They all do, you know, all the grand ladies of Saudi Arabia. They think it very odd that I spend so much time basking in the sunshine."

I was off and running, like a racehorse when the gate is opened;

I tried in a few minutes to give Gordon the whole of my Riyadh life story and, as is always the case, a flood of details emerged—the washing machine, the video cassettes, Ahud's pampered rabbit, even Mishaal's haircut; the details might have seemed to drown the important points except, as Gordon well understood, it is on details a case is built and of details our lives are composed.

"Look . . ." he said, interrupting me in mid-flow, "do they let you out of this place for dinner? I'm staying at the Inter-Continental for a few days and if you're able to escape this evening we could dine together."

My impulse was to accept happily but I had to take into account that I was no longer Rosemarie Buschow of Hamburg and London, woman of independence and self-sufficiency; I had become an inhabitant of the women's palace in Riyadh. Over and above my own conscience, over and above my own judgment, over and above my own desires, sat Mama Sarah. I told Gordon I would ask Princess Moudi for permission to dine with him and he gave me his telephone number at the Inter-Continental on a piece of paper I later hid with my contract in the band of my hat.

"Oh, Gordon!" I called, as he was turning to leave. "Did you happen to telephone me here the other day?"

He considered the question.

"No," he said. "No, I did not. Why do you ask?"

"Nothing," I told him. "It's nothing important."

But I felt the tiniest prickle of alarm.

Whenever I wanted something for the nursery or for Susu I went to Princess Moudi full of confidence and ready to fight if I had to, but this was the first time I had something personal to request and I felt very shy.

"Am I disturbing you, Princess Moudi?" I asked, when she replied to my knock on her bedroom door. She looked surprised at my meekness: her falcon had become a sparrow before her very eyes! Princess Moudi was in her nightgown, reclining on a chaise longue in the corner of her bedroom and waving her hand in the air languidly to help the nail polish dry. A few servants crouched on the floor around her. There was the immense new bed with its canopy, dwarfed by the vastness of the room. Over the dressing table, the armchairs, and the chaise longue itself were more billowing canopies, giving the effect of a film set for a desert epic. Princess Moudi listened attentively when I explained about Gordon and his invitation to dinner.

"He is a good, good, good friend?" she asked, looking at me speculatively.

"He is a friend," I replied firmly and added with a flash of my customary feistiness, "in my country, men and women are permitted to be friends."

She shrugged and blew on her fingernails.

"Of course you can go, Rosemarie," she said. I suppressed an urge to jump up and down the way Princess Mishaal did when she was happy.

"Ahmed will drive you there and you can have him wait or tell him when to come back for you. Esher will sleep on a mattress in the nursery until you come back. Yes, yes, sure," she said, and I saw that she was really happy, even thrilled, as if she were taking vicarious pleasure in my dining out with a man: a treat denied her by custom and protocol as embodied in Mama Sarah.

"About Mama Sarah . . ." I said.

Princess Moudi considered for a moment.

"When you go out, if she sees you—she *will* see you because her door is always open so she *can* see—when she sees you, you say this: 'Say-dal-eeya.' Understand? That means 'chemist.' You say 'Saydaleeya. Saud. Saud.' Okay? Good. Otherwise she will be angry . . . with *me!*"

She laughed like a mischievous schoolgirl.

"But I'll be in evening dress. Will she really believe I'm only going to the chemist?"

Princess Moudi waved her hand. "Sure. Sure. Why not? We always dress in long gowns. My mother sees us like that all the time." She turned to her servant and she spoke in Arabic.

"Sheikha Rosemarie is going out," she said.

"Rosemarie," she called as I was leaving.

I turned and walked back to the chaise longue. Princess Moudi blew on her nails, looked up at me. When she finally spoke it was not a command she uttered but an entreaty.

"Rosemarie, before you go out will you come show me how you look?"

The door was wide open. Mama Sarah's unblinking gaze fixed upon the corridor. Her finger pointed toward me in pinning accusation.

"Where are you going? Where are you going?"

She rose and walked toward the open door.

"Where are you going?"

Just as happened when I was approached by a London policeman on the most routine and innocent of missions, I felt guilty. I swallowed. I braced my shoulders.

"Saydaleeya," I said. Being honestly guilty made my voice convincing. I looked straight into her shrewd, suspicious eyes. "Saydaleeya. Saud, Saud."

She considered. She nodded. She waved me out of the palace to the waiting car.

I would defy any woman on earth to resist the tickle of vanity I felt when I stepped out of the Mercedes and walked into the lavish lobby of the Inter-Continental Hotel. One or two wives were sitting there but most of the crowd was composed of businessmen from every country in the world, drawn to Saudi by the scent of oil and money.

"You know," Gordon said after he had come downstairs in answer to the desk clerk's summons, "men come to the desert for many things. They come for money. They come for adventure. They even come"—he paused and looked around at the hotel lobby with its potted plants, its upholstered chairs, and its chandeliers—"to get away from it all. But I may be the first man in the entire history of Saudi Arabian commerce with the West who has come here and got himself a dinner date with a beautiful blonde!" Gordon's delivery was so serious it was a moment before I realized he had made a joke, and then he watched me, poker-faced, but appreciating my laughter.

"A colleague of mine is here," Gordon told me, "and I've asked him to join us. He just arrived a little while ago from Kuwait."

Again, Gordon paused. I was beginning to realize that pauses were as essential to his conversation as words.

"By taxi," he said.

In the luxurious, candlelit dining room Gordon and his colleague, Robert, ordered filet mignon that the menu assured us had been "imported fresh by air" and would be "cut in front of you." When the meat arrived, it was served just as gold was in the souk, weighed out and paid for by the ounce. I chose Arabian Gulf shrimps and then a delicious fillet of local fish sautéed with almonds. We lashed out on two bottles of sparkling apple juice and it was only this non-vintage beverage that prevented me from imagining I was in a fine Parisian restaurant. With a little persuasion the men agreed to end the meal with a dessert I selected as most appropriate for northerners in the desert: baked Alaska.

Before, during, and after our meal I shamelessly dominated the conversation with stories about life in the women's palace.

"Do you realize, Rosemarie," said Robert whose Scottish burr made a drumroll of my name, "you're having a most unusual experience. You do realize that not many women from the West have penetrated the sort of place you're in. And no men ever have. Or none who lived to tell the tale."

"Speaking of tales to tell," Gordon said, "if you two will give me your undivided attention, I'll tell the tale of 'How I Tried and Nearly Failed to Find Rosemarie Buschow.'"

Possessing the single piece of information that I was at the palace of Princess Moudi in Riyadh, Gordon told us he managed to communicate this scanty direction to a taxi driver who took him on a long and expensive ramble ending in front of a desert stronghold on the very edge of Riyadh, constructed in the traditional material of mud and wattle. Its crenellated towers rose above a grove of palm trees that had been planted in straight ranks, stiff as soldiers, to shade the building and screen it from curious eyes. In the mud-daubed wall that surrounded the main building Gordon found a heavy, wooden door, its hinges anchored deep in the masonry. Two male servants who answered Gordon's knock spoke no English and they looked at him suspiciously as he repeated "Princess Moudi!

Princess Moudi!" Behind them Gordon saw through an archway
into a cloistered quadrangle that was deep and deliciously shaded.
Finally, the servants beckoned for him to enter and he followed
them along the quadrangle and into a complex of corridors bringing them finally to a cool, vaulted room that was very dark, the
only light coming through slits in the thick walls and from a suspended lantern of cut brass. Here, the servants left Gordon alone,
one of them returning presently with a robed and veiled woman.

"In that dim, silent room, standing before the inscrutable figure
of that woman," Gordon said, "I had the impression I needed to
make myself understood not just across the barrier of language
differences, but across the barrier of history itself. I had the curious
and alarming conviction that somehow I had stepped back into another age." Courteously, though without a word of mutual language, the woman made it clear that Gordon had come to the
wrong place and he was expected to leave immediately. She then
melted into the shadows of the corridor that penetrated deeper into
the palace while the servant led Gordon out, this time through
what appeared to be a tradesman's entrance.

"I stood blinking in the hot sun outside the walls. I had returned
to my own world but I could feel the maze of centuries unwinding
at my back, chill and silent like the corridors of that old palace."

I sat quietly, pleased that Gordon had understood and described
for me the jumble of time—past, present, and perhaps the future
too—which is part of the Arabian experience for a Westerner.

"After that," Gordon said, "your palace when I did find it at
last, looked downright modern!"

Robert had been bursting to say something for a few moments
and he leaned over at last to speak to me softly.

"Don't look now, Rosemarie," he said, "but that tall Arab sitting
near the window to your left has been staring at you ever since we
came in."

I turned my head slowly. There, at a neighboring table, was a
young Arab, distinctive because he was very handsome and also because not a day went by that I didn't see him at the pool, watching
me covertly, looking away quickly as soon as he saw himself noticed. I had long ago decided who he must be.

"Oh, that man," I said in my most blasé and world-traveled tone, "he's the secret policeman assigned to me."

It was common knowledge in the foreign community that all visitors to Saudi were kept under surveillance for any moral or political breach of local custom. I found it quite thrilling to have a secret policeman assigned to me, and I even toyed with the idea of sending a glass of apple juice over to his table with my compliments. Fortunately, I did nothing of the kind! The very next day a bevy of western models descended on the Al Yamama pool to work on their suntans before going into the desert for fashion photos. While the nymphs cavorted by the pool my very own "secret policeman" was so enchanted by them, I could have drunk a bottle of whisky and distributed revolutionary leaflets with no trouble at all. The omniscient Mrs. Smythe finally told me that my dashing Arab "tail" was actually a well-placed member of the foreign office who liked to look at women.

Nevertheless, on that night with Gordon and Robert at the Inter-Continental, the handsome Arab in his role as a spy added a lot to the mood of joyous, innocent romance.

"Cinderella!" Gordon said when I asked him yet again what time it was. I had promised myself to return to the palace before midnight and I sighed, as Cinderella probably did when she saw the minutes of her magical night melting away.

"Eleven o'clock already!" I said. "Just another hour and the Cadillac turns into a camel . . ."

My lament was interrupted by a familiar figure coming toward us purposefully; it was the jewelry merchant, Winston Stuart, who had sat next to me on the airplane. Walking behind him was a short, stooped Arab who kept his head lowered and darted glances from side to side as if he thought ambush or arrest was imminent.

I made my introductions and Winston introduced his Arab companion, who mumbled something and took a step backward away from us, his eyes downcast.

"Well, well, well. I thought by this time you'd be locked up in a harem someplace, but here you sit, suntanned and surrounded by men. Unbelievable!"

"Why is it so unbelievable? I told you on the plane, I'm employed as a nanny in the household of Princess Moudi Bint Mohammed Bin Abdul Aziz . . ."

The small Arab looked up at Moudi's name, his glance passed quick as a rapier and bright with avarice across my face and then he looked away again.

"Well, well, well!" Winston said again, "And they let you out, too! They must trust you a whole lot. Rosemarie, we must meet again. Can I contact you, care of your princess?"

In his blue eyes there was the same glint of self-interest I had seen in his companion's eyes. My initial pleasure at our meeting began to fade, and Gordon, sensitive to the most subtle currents, made it evident by gestures and general attitude that we were soon leaving and, no, we would not invite Winston and his friend to join us at our table. When the Englishman looked at Gordon, his face resumed its customary expression of bland honesty.

"Rosemarie. I'll talk to you now like an uncle," Gordon said after Winston and his companion had left us. "You may find yourself in a vulnerable position as the only member of an enormously rich household who is relatively free to move around in public here. Remember, the foreigners you meet have not come to Saudi for a holiday! They have come driven by greed and ambition similar to the kind that drove men to California in 1849 and to the gold-strikes of the Yukon. This place is highly competitive, especially for luxury merchants like Winston. Private homes of Islam are closed to them and every contact becomes like a vein of gold: to be exploited until it has run out. So, watch yourself, Cinderella. And I'll give you one more tip, if I may. Every foreign businessman needs an Arab sponsor before he can do anything in Saudi. If ever you're in doubt about the quality of the Westerner you meet, take a good look at the Arab who is with him. Will you remember all that?"

"To hear is to obey, Uncle Gordon," I said.

Ever since the last days of April, hints had been flying around our household that Princess Moudi and her entourage would soon be going to Europe. A few days after my dinner with Gordon and

Robert, Moudi came to the nursery to see Susu. She seemed unusually excited and her dark eyes sparkled.

"We're going to Europe!" she said. "It's fine! It's good! Okay, Rosemarie? A fortnight in London, a fortnight in Paris, a fortnight in Geneva, and a fortnight in Rome! London! Paris! Geneva and Rome!"

She squeezed her hands together under her chin as if to keep from applauding, and then she made a great effort to sound like the head of a household.

"Try to get ready soon, Rosemarie," she said in an imitation of dignity. "Don't pack anything much for Susu. We'll buy everything brand-new when we get there." Moudi struggled for an air of mature responsibility, but her slim, well-kept hands had their own ideas; they flew together under her chin and she laughed out loud.

"London! Rome! Geneva! Paris!"

Princess Moudi noticed a worried glance I cast to the corner of the room where my battered suitcases were stacked.

"Rosemarie, tomorrow go to the souk. Buy suitcases. Yes! Buy all the suitcases you want. Buy beautiful suitcases, Rosemarie. From me to you, a gift, Rosemarie, because we're going to London!"

Moudi's delight lingered in the nursery after she had gone. Susu chuckled and kicked with glee before he finally dropped off to sleep. It was only after the baby slept and I stood out on the balcony breathing the clear, dry air I realized that I was afraid. Four months had passed since my departure from London and a year since Stephen's death.

"Only four months," I whispered to the evening star and it sparkled back at me. When Stephen was traveling and we had to be apart, we used that very star as our contact point as if it were the apex of a triangle, joining us in our two separated corners.

"Four months isn't long enough," I said aloud.

Then I remembered something Robert had said when he and Gordon and I were discussing life in Saudi, and the memory of his words made me smile back at the evening star.

"For us Westerners," he had said, "one year in Saudi is like seven years at home!"

My four months had passed as years would have done in the West although, paradoxically, the speed of the passing months in retrospect amazed me. But then, hadn't the speed of passing years astonished me in London? Months, years, or forever, it didn't matter; I knew that life had started to grow around the pain, to enfold it and to change it into sweet memory.

chapter 10

I had finished packing for Susu and me before the servants had so much as dusted off the princess's suitcases. Jawahir and Anud were accompanying us on the European trip, little Ahud was going to visit her grandfather Prince Mohammed, who was staying in Sweden, but the sly child Hessa was to come with us. As our departure drew closer, it seemed to me less and less was being accomplished in the flurry of excitement. Every few hours one royal princess or another would pop her head through the nursery door and sing, "Three days more and we go to London!" "Two days more and we go to London!" "One day more and we go to London!" In the meantime, aside from the packing, there were Susu's first passport pictures to be taken, and then his vaccination, which left him feverish and unhappy. When I had the temerity to suggest to Moudi and Jawahir that we delay our departure for two days until Susu was fit and, incidentally, until there was a direct Riyadh-London flight instead of the convoluted route we had to take through Jeddah and Geneva, they were scandalized.

"No, no, no, Rosemarie! Oh no!" Jawahir cried, her distress helping her find the unfamiliar English words. "Oh no! One year, it is one year we wait and wait for this trip and we cannot wait more!"

"Not one day more! Not a minute!" Moudi added.

Moudi finally agreed that she and her sisters and their servants would fly ahead to Jeddah and I could follow the next morning with Susu.

Departure day began with a reversal of the customary Saudi tai-

diness. Instead of coming late as usual, the car to take us to the airport arrived two hours early. I was sorry about the chauffeur's
aberration mostly because it meant I had no chance to say good-bye
to Nedula and since I knew we would return to spend the summer
months in Taif, I was not sure when I might see the child again.
Esher and a wrinkled old servant I called "Mama Sayida" accompanied Susu and me and waited with us at the airport until our
flight was called. I listened to their chatter and I was pleased to
find that my Arabic had improved to such a point I was able to understand the gist and the spirit of their conversation, and to
translate it loosely.

"When I joined the family I was a child. I was a slave," the old
woman was saying. "You young women these days, you don't know
what real work is. Praise be! How we worked in those days! We
didn't sleep all day in the shade, no, no; or eat a morsel before our
masters had been fed. We woke with the sun and slept with the
sun, and all our hours between were work, work, work! We had
only brooms and our two hands and our two feet. If we made a
mistake or did wrong, we were not forgiven. You young women
. . ." She pulled her abaya over her face and turned her head dis-
dainfully from Esher who was listening with grave attention.
"What do you know of obedience, you young women? What do you
know of work in sun and rain? You chatter with the men and flash
your eyes. But I was a good slave!"

It was these final words delivered in a tone of noble pride that I
carried with me on the first lap of my journey home.

After very nearly boarding the wrong plane—had I not on an
impulse asked the steward at the top of gangway where his plane
was going, Susu and I would have had an unscheduled visit to Kuwait!—we finally arrived in Jeddah. There we were met by an airport official and escorted to the VIP lounge for women. My passport was once again with other travel documents for our party in
Princess Moudi's safekeeping and the official was naturally very suspicious of me, checking regularly to make sure that the western
blonde without any papers at all had not done a bunk with the
baby she maintained was one of Saudi Arabia's most important

princelings! When there were but four or five minutes to takeoff
and still no sign of Princess Moudi, I began to share the official's
concern. It is my nature not only to be on time for airplanes, but
even to be a little early; I don't think my punctuality is a sign of any
deep insecurity so much as an indication that I am accustomed to
traveling economy class and to paying for my own ticket. Not so
Princess Moudi! She and her party arrived with literally seconds to
spare and then, while the pilot idled his plane on the runway, they
exchanged hugs and kisses and farewells with all those who had
come to see them off. When we finally mounted to the first-class
compartment, every passenger turned to see the people important
enough—and arrogant enough—to delay a flight from one continent to another.

At the entrance to the plane, Moudi dropped her abaya and took
Susu out of my arms; then she walked unveiled and proud, carrying her handsome son, down the center aisle to our seats. The moment we were seated, she gave Susu back to me.

Although Jawahir managed to doze in her seat, Moudi could not
sit still. She kept jumping up, pacing the aisle like a nervous child,
while her baby son, a true nomad, stayed peaceful and well-
behaved. Before we landed in Geneva, I saw Moudi confer with
a dark-skinned, middle-aged man who had joined our party in
Jeddah; he had the embarrassed, defeated air that often marks men
attached to groups of women. When Princess Moudi returned to
fasten her seatbelt for landing I asked who the man was.

"Him? Oh, that is Mister Al Jowahir. He is our . . ."

She made a gesture with her hand.

"Our . . . what should I call him? Our man with money and
passports. He pays in the hotel, he pays our meals, he goes with us
to restaurants. He is our . . . our . . . you understand, Rosemarie?"

"I understand perfectly, Princess," I said. "He is our watchdog."

Princess Moudi thought my phrase so funny she woke Jawahir to
tell her, and poor Mr. Al Jowahir cringed in his seat while the
princesses laughed uproariously. In Geneva, Hessa, Jawahir, Anud,
and Moudi left the plane to invade the duty-free shop like a parcel

of schoolgirls in Woolworth's while I took Susu out on the tarmac
to have his first sniff of Alpine air.

We were the first passengers off the plane in London and, once
again, Princess Moudi took Susu; but this time she asked me to
carry her boarding-case, a square, large valise similar to the cases
models carry on location only much, much heavier, practically pulling my arm to the ground with its weight.

"What on earth do you have in here, Princess Moudi? Rocks?" I
asked.

"My jewelry," she replied.

As we left the plane, Saudi Airline staff lined up in a guard of
honor; behind them was a row of officials from the Embassy; one of
the gentlemen gallantly took Moudi's jewel-case and nearly stumbled under its weight. I was unfamiliar with the protocol of VIP
arrivals and it was only when we were ensconced in our black limousine, rolling toward London with Mr. Al Jowahir and our mountain of luggage following in another car that I took into account
that I was home again. The landscape unfolding outside our windows was the tender green of a balmy English May. How thirsty
my eyes had been for green! And for the sight of chestnut trees,
and the washed, green fields where cows grazed, dumb and unaware that the grass they munched presented a kind of miracle to
my parched eyes.

As soon as we pulled up in front of the Inter-Continental Hotel
at Hyde Park Corner, Princess Moudi took Susu again in his basket, sweeping with him out of the limousine and through the flurry
of greetings in the lobby with all the nonchalant self-assurance of a
Hollywood star. As I would learn, Moudi's approach to Europe was
consistently theatrical because Europe was as much a fairy tale for
her as her country had been for me. For Moudi, Europe was a pag-
eant to observe and in which to be observed, a stage on which to
walk unveiled, sometimes even in blue jeans and a Zandra Rhodes
top, a place in which to shop and to play; but not a place to be
taken seriously, since it was not in these western capitals that the
fate of an Arabian princess was determined. On the other hand, for
me, the first days of our stay in London entailed more than the

usual sorting out of chaos since Moudi was now even less concerned
with practical considerations such as sterilizing baby bottles, supply-
ing baby food, and arranging sleeping accommodations.

"Rosemarie, you are not in London to amuse yourself!" she said,
when I suggested that a small double bedroom was not what I
found an ideal nursery for Susu and me to share. As always, by
being bossy and stubborn I got my way in the end which, in this
case, turned out to be a delightful studio room of comfortable pro-
portions on the sixth floor, just down the hall from the princess. It
was a long time, however, before I managed to establish the homey
comfort which is so important to those of us born neither to a great
fortune nor to the nomadic tradition.

Jennifer was out and I left a message at her office that I was at the
Inter-Continental Hotel; then I rang European Ferries and spoke
to the people I had worked with and whom I found myself deeply
wanting to see again. Everyone agreed to ring me back when I was
settled and pay me a visit. However, during the next days I had no
replies from anyone at all, not even Jennifer, and I began to feel
very sorry for myself, profoundly unloved, a virtual stranger in my
adopted homeland. Each time the phone rang in my room—and it
rang often because the royal party transferred all calls to me while
they slept, when they were out, or whenever they had language
difficulties—I raced to the apparatus like a lovesick teenager, but it
was never for me. One night long after midnight, the telephone
rang and I seized it with the alarm a late-night call always pro-
duces.

"Hallo there," said a sultry, feminine voice. "May I please speak
to Prince Saud. My name is Yolande and I have a very urgent message for him."

"Yolande," I said, controlling my laughter, "if you have anything more urgent to say than 'goo-goo,' I think you'd better wait a
few years. Prince Saud is four months old."

After a dozen similar phone calls I undertook to have any calls
for Susu from strange women stopped at the switchboard. It was in
making this arrangement that I learned that my own calls had not
been put through to me simply because nobody in the hotel had the

faintest idea who I was, since our room had been booked in the name of Prince Saud Bin Abdul Majeed Bin Saud Bin Abdul Aziz.

In the following days I came to realize how many friends I had in London and the West, friends who remembered me and who had waited patiently for me to work my way out of the depression and isolation that followed Stephen's death. My phone continued to ring incessantly but now it was no longer Prince Mohammed calling to talk to his daughters, or Mama Sarah shouting her familiar "Moudi . . . Moudi . . . Moudi!" across the miles between us and Riyadh, or jewelers, dressmakers, and hairdressers phoning about appointments, or invitations for the princesses; now the calls were for me. So many calls were coming through that I took the telephone off the hook one weekend in self-preservation and was rewarded with a Telex from an old friend of Stephen's and mine in Washington, complaining he had been unable to get through to me because my phone was apparently off the hook.

"Rosemarie, what have you done to yourself? You look wonderful," Princess Moudi said on one of her flying visits to our makeshift nursery. Outside my window a few fleecy clouds drifted lazy as fat sheep: outside the hotel door the gardens of Hyde Park spilled over onto the paths where children played hopscotch while mothers pushed prams holding babies no more plump or bonny than my own little prince.

"Princess Moudi," I told her, "I'm happy."

Our fortnight in London became a month, then more. It was the glorious summer of 1976, when for once the English themselves could not complain about their weather. Unlikely though it had seemed at first, the Inter-Continental Hotel had begun to feel like home and the staff like familiar friends. Susu and I went for walks, fed the ducks, and lolled in the parks. One of my happiest mornings was spent in the offices of European Ferries where I basked brazenly in compliments on my dress, my suntan, and on my baby boy who behaved beautifully—indeed, like the prince he was!

The princesses woke earlier in London than in Saudi, just in time for lunch, as a rule, when Susu and I were returning from our morning outing. They then dressed and went for a meal to the hotel coffee shop which they preferred to a restaurant because there was a constant flow of people passing through whom they could watch, as if the lunchtime crowd were a fashion parade laid on for their benefit. I took Susu to see his mother every afternoon and I noticed that her room was becoming perceptibly more crowded from day to day, her wardrobe literally overflowing with new clothes, and boxes stacked in so many towers that I could not push the pram into the room after a while, but had to stand chatting from the open door.

"Rosemarie. Rosemarie!" Moudi said one afternoon in her most ingratiating tone. "Would you do me a little favor? Would you count how much money is in this envelope? I am so bad at it."

I took the brown paper envelope from her hand; it was crammed full of twenty-pound notes. Because the child Hessa was crouched in the corner watching me with crafty eyes, I used scrupulous care, as I counted the notes out loud while Moudi fidgeted and looked bored.

"That's all! Enough, Rosemarie! I must hurry or the shops will close. How much have you counted out so far?"

"Twelve hundred pounds, Princess Moudi," I said, looking at the notes in my hand. "Twelve hundred pounds!"

There it lay in my hand, a sum larger than the average English family spends on food for a year.

"Put it in my handbag, would you, Rosemarie? Hurry, hurry! The shops will soon close. And maybe you'd better give me another bunch just like it."

"Another twelve hundred pounds, Princess?"

"Oh, Rosemarie, please!" she said from the mirror where she was examining her eye make-up. "Please, do hurry! Jawahir is waiting for me and the shops will soon be closed."

The next afternoon, Princess Moudi asked me to take Susu to Harrods and buy him an entirely new wardrobe.

"Here . . ." she said, handing me two twenty-pound notes. "Will that be enough?"

When I looked a little doubtful, she immediately gave me ten notes more.

"But that's over two hundred pounds!" I exclaimed.

"Not enough . . . ?" she asked and I truly realized the extent of her royal ignorance about those bits of paper for which the rest of us labor hard and long.

"Buy him the best of everything," she said.

With these words in my ears, I wheeled Susu's pram into a taxi and set out for Harrods. All the way there I discussed ethics with Susu who cooed and gurgled his appreciation of my philosophical pondering.

"First of all, Susu, I am spending this money on you by order of your mother. I am only an agent. I am not spending this money on myself. Second, Susu, if I do not spend it on you, someone else will spend it on herself: Ahud will have yet another hand-made play-pen or your mama will buy you another useless, dangerous, expensive toy. Now, tell me, is that sophistry, Susu?" Susu, sitting on my lap, reached up to tug my hair and assure me that I spoke perfect reason as far as he was concerned. "And besides, Susu, if I don't spend this money it won't go to the needy. If I try to give it away to a beggar, we'll probably be arrested, and if I deposit it with a charity your mama will not believe me, or she'll laugh and give me some more." Susu blinked his big dark eyes and looked wise.

"And there is one more thing, Susu," I said, leaning down to run my cheek over his silky hair. "I love you so much that I'm afraid I really do want you to be the best-dressed baby in the world!"

Restraints of conscience had dissolved by the time our taxi arrived at Harrods and I relaxed into the sinful, delirious pleasure of buying absolutely anything that caught my eye for Susu.

"How many children do you have, madame?" the salesperson asked me as I piled packages into the pram.

"Just this one," I said, nodding approval of a romper suit that cost £30. "But he is a real little prince."

Moudi had told me I could invite friends to dinner at the hotel, and she had even added unsolicited permission for us to include alcohol on the bill. Room service had become a sort of mother figure for me as I chose, most nights, to order dinner in my room.

"Well, I think you're nuts, Rosemarie," Jennifer said one night when she was visiting me. "This hotel is supposed to have one of the best restaurants in Park Lane. Why sit up here night after night with your steak and salad? I promise you, you've lost more than enough weight in Saudi since you've been away. I could do with a few months of that Arabian diet myself," she said, turning in front of the mirror and, with some difficulty, holding her stomach in.

"But I don't like to take advantage . . ."

"Listen to me, Rosemarie, your princess won't be pleased at all if you starve to death. Also, from what you've told me she won't go broke if you put a few extra quid on the hotel bill . . ."

"Yes, but we're two women . . . alone . . . in a famous, expensive restaurant!"

"Precisely, Rosemarie, precisely!" said Jennifer. "We are two women, two grown women. We are not two little girls. Why shouldn't we eat as well as the male chauvinists do?"

"You know, Jennifer, you're absolutely right. Here I am, a grown woman, and I have never been in a restaurant on my own! Isn't that ridiculous?"

I wasn't really feeling as brave as I sounded or as brave as I looked when, carefully dressed and made up I finally brought myself to cross the threshold of Le Soufflé restaurant as a woman on my own; or, to be honest, a woman on my own with Jennifer. By the end of my first evening in that ambience of good food and discrete elegance, M. Pacaud, the maître d'hôtel, and his staff had made me feel so cosseted I never again hesitated about dining at Le Soufflé with a friend or on my own. In the next weeks of our prolonged London stay, table 22 became as familiar to me as my own dining-room table when I lived in London.

"We have carved your name on the table, mademoiselle," M. Pacaud told me and for a moment I knew how Moudi felt when she entered a crowded room as if it were all her own.

Susu and I joined Princess Moudi one afternoon to visit Prince Abdul Majeed's mother, who lived in London after being one of the forty-odd wives of King Saud. Susu's paternal grandmother lived just across the park in Cambridge Square, and I would have chosen to walk there, but Moudi insisted we take her yellow Mercedes parked permanently in front of the hotel while its Arab

chauffeur was permanently installed in the lobby, ostensibly needing neither sleep nor solitude of his own. The house was modest, a
far cry from the Arabian palaces of royalty, but it was comfortably
furnished and Susu's grandmother was a kindly woman in her
fifties, bespectacled and a little westernized in her dress, I thought,
but sharing Mama Sarah's fondness for poking Susu in the stomach
and covering his mouth with kisses. One of Moudi's sisters-in-law
was there too, an attractive young woman who was studying foreign
affairs in London and whose modern, forthright attitude made
Moudi's glamour seem dated and old-fashioned. The two younger
women left the room on some errand and I found myself alone
with Susu and his grandmother. She and I treated each other to
the wide, pained smiles that characterize a couple of strangers who
are trapped alone together with a common interest but no common
language. Susu did not help matters by falling abruptly and deeply
asleep. There was a limit to how many times his grandmother and
I could look at him, smile, look at each other, smile, then look back
at him.

Suddenly Susu's grandmother rose and gestured for me to sit still
while she left the room. She returned in a moment and, to my
horrified embarrassment, she was holding out a handful of eight or
ten five-pound notes! When I was reluctant to accept the money,
she tucked it into my hand, pointing toward me and smiling in
such a cordial way that I reminded myself these slips of crumpled,
dirty paper had not the same practical or emotional complications
attached to them by the rich Saudis as by us. I was not receiving
payment due, or a bribe, or even a tip; I was receiving a well-
meant, if tawdry, bouquet.

It was as we returned through the park that Moudi told me she
had been very nervous of meeting her former mother-in-law because nobody had yet dared tell the older woman about her son's
divorce. Moudi was quiet and looked out of the window of the car
at Londoners shopping for their groceries, rushing home to make
dinner for their families, or hurrying to earn the money that paid
for dinner. She was frowning and biting her carefully manicured
thumbnail; she resembled a child defeated by a problem in long di-

vision, trying to excuse herself, trying not to cry. Although my urge to comfort her was strong, it was Moudi who spoke first.

"You've loved a man, Rosemarie," she said, making a statement of the words, not a question.

"Yes, Princess Moudi, I have."

"And he is gone."

"Yes, Princess Moudi. He is gone."

She said no more and by the time we reached the Inter-Continental she was perfectly self-possessed and ready to make her entrance.

"What a lovely, adorable babykin!" the well-dressed American woman in the hotel lift said. "And what gorgeous big dark eyes." She looked up at my blond hair, back to Susu, then at me again with a perplexed expression that made Jennifer, who was with us, choke with swallowed laughter.

"He doesn't look like his mother, does he?" the American woman said at last.

"No, madame," I said, "He takes after his father, one hundred per cent!"

"Do you know, old chum," Jennifer said later when Susu was tucked away for the night, "you've got ever so much funnier than you used to be. Ever so much more relaxed."

I knew Jennifer well enough to know she was leading up to something.

"Yes . . . ?"

"I mean, you'd never have talked to a stranger before the way you did in the lift. You're bolder than you used to be. And you look an absolute knockout with that suntan."

"Come on, Jennifer, what are you driving at?"

"After dinner tonight," she said, "let's go to the Inter-Continental discothèque!"

While Jennifer was dancing with a tipsy diplomat from an Arab country, I looked out across London: a fan of lights against black velvet. The disco was at the top of the building so I could even see the last red double-decker bus meandering down Kensington High

Street, no bigger it seemed from where I sat than a child's toy. The love I had for the great city, just as once it had blended with my love for Stephen, now enhanced the feeling I had for Susu, my little prince, who slept peacefully in our nursery where I checked on him at half-hourly intervals during the night.

"Will you have a drink?" Jennifer's partner asked when their dance had ended.

"An orange juice for me, please," I said.

"I'll buy you an orange grove!" he replied.

"I'll have a glass of wine," Jennifer said.

"And I'll buy you a vineyard!" was his reply, the elegance oddly punctuated with a hiccup.

We sipped our drinks and after a few minutes we were joined by another Arab whom Jennifer's cheerful partner introduced as Ahmed, a Libyan from a very celebrated family. I did not want to dance, but Ahmed joined us at our table and I was pleased to see he took only soft drinks, showing a principled religious character rare enough, I'm sorry to say, among Moslems traveling abroad. I don't disapprove of drinking, but Islam is sworn to abstinence and I disapprove of vows too lightly taken. When Ahmed invited me to dinner the next night, I was about to refuse gently but Jennifer not only accepted for me but offered then and there to babysit with Susu, leaving me with no excuse.

"Good!" Ahmed said. "I'll fetch you at seven o'clock. I have a flat in Kensington with a kitchen and a cooker."

"Well, well, what happened?" Jennifer asked when I got back around midnight.

"You know I didn't want to go, Jennifer, you know it was all your idea. I want to remind you about that before I tell you what happened."

Jennifer looked stricken.

"But he seemed so nice, and he didn't even drink . . ."

"We got to his flat in Kensington around nine o'clock, having stopped off first for a few quick Coca-Colas in the Royal Garden Hotel. Have you noticed that Arabs in London prefer the big hotels? They don't seem to like the pubs or those bistros in Chelsea and Soho. They must feel more at home in those palatial hotels. Maybe it's the chandeliers . . ."

"Yes, yes, yes," Jennifer interrupted. "But what happened at Ahmed's flat?"

"We had some more Cokes and we talked. He told me the flat belonged to his brother, Sayed, who was coming over soon to take up an appointment in the Libyan Embassy. Ahmed is going to Brighton for a course in English and then to Pakistan where he is taking a pilot's training course . . ."

"Rosemarie . . ."

"Where was I? Oh yes, we had some Cokes. I was a little nervous but he was very much the gentleman. Around ten I got so hungry I could hardly stand up. From what he had said about the kitchen and the cooker I figured I was going to have to make our dinner, but I was too hungry to complain. So I said, 'Ahmed, I'm starving. Where is this kitchen and cooker you talked about?' 'Well,' he said, 'the kitchen is through that door, but the cooker is asleep. I'll just go wake him up!' And he did. The 'cooker' turned out to be a Sudanese servant who made us a terrific meal and, by the way, made a pretty ferocious chaperone being in the region of six feet tall with ritual scars all over his face."

Moudi's rooms had become nearly impenetrable; even the chambermaids had difficulty maneuvering around her purchases which now included a pair of spaniel puppies for Hessa. The dogs frolicked and somehow survived among all the boxes and packing cases, doing unspeakable things to the carpet which, I assume, the royal party was quite justly charged to replace on their final bill. One of the poor creatures did not survive his journey to Saudi, but the other joined the rabbit at Ahud's table and somehow endured Hessa's alternating affection and neglect. As our days passed far beyond the original limit, we never spoke about imminent departure but we knew that each happy moment was borrowed from a diminishing store. Sometimes, Moudi would ask me to purchase gifts she hadn't time to find—a dress for one relative, for example, on which Moudi told me to spend £1,000—a sum that outclassed everything I saw until I finally settled for a gown costing a mere

£500—and although Moudi hardly looked at the change I brought back from these expeditions, I was scrupulous about keeping bills and accounting for every penny. Not only am I honest by conscience and training, but I knew the eyes of Hessa were on me; like all people who are themselves out for the main chance, opportunism seemed natural to her and she was speculating on just what profitable game I might be playing. Like all honest people, I expected to be treated honestly. One morning I happened to look down in the hall inside my door to find a key lying there, apparently dropped carelessly. On some paranoid impulse, similar to those I felt in the palace of Riyadh, I tried the key in my own door. It fitted perfectly. Princess Moudi herself was the only one of our party who could have ordered a duplicate key to my room and although I never spoke about my discovery, the memory of it hurt me deeply, adding fuel to the explosion between Moudi and me when it finally happened.

I was hanging Susu's clothes in his wardrobe. He was asleep, the day was warm, I was pleased to be in England, yet I had recently noticed a niggling discontent, like a single nettle in the garden that must be seized and pulled out before it spreads: it was the thought of returning to Saudi from this, my own world where I was at home and safe, where I spoke the language and had friends, where I even had been given back my own passport to carry in my bag— albeit, not so much as a symbol of freedom as proof of my exemption from V.A.T.! Yet, the desert too had laid a claim to part of me and so I was being, if not quite torn apart, stretched between my familiar culture and the alien ways of Arabia. It was during one of my moments of impending personal crisis that Moudi chose to enter the "nursery" and deliver her infuriating message.

"Rosemarie, I must tell you something," she said, using the imperious tone that suited my mood very badly just then.

"When we leave Europe, we are going to Taif."

"Yes, Princess Moudi . . ."

"Well, in Taif I have no room for you and Susu."

She did not look at me, but strolled as if unconcerned to the window where she showed uncharacteristic interest in the habits of the London pigeons.

"You have no room for us? Is that what you said?"

She whirled around, her head high and stiff.

"Well, how was I to know I would be on my own again? I'm no teller of fortunes. Do you think I expected to be living in my mother's house again? My mother's house is not big. Is that my fault? Is it my fault I'm divorced?"

Her anger, although I knew logically it was not really directed at me, aroused my anger which was not really directed at her.

"I do not care a fig whose fault it is, Your Highness. And I am no fortune-teller either. But I do have a contract with you, and that contract promises me . . ."

"I know! I know! I know all about that contract of yours. That piece of paper that carries a signature not even my own. Well, it's up to you. If you come with us to Taif, you and Saud will share my dressing room. In the daytime you can use my own room. That's all I can do. Leave it or take it!"

"Your room in the daytime, Princess Moudi? Do you forget that you sleep all day long? Do you know what it is to cope with servants who speak no English? Who do not trust me? To cope with meals that make me ill? Then, to have no corner I can call my own to be alone in?"

"Alone? Alone? Alone?" she shouted, her voice shrill with anger.

"Why do you need to be alone? To be alone is bad, bad, bad!"

"No! To be alone is good, good, good!"

Even to me, my words sounded silly, but instead of laughter I felt myself on the verge of tears.

"Princess Moudi, please," I said, struggling to stay calm, "let me think about it."

She contrived on leaving to slam my door so hard it bounced open again, as if to say she was angry. She was gone—but the door was still open.

"Well?" Jennifer asked. "What are you going to do?"

I felt M. Pacaud's worried eyes on me as I failed to do justice to his *chateaubriand*. I reached for my glass of wine.

"I'm going to give in my notice. I'm going to stay in London." Wine spread its warmth and false courage; I reached for the glass again.

"I'll get a job. Maybe European Ferries would have me back again. I've saved a little money. I'll find a place to live . . ."

Jennifer said nothing, and I fell silent too, remembering with the clarity of a pain, stars heavy in the desert sky and sunshine so intense that heat became a curious new dimension. I remembered Nedula, for whom I had bought some books already packed in my suitcase, and I even remembered Mama Sarah's scolding voice with rueful affection.

"Oh, I don't know, Jennifer. I just don't know. I've always done what I must do in life, but I don't know what I must do this time. I'd like to do what I want to do, but I don't know what I want to do. Enough!"

I brought my hand down on the table. M. Pacaud glanced my way and sent the waiter to refill my glass.

"I'm staying in Europe. I belong here. I'm a European. I've decided and that is the end of it."

Yet, if I had decided, why did my heart fly in that moment to Jeddah, to Prince Mohammed's garden bathed in the moonlight that changed the red and coral flowers to black and set the pale flowers glowing? Why did I long to see with my own eyes, as I had seen in books, the dark gold fortresses, risen from the sand, preserved by the dry heat of the desert to outlive their architects and to become part of the remote landscape on which they stood?

"I've decided," I said, pushing away my full plate. "I stay in London!"

Jennifer waited at the table while I made my regular check on Susu.

I opened my door and entered the warm aura that surrounded Susu and filled the room. He lay curled on his side; his cheek was soft and his long lashes swept it with their tips. I replaced the blankets he had kicked away and he stirred as if struggling to awake and say "hello," but he wasn't strong enough to fight sleep and he settled back with a sigh of absolute trust. He had gained weight and he had grown; awake, he could roll over by himself and his reflexes were all bright as new buttons. I had not a doubt in the world that Susu loved me and knew me even better than he did his own mother.

"My little royal handful," I whispered to him. "My charmer. My baby. My dove."

Then, as if a sheet of glass had broken in front of me and I could step forward, as if a waiting storm had come at last, as if I had regained one of my senses after having been deprived of it by an accident, for the first time in more than a year, I cried.

"I'm going back to Saudi Arabia," I told Jennifer when I'd returned, peaceful, with my face repaired. "Susu needs me and I love him." She filled our glasses herself, too quick and eager for the hovering waiter.

"I'll drink to that, Rosemarie Buschow!"

That night as I went back to my room I met Princess Moudi in the corridor; she was wearing one of her magnificent nightgowns as she did at home, unaware or uncaring that in big hotels of the West guests are usually more modestly attired.

"Rosemarie . . ." she began.

"Princess Moudi, I'm sorry I was so angry. I would like to go with you and Susu to Taif. We'll see what we can work out when we get there."

"Ah!" she said, and clapped her hands together.

Her smile was dazzling but in her eyes a serious thought was being born; it struggled, was suppressed, then finally burst free.

"Rosemarie," she said.

She paused.

"Yes, Princess Moudi?"

"Rosemarie," she repeated, "Rosemarie. Thank you."

"A gift for you from Susu," Princess Moudi told me a few days later, handing me a box with a very important label.

She watched me as I opened it to find a wristwatch of white gold set with moonstones and diamonds.

"My goodness, Rosemarie," Jennifer said the next day, "that watch must be worth a couple of thousand pounds!"

"No, Jennifer, you're wrong. This watch is worth much, much more than that."

I entered Princess Moudi's suite as usual to bring Susu for his daily meeting. The entourage was there, all of them looking glum; even the puppies huddled in a corner behind a mountain of Harrods boxes.

"What is the matter? Why are you all so miserable? It's a beautiful day."

"Oh, Rosemarie, Rosemarie. It has come. My father has telephoned from Sweden. He says we must leave immediately for Paris and then right back to Taif. Ugh!"

Everyone muttered and groaned as I had noticed they always did when Taif was mentioned.

"Not a day longer than is necessary," Moudi said. "Not a minute longer than we need to pack."

"Well, Princess Moudi," I said, looking around at the clothes, furniture, jewelry, and animals we had acquired. "That could take a year or two."

She wouldn't smile.

"Look, Princess Moudi," I said, "why don't you telephone your father and tell him we won't go to Paris but we'll spend the extra two weeks right here in London."

"My father does not want us to stay here any longer," Moudi said. She sighed. "My father says there are too many Arabs in London."

chapter 11

In Paris our Mercedes was black instead of yellow. The princesses were less happy than they had been in London; too many other people were making stunning entrances, and the great *maisons de couture* with their austere, nearly religious approach to fashion, didn't suit Moudi as well as the Bond Street boutiques or Harrods where nobody sneers at the eccentricities of the rich. If the Parisians were not especially impressed or charmed by Arabian princesses, it was largely because they were so busy impressing and charming each other. Moudi had even once to send me with a five-hundred-franc note to sweeten the temper of a hostile waiter in one of the Bois du Boulogne's pavilion restaurants. Apparently she judged correctly the price of a Parisian waiter's haughtiness, for he immediately became a true Ganymede and our humble servant.

Although none of us enjoyed Paris as much as we had London, the princesses preferred it to Taif and so we managed to extend our two-week stay to one month before the inevitable summons from Papa Mohammed. That very morning the princesses had been on a shopping spree; they sat on the floor of Moudi's suite surrounded by wall-to-wall Cartier bags and boxes as they compared their purchases, swapping and giggling like children in a sweet shop. After Papa Mohammed's call, however, diamonds turned to ashes and the carefree mood to gloom. It was Jeddah, then Taif, for us, no nonsense! And we were to be there in good time for Ramadan, which began that year on August 20, 1976.

Some of our luggage had been sent to Saudi direct from London, but we still had eleven suitcases just for Susu and me, seven huge trunks for the princesses, and a small Himalaya of valises for Moudi alone. I knew I really was back in Saudi Arabia when we arrived at ten o'clock at night in Jeddah, but our vast collection of luggage did not. Later we found everything had been accidentally shipped straight to the villa in Taif where it sat on the balcony, since nobody had the courage to tackle it.

The August heat of Jeddah wrapped itself around me and squeezed hard; my cotton traveling suit was immediately plastered to me with the humidity and Susu awoke in my arms to rage at his native climate. Before going on to Taif, our party was to spend a night in the palace of Mishaal's father, and the warmth of our welcome by the assembled household made Jeddah's midsummer weather seem cool by comparison. Even Fauza with whom I had had a wary and superficial relationship threw her arms around me and hugged me with a genuine affection I have never seen so spontaneously expressed anywhere in the world as among Arab women. Only the malevolent Zuchia, fatter than ever, ignored me pointedly. I thought then, among the women, as I had often thought before in Saudi, of those nomadic tribes wandering in their wasteland where each meeting with friends, with relatives, with strangers, is a chance encounter and a kind of miracle. When Susu had been fed and had fallen into a deep, exhausted sleep, I went to join the rest of the women for dinner laid outside on a carpet. Despite the heat of the night I was pleased to see that the Arabian stars were out in all their customary glory. Suddenly, from the circle of women I was about to join, a slim figure hurled itself before me and I found myself looking at Mishaal's face, happy and beaming, although I noticed there were shadows under her big, dark eyes, as if she had not been sleeping well in the summer heat. Mishaal twirled in front of me.

"Rolls-Royce! Rolls-Royce!" she said, which was as close as she could come to pronouncing my name. "London . . . London . . . my darling London!"

She laughed and blew kisses into the air, then took my hand and made me sit next to her on the rug where she ate from my plate, dipping her fingers into my food as if we were sisters. When I began to tell Mishaal all about our stay in London she listened with an intensity that seemed to penetrate my words and go straight to their meaning, and I forgot that my eager listener understood barely any English at all. She began speaking to me then in bursts of Arabic while in my turn I listened, enchanted by the lilt of her voice although the words were too rapid for me to fathom. I looked at the others, servants and mistresses, gossiping around us, and I looked back at Mishaal's pretty, animated face; suddenly, I had the odd conviction that I too had been a traveler in the desert night and it was to this campfire I had come at last.

Next afternoon Susu and I took the plane to Taif; the princesses were following later by car. Moudi had told me Taif was a resort in the Al Hiraz mountains northeast of Mecca, and the image conjured up in my northern imagination was of cool, green forests and streams meandering down hillsides. However, from the airplane I looked down at mountains, to be sure—but in the colors of stone and terra-cotta with purple shadows caught between the formations so it seemed the earth's surface had been subjected to a devastating convulsion that left it with a beauty of its own, but forever barren.

A servant met us at the plane and drove us to the reception building. As soon as we got out of the car, two figures veiled in black hurried from the entrance and it was not until I saw the familiar, bony fingers reaching for Susu that I recognized one of them as Mama Sarah.

"*Habibi! Habibi!*" she cried: "My love! My love!" And "*Ya ruhy! Ya alby!*": "My soul! My heart!"

These endearments were delivered with a storm of hugs and kisses that Susu received more or less stoically. The dashboard on Mama Sarah's big American limousine was equipped with more gadgets than a jet's flight-panel including a flashing green sign commanding us to fasten our seat belts. After a hasty investigation I discovered the car had absolutely everything . . . except seat belts. From our cocoon of air conditioning, I looked out the window at the encircling mountains of rock and the expanse of sand, sand, sand, with here and there a tuft of grayish vegetation. Suddenly Mama Sarah, who was sitting in the back with her servant, leaned forward and spoke a sharp command to her driver who stopped immediately, reversed, then turned the car and drove straight into the wilderness for about two hundred yards before coming to a halt. The two women got out of the car and began pacing among the low-lying bushes and dry grass as if they were looking for a lost earring or a succulent wild cactus. The shadows of the black-robed figures were attenuated and the cloudless, cobalt blue canopy had darkened slightly in readiness for sunset that had already tinged a corner of the sky with softest pink which grew deeper before my eyes, glowed, then blazed and swiftly flared into orange-red, covering the entire sky and bathing us in its radiance. Mama Sarah and her companion had stopped their ramble, they stood silhouetted, watching the fire overhead as if waiting for a signal; then without exchanging a word or sign, both women covered their heads with an extra flap of their abayas and, old as they were sank easily to the ground where they bowed their heads in prayer. They were as dark, as simple as the mountain stones and they prayed the way birds sing or lizards bask in the heat. Watching them, I felt again that stirring sense of space and peace that is the Arabian peninsula's most seductive feature and as much a part of its landscape as any cliff or sand dune.

Not everyone shared my reverence for the wilderness. When Mama Sarah insisted that one or more of her daughters accompany her on a retreat into the desert, their moans and groans were heartrending, and they always returned in their own cars, exhausted, before nightfall, leaving Mama Sarah and a servant or two to sleep under a tent.

The villa in Taif was just enough for Mama Sarah and her own servants, so when Susu and I, Jawahir, Moudi, and all her household descended upon it, the place took on some of the least appealing characteristics of bedlam. A large hall on the first floor served as our living room, where in the evenings everyone sat on the floor to gossip and to commiserate on our shared discomforts. Moudi's dressing room had been turned into Susu's nursery and, to my astonishment, I realized I had been given Princess Moudi's bedroom for myself. The only bathroom for the entire party was next door to Susu's cot, so the to-ing and fro-ing all night, although it

did not awaken *him,* kept *me* awake worrying about whether or not
he was being awakened! The villa had none of the orange groves
and splashing fountains I had imagined; indeed, its grounds were
composed of a few hundred yards of surrounding desert enclosed in
the eternal, ubiquitous wall with a couple of sparse pepper trees
growing untended. Anud, of a more practical turn than Moudi,
had taken a villa for herself and her household across the sandy
road from ours. Next door to her was the villa of a high-ranking
government official who had a sentry at his gate. One day when I
was taking Susu to visit Anud I saw the young uniformed guard on
his feet but sound asleep with his head and one shoulder leaning
against the wall; on the opposite side of the entry arch from this
weary figure, in precisely the same position, and asleep, leaned a
heat-stricken billy goat.

What Piranha fish are to the far reaches of the Amazon and
leopards to the Kalahari, so mosquitoes are to Taif! After a sleepless night of whining air attacks, I found that poor Susu was in a
dreadful state: red and swollen and in an understandably bad
temper. Moudi was asleep and the servants were all lethargic or
hopelessly obtuse; even Esher had grown too lazy to remember her
few words of English, so I took Susu under my arm and stormed
Mama Sarah's rooms. The old woman could not hide her surprise
to find me at her door since she was wise enough to have noticed
that I elected to keep out of her way, bringing Susu to see her only
by appointment or request. I showed Mama Sarah Susu's welts and
she clucked her tongue in sympathy, then she looked at my dis-
traught face and in her dark, clever eyes was a perceptible soften-
ing. I put Susu down on the carpet and she saw him crawl in his
new and imaginative way: up on one side, down on the other. She
laughed when Susu's circular expeditions ended always at my feet,
where he tried to pull himself up by the hem of my skirt. I took
Susu in my arms, cuddling him and exclaiming over the worst of
his mosquito bites. Mama Sarah was watching me shrewdly with
her head to one side.

"Mama Saud! Mama Saud!" she said suddenly, pointing her
long bony forefinger at me and she cackled with laughter.

I laughed too and nodded my head. "I suppose I am," I said.

Mama Sarah stepped forward and did something I knew she had been wanting to do since the day we met: she took a strand of my blond hair and rolled it between her dark fingers as if to see whether the color would come off; then she pointed out of her window to the dazzling sunlight. I smiled and nodded my head again.

"Yes, yes, Mama Sarah," I said, "it is the sun that colors my hair, not a bottle from the chemist! No chemist! La, la, Saydaleeya!" She did not understand the words, but she seemed to grasp their meaning, and she was pleased.

Later that day the old servant, "Mama Sayida," who had seen Susu and me off when we were bound for Europe, arrived in the nursery with mosquito netting which she helped me drape around Susu's cot; then to my grateful surprise, she took the netting that remained to make a canopy over my own bed, obviously by order of Mama Sarah. I was touched and from that time forward, although Mama Sarah and I could not say much to each other, we met with the unspoken, cordial understanding of two caretakers in a house full of feckless children.

Although Taif is only the sixth-largest city in Saudi, in the summer it is a favorite resort; even the government keeps a special summer center there, and Saudis come from everywhere to spend the religious month of Ramadan in their native mountains. Neither accommodation nor supplies was up to the seasonal influx; equipping the nursery, stocking Susu's food, finding all the small things that make existence bearable for a European nanny in Saudi Arabia, finally defeated me. When I complained to Moudi she responded with her usual solution to life's problems.

"Take money. Take the car. Take Zuchia. Go to Jeddah and buy anything you need."

Zuchia's girth on our shopping expedition to Jeddah was enhanced by rolls of money wrapped in tissue and stuffed into her bodice. To my relief, Ahmed One, whom I had renamed Ahmed-the-Killer since his involvement in a very serious crash while we were in London, was unable to drive us to Jeddah and we were assigned Anud's driver, Abdul Rahman, who was much the more proficient chauffeur and might even have squeaked through his test in England. I debated about whether to sit in the back seat and pray, or sit in the front seat and see what was coming; but I am not a fatalist by nature, so I decided to stay close to the driver where my tempering influence might do some good. Zuchia sprawled out on the back seat of the car, turned her face away from me, and fell asleep, or pretended to.

The road to Jeddah from Taif had been built by German engineers; it was an extraordinary road, winding through a landscape of rare splendor. The great mountains, without cloaking forests or distracting waterfalls, were stark, ancient, and powerful: earth's muscle and sinew. Sometimes we drove between dark walls to emerge on a ribbon of road clinging to the mountain with on one side a sheer drop to a floor of sand and jagged peaks. At most of the hairpin turns there was a wrecked car to remind us that even the best German engineers, though they may defeat cliffs and mountains, cannot circumvent mankind's impatience to get where it is going.

We were on the road into Jeddah with nothing on either side of us but desert and naked rock formations. About an hour earlier we had passed the control checkpoint for the trans-Arabian highway into Mecca—the quickest route from Taif to Jeddah—but because I was a European and unwelcome in the holy precincts we had to take a secondary road skirting Mecca and then rejoining the major highway after a detour of almost three hours. Annoying though it was to extend our journey like that, I was not in the least tempted to cheat or hide in the boot; I had been told that Europeans who were caught inside Mecca, which is, along with Medina and Jerusalem, one of Islam's holy cities, were turned loose on foot outside the city limits to fend for themselves in the desert and to hope somebody would give them a lift. So I watched the hot, dry landscape pass and I planned the purchases to be made in Jeddah.

I had just begun to doze when I was brought sharply awake by the spluttering of our engine. Immediately Abdul Rahman stopped the car and got out to investigate. When he lifted the bonnet, a geyser of steam shot straight up into the air. He returned to the car, muttering in Arabic sentiments I could not translate but I knew echoed my own. We waited for a few minutes while the engine cooled and then drove on for about ten minutes before the car spluttered again. This time it lurched to a halt, responding to Abdul's ministrations with deep, fatal coughs. It was half-past one in the afternoon and the landscape around us shimmered the way paper does just before it catches fire. The air conditioning was *kaput*, of course, and the inside of the Cadillac was beginning to feel like something cooks do to potatoes. By now Zuchia had awakened, her face swollen with sleep and bad temper. Abdul tried to start the car again; he got out and looked under the bonnet once more; but finally he shrugged and walked into the shade of a nearby boulder where he hunkered down on the ground, clearly intending to wait there for a miracle. Grunting, Zuchia pulled herself out of the back seat and, wrapped in her abaya, she joined Abdul to crouch in the sliver of shade and stare impassively at the sand in front of her. In a moment, I was forced to join them and each, without looking at me, shifted a few inches to free enough shade for my head.

Time, I learned then, does not melt in the desert sun, it turns to stone. The Arabs waited, I waited, nobody spoke, and while they thought their Arabian thoughts, I found myself remembering the sparkling *vin rosé* I'd sipped just a few days before in Paris and the ice cubes tinkling in my glass at the Inter-Continental discothèque. So sharp were my memories of things wet and cold that they were becoming more solid to me than the Saudi rock at my back and I knew I'd better do something fast because my companions in this arid adventure were obviously immobilized. I dragged myself to my feet and forced myself back through the sand to the edge of the road where not a single car had passed since our breakdown.

"Keep moving! Keep moving, Rosemarie!" I told myself. I wasn't absolutely sure whether incessant motion was survival strategy for the desert, but at least I knew as long as I could move I was probably alive. I muttered to myself, pacing back and forth, trying hard to think of what a joke all this would be to tell Jennifer some day; trying hard not to think about all those who had lost their way in this white-hot wasteland to wander parched, frightened, until they saw the phantom of an oasis, the memory of a lake, the semblance of water, and followed the mirage of safety and succor that led to heat prostration and death.

With the smallest of "pings," the strap of my plastic sandal, stretched by the sun, just gave out. Then, for all of half-an-hour in actual time and about a century of my time, I hopped from foot to foot in the burning sand, resting for moments on top of my leather handbag like a sunstroked stork . . . until I saw a car approaching; I thought it might be a mirage but I took no chances and all but threw myself in the middle of the road to stop it. The car contained a Swedish couple and their young son, also detouring around Mecca, and pleased to give us a lift into Jeddah.

Two hours later, the first ever barefoot blonde to be sighted in the souk of Jeddah, I finally found a pair of sandals to fit my swollen, burnt, and aching feet. We spent the night at Prince Mohammed's guesthouse, where the servant, Sudani, received us royally. After I had telephoned Princess Moudi with detailed instructions about Susu's care, I let the gentle scents of the garden heal my thirst-stricken memory of that day. The next evening, however, to my distress it was Ahmed One—Ahmed-the-Killer—who came to fetch us back to Taif, so I had hours of hairpin turnings to ponder whether death by sun's burning was preferable to death in a wrecked car.

"Ahmed!" I screamed as we screeched to a halt just inches away from the looming hulk of a camel which was the first and almost the last camel I'd seen in Saudi.

"Ahmed!" I said, "Ahmed, next time I'll ride the jackass instead of letting you drive the car!"

Until Papa Mohammed arrived for Ramadan in Taif, Susu and I took a daily ramble in the gardens of his villa which was a luxuriant contrast to Mama Sarah's compound. Taif is renowned for its roses and in Papa Mohammed's garden they grew in a profusion of white, pink, yellow, orange, and deep rose red. I always picked a rose for Susu to give his mother when we returned; however, when Susu and I crossed a cloister where grapes hung heavy overhead from their arbor, and found ourselves in a small orchard of pomegranate trees, I did not give way to the temptation to steal one of the ripe fruits for myself. The Saudis say pomegranates cure dysentery and not long afterward I was to regret my honesty.

Television sets as well as video and stereo equipment were all delivered in due course from Riyadh to blare all night long in the hall outside my door, but the boredom that infected our household was so deep it was nearly tangible. Most days, however, in the late afternoon there was a flurry of animation. The princesses put on their best dresses and primped themselves in front of their mirrors until each tress and brush-stroke was perfection; then Moudi called for her car and she, with Jawahir and a few favorite servants, drove off into the mountains, returning an hour or so after dark.

"We go to see the sun set in Shafa," Moudi said, when I asked about her mysterious expeditions.

I looked at her long dress from the Dior Boutique in London and her flamboyant eye make-up.

"Forgive me, Princess, do you go to see the sunset or to let the sunset see you?"

Always quick to understand a joke, even in English, Moudi laughed uproariously.

"You come too this afternoon," she said. "Esher will feed Susu."

We piled into the car and traveled the asphalt road that zigzagged straight up into the mountains; shadows were lengthening and hawks circled high overhead. To my surprise, we had gone only a few miles along the sandy cut-off when we joined the tailend of a cavalcade of cars all apparently bound for Shafa and the sunset, although Shafa, when we finally arrived, was only a barren plain strewn with boulders, hardly worthy of Moudi's best gown.

The sunset, when it happened, was magnificent, beggaring any postcard sunset I had ever seen; but it was not really the celestial display that brought Moudi and her sister to Shafa most evenings. Shafa was one of the rare places where highborn Arabs, men and women, could flirt discreetly. In some of the cars parked near us were princes, men of property and distinction, men with eyes in their heads too, to glance through the window of a limousine where a princess had carelessly let her veil drop. The game carried small risks—sometimes it was not the prince ensconced in his Cadillac but only his chauffeur who had borrowed the car for the evening— but it was very innocent and, I couldn't help but think, for a woman of Moudi's age, the mother of a child and daughter of a royal house, it was a pretty silly game.

The princesses took their tea from a thermos flask on a carpet the servants unrolled by the side of the road and they basked in the golden, rose, and violet tints of the sun, while I watched them and wondered for how much of their own fate they were themselves responsible. Other Saudi women from rich families had gone to universities in England, Paris, or America; could Moudi and Jawahir not have done the same? Had it been Moudi's choice, I wondered, to rely for security of soul upon her beauty which must one day fade as the sky would soon fade overhead? And Jawahir, whose world was for a few fleeting moments at this hour every day bathed in the deep purple she loved so much, was she going the way of her older half-sister? I thought then of Mishaal, the youngest of the three princesses, already married and virtually abandoned by her husband who preferred life alone in the West, would that merry child come here to Shafa someday the way Moudi did, still playing a game happier women outgrow sooner?

I was not bored in Taif. How could I have been bored, when Susu's progress was so engrossing as he began to hoist himself on furniture, craning his neck to look around, and as he discovered his fingers, discovered his toes, and began to understand more of the world around him. I did, however, miss my daily swim very badly and I was delighted when Princess Moudi said she had heard that there were some swimming pools near Taif attached to the installations of European engineering and development companies.

It was a bright, hot afternoon a few days before the beginning of Ramadan when Ahmed Two and I set out into the desert to find a swimming pool. The first installation we tried had a European guard at its gate who told me harshly that because of my connection to a Saudi household, I would not be welcome in their swimming pool.

"But you aren't colonizing Saudi Arabia," I said. "You're being paid to do a job here! How can you discriminate against your employers?"

With a look of loathing, not unlike the one I sometimes surprised on Zuchia's face, the guard clanged the big gate between us and turned on his heel.

Educated by this experience to a form of prejudice I had not encountered before in Saudi Arabia, I didn't bother to reason with the guard at the second installation we visited, but, leaving Ahmed Two and the car at the gate, I sailed past him into the big-fenced quadrangle that was the very replica of a prison camp in the middle of the desert. I found two English-speaking men sweating over a piece of machinery in one of the garages and they gave me enthusiastic permission to use their swimming pool, an incongruous luxury in the center of their forbidding compound.

Unlike the international lawyers, merchants, and businessmen who were to be found at the Al Yamama pool, I now met the engineers, construction foremen, and laborers, most of them driven to Saudi not so much by the dream of great wealth as by a nightmare at home.

"Take that guy over there for instance, Rosemarie; that skinny blond guy reading an old *Time* magazine. Well, he was in jail back in England for two years. Used to be a teacher, but jailbirds aren't too popular in the education system over there, I guess."

My gossip and guide to European desert society was an American named Frank; he was a giant of a man with a sunburnt face, and a distinct line on his arms—white above, red below—marking the edge of the short-sleeved shirt he usually wore. His chest and back were just flushing pink in the sun. Even under the deep sunburn on his face I could see a tracery of red-blue veins.

"Well, he does his year or two out here and then when he goes home, maybe the dust has settled. See that heavy-set guy over there? Comes from Detroit. His marriage just went bust, she left him and took the kids. Then he gets laid off from his job. So what does he do? Comes out here to get away from it all, and to pay off his alimony."

"What about you, Frank?" I squinted up at him from my chaise longue. "What's your problem?"

"Me? Hell, I'm an alcoholic. Yeah, no kidding. Drink like a fish."

"At least you can't drink out here. The Saudis don't allow it."

He snorted with laughter.

"You kidding, Rosemarie? See that bungalow over there? The third one from the left; well, we've got the cutest little bar you'd ever want to see in there. Plenty of homemade booze and sometimes we manage to smuggle in the other kind. Got a good stereo system there too. Everything but broads. Want to see?"

"No thanks. I'll take your word for it. But what happens if you get caught?"

"We don't get caught, Rosemarie. In this country, guys who break the law—not just us, Saudis too—they're a dime a dozen. It's the dopes who get caught. In this country you aren't punished for breaking the law—hell, everybody expects that—you're punished for getting caught. There's a subtle difference there, you know what I mean? In the spirit of the law, you might say. Like, I hear there's a bunch of guys at another installation, got drunk and started singing a rude song from an Israeli tape; going on about the Saudi religion. Now, getting drunk, that's not so bad, but getting caught singing songs at the top of your lungs about the Prophet Mohammed, that is not cool. That is plain stupid. I hear they're sitting in some stinking jail in some small town now under sentence of execution . . ."

"Oh, get out, Frank! That's ridiculous. People don't get executed for such things."

He shrugged, and smoked quietly for a few minutes.

"They cut off their left hands," he said, "for thieving."

The sun was beating down like a whip; I shifted my chair over into a sliver of shade cast by a desiccated tree.

"You know," I said, settling back again, "I've sometimes thought that having a hand cut off, a quick, sharp punishment like that, is better than rotting in jail for seven or eight years . . ."

"You're wrong," he replied quickly. "Let me tell you why, Rosemarie. See, these guys in Arabia, their hands traditionally have different duties. Like, their right hand is for good, clean things and their left hand is for . . . well, an Arab never uses his left hand for eating. Need I say more?"

I sat up and looked at him; he had just explained something I had noticed that had been puzzling me. Also, I suddenly understood to some degree at least Zuchia's looks of disgust in my direction at the dinner table.

"O.K.," Frank continued. "You cut off a guy's left hand in this country and you are doing worse than putting him in prison for seven or eight years; you are condemning him to a whole life of what he and all the others see as filth and degradation. Get my point?"

"Still," I said, "at least he's alive."

Frank lit another cigarette, and cast a glance toward the bungalow-bar. He shifted in his chair, sighed, and settled back. When he spoke, his voice was soft, almost as if he spoke to himself.

"A few weeks ago I was out with my buddy working on this water system we're installing. There's the two of us—he's a Swiss but he speaks good English—and in the back of the car is our Arab interpreter. So we drive into this little village in the middle of the road; hell, it's not a real village, not a real road either. Just a bunch of mud houses and a dust track with goats, a few chickens, the usual. But the place feels funny, too quiet, maybe? I don't know. I'm not good at that kind of thing. But it was quiet and it was funny, like a fairground when it's closed. Anyhow, it was creepy, really empty. Except there are these dogs sniffing around. So I get out of the car to stretch, and I walk around, and I walk over to these dogs, and what they're sniffing at . . ." he drew on his cigarette. "They're sniffing at a great big puddle of blood."

I shuddered.

"An animal . . . ?"

"The interpreter gets out and goes to talk to an old geezer standing in a doorway; then he comes back and he tells us nothing at first. Like, he doesn't want to tell us, you know what I mean? After a while, he tells us that a woman was just stoned to death in that

village which is the penalty for going with a guy who isn't her husband . . . and getting caught."

I sat up and looked at him; despite the heat of the day, I felt an
icicle down my spine.

"It seems like they dig this big hole in the ground and they bury
the woman to her waist. Then this wagon full of rocks comes in
and if the driver is feeling good, or maybe if somebody has slipped
him something, he just drops the whole load of rocks on top of her.
Otherwise, our interpreter said, everybody in the village grabs a
rock and starts throwing them, until . . ."

I thought of Prince Mohammed's gentle smile when he held Susu,
of his fragrant garden; and then, for some reason, I thought of the
vast desert that stretches to Oman, and of its shifting, undulating
dunes where only the Bedu and desert Arab has the firmness to
prevail. Out of that merciless tract came many of the judgments of
Islam.

"No. I can't believe it," I said at last.

Frank shrugged and smoked his cigarette in silence for a while.
A Saudi attached to the installation approached the swimming
pool on some errand or other.

"Get the hell out of here!" Frank screamed at him in a rage
compounded of frustration, thirst, and homesickness. The veins
swelled in his neck. "You don't let us see your women!" he shouted.
"Why the hell should we let you see ours?"

Ramadan, the month of penance and fasting, had begun and Papa
Mohammed had taken up residence in his villa, visiting us at regular intervals when he was given his usual royal reception by Mama
Sarah and her household. A town crier passed several times daily
through the streets of Taif to remind the faithful of their duties to
Allah although some, like Mama Sarah, needed no reminding. The
old lady grew more gaunt from one day of fasting to the next; her
gaze rested lethargically on things close by but seemed to penetrate
further and further distances as if she searched the horizon for a
sign or a visitor. "How my mother suffers for her God!" Moudi
said one evening. She herself suffered less keenly, being accustomed

to sleeping all day and taking her food at night. During Ramadan the first light meal after sundown was composed of water, dates, broth, and a mince-meat pasty, then a bigger meal was taken around midnight and a snack before dawn; these were more or less Moudi's customary eating habits. Moreover, menstruating women are exempt from the severities of Ramadan and can collect their fast days to make up later. At least one of our women owed more than fifty days accumulated in the past which she kept promising herself to repay.

I tried not to be seen eating by the household staff who had all their duties to attend to despite fasting and reached, every day around five-thirty in the afternoon, an agonizing low-point of temper and efficiency. In fact, I too ate so little that it came as a shocking surprise to realize one day that I had the fever, the dizziness and the general malaise that indicated another attack of the usual stomach trouble. This time, however, it was not just an attack on my system; this time it was war! And a war I very nearly lost to the invasion of minute and vicious organisms out to get me.

"Rosemarie! You look terrible!" Moudi said in the nursery where I had just managed to give Susu his early morning feed despite a tendency of the world to spin with alarming speed on its axis. "I am going to call the doctor. I am going to call the doctor of my uncle, the doctor of King Khalid!"

I will never know how I got through the next hours, sick, dizzy, alternating between hope that the doctor was soon arriving and conviction that I had hallucinated Moudi's visit. In fact, the princess had gone back to bed, meaning to call the doctor when she awoke; and, as it turned out, King Khalid's doctor was not yet in Taif. Or at least that is what I pieced together later. The only thing I was sure about at the time was that I put my head down for a moment in my room and awoke after a couple of hours in the emergency ward of the Taif hospital. I managed to request—or possibly to demand—that a servant be sent from the palace to take down details of Susu's regimen. Then I dozed off, or so it seemed, and woke up with a glucose drip in my arm and a hazy memory of having been requested by the young doctor to leave any valuables at the desk.

"But doctor," I had said, "nobody steals in Saudi!"

"True. True," the young man replied, "but this is a hospital and foreigners are employed here and they steal . . ."

In a dream, or maybe in fact, I asked the doctor if foreigners too were deprived of their left hand for thieving? "Everyone is punished . . . for getting caught," came the reply, but it was in Frank's voice and it set me out on an uneasy dream.

There were no Saudi nurses in the hospital since the women were forbidden to come into contact with men to whom they were not related, so the staff was made up mostly of Egyptians and Lebanese who were motivated by greed more than they were by humanity. They could not bully me, as I heard them bully other patients, but they had no scruples about neglecting me. Sometimes they simply forgot to remove the needles when my glucose drip was empty, sometimes they gave me twice as much as I needed; and every night they gathered outside my room to have a noisy old gossip. Being privileged, I had been given a room next to a bathroom and this meant the less privileged all passed by the foot of my bed to get to the only toilet facilities; augmenting this parade were the curious who had heard about the unlikely presence of a fair-haired European. As I came more into my senses, I took note that the transom between my bedroom and the communal bathroom had no glass in it and squadrons of flies were passing merrily back and forth.

"Poor Rosemarie! What can I get you? Anything! Anything you want! Just name it!" Princess Moudi said on the phone.

Whatever magnificent gifts she had in mind, I asked only for mosquito netting and fruit juice. Ahmed arrived a few hours later to rig up a tent of netting around my bed and to leave me a crate containing ten large tins of each and every juice Libby's had ever managed to extract from any known fruit! Moudi also offered to have my meals sent in, as I noticed they were to other affluent patients; however, this offer I rejected since it seemed to me it was thanks to those meals I had come into the hospital in the first place. When I was allowed to eat and the nurse brought me a bowl of soup, she left it just beyond the reach of the glucose drip to which I was still tethered; she then scolded me for not eating my lovely soup, and finally she played tug of war with me over my mosquito netting. My complaint to the doctor got me a transfer to the so-called "royal suite" where I did at least have my own bathroom; it also incurred the hatred of the nurses who found petty ways to retard my cure.

"You see, Miss Buschow," my doctor said, "the ordinary Saudi peasant woman would never complain. She wouldn't know how to complain. She wouldn't even know she was being badly treated."

I understood him for I had watched the ordinary peasant women being examined while veiled and fully-clothed, their husbands standing behind them to answer any questions the doctor asked as if the woman were a dumb animal, capable of suffering but not of judging or of communicating. These were not women who complained, I could see that, or who defied authority and, watching them, I had to wonder if in a sense they were better equipped for the society to which they had been born than were my rich, royal princesses. If a society demands that half of its citizens, in order to live in peace, should live without choice or alternative, how far must it change before it can become—for better or worse—like twentieth-century western societies?

"How is Susu?" I asked Moudi on the telephone one morning.

"Susu is very good. A real little Arab boy now," she replied. "He stayed up to watch television with us until three in the morning!"

"I must get back, Doctor, right away," I said. "I've got to take care of Susu."

The doctor shook his head and looked disapproving.

"Please understand, Doctor, just between us, not a woman in that place knows how to take care of a baby. I can't think what will happen to Susu if I don't get back. He needs me."

Later, Princess Moudi mentioned to me how pleased Papa Mohammed was that I had discharged myself from the hospital out of concern for Susu.

"But how did he know that?" I asked, realizing even as I spoke that the only person who could have relayed to Papa Mohammed the reason for my haste to be out of the hospital was the nice young doctor in whom I had confided.

"My father knows everything," Moudi said.

My strength returned and soon the period of my illness was a memory darkened by feverish dreams I could not recall in detail beyond an impression of menace, violence, and grief.

chapter 12

Ramadan is the ninth month on the Mohammedan calendar and it seems to last twice as long as any other. The sigh of relief that blew across Islam when guns were fired in the streets to announce the end of the great fast was nearly audible. In our household only Mama Sarah remained calm, having fasted to the very end and assembled her household even on the very last night to pray in the garden under the pale, cool moon. The end of Ramadan was the snapping of a bowstring: laughter was heard in the house again and snatches of song, appetizing food appeared from the kitchen and at night fireworks were hurled against the impassive stars. Papa Mohammed was leaving for Europe so we were all invited to assemble at his villa to celebrate the end of the holy time and to say our farewells.

Susu and I had been visiting Papa Mohammed regularly during Ramadan and the old man was becoming increasingly fond of his grandson, dandling him on his knee and even letting him tug his beard quite hard. Although the prince never spoke to me directly, I sometimes saw him watch Susu and me with the same surprised appreciation now apparent in Mama Sarah's attitude toward me, as if to say: "You are not one of us, but see how you love one of our children!" Once, on my way out with Susu, a servant was sent by Papa Mohammed to catch me up at the door to our car and hand me a roll of riyals worth about three hundred pounds. I never really made peace between my conscience and these handfuls of money the Arabs doled out because I could not rid myself of the western bourgeois feeling that money is of the marketplace and

can never carry affection or significance beyond common payment
of a debt owed.

The visit to Papa Mohammed before his departure was obviously
special and our household was in a storm of preparation and self-
beautification. Moudi seemed particularly eager to please her father; she tried on dress after dress, selecting and rejecting, and she
asked me to see that Susu was more splendid than ever. I had a
strong impression there was a motive to Moudi's eagerness to please
her father, but I did not suspect what it might be. Finally, Susu
and I stood in the nursery ready for Moudi's inspection, which we
barely passed, because Susu kept kicking off his slippers and tug-
ging off his little white socks to liberate his toes.

"Remember, Princess, when you told me your father would not
be King of Saudi Arabia because he disliked wearing shoes? Well,
apparently his grandson has inherited that tendency!" Moudi's
laugh had a hysterical edge to it, as if she were a woman about to
lay a big wager on the gaming table.

Cars filled the drive of Papa Mohammed's villa, and the big
balcony, furnished with carpets and garden chairs, was laden with
people. The moment I appeared with Susu, Mama Sarah, veiled as
ever in the presence of her former husband, motioned for us to
come sit next to her in a shady corner. One by one each of the
daughters and grandchildren was called to Papa Mohammed for
a hug and a kiss. When it was Susu's turn, I deposited him on his
grandfather's knee and he sat there looking interested for a moment
before bending down quick as a flash to pull off his slippers and
socks so he could wiggle his toes before an enraptured audience.

"Rosemarie says he is just like you!" said Moudi, who was standing behind her father's chair. "He hates wearing shoes. She calls
him 'little Papa Mohammed'!"

Everybody laughed, including Papa Mohammed, and Moudi
gave me a conspiratorial wink. Before the laughter had quite died
away, I saw her lean down and speak softly but urgently into her
father's ear; the smile faded on his face, he looked intently at Susu
and his brow was heavy with concern. He spoke a few words softly
to Moudi, then he nodded, and she motioned to me to come and

take the baby back again. As I lifted Susu, I glanced up at Moudi and saw her eyes ablaze with triumph, quickly suppressed.

Although I was not among the family by blood, I felt a real kinship to them, especially when Mishaal, turning from her grandfather's embrace, caught my eye and fluttered her fingers at me in the whisper of a wave. Then Prince Mohammed left the balcony for a moment, returning with his hands full of small boxes. This time, instead of an embrace each member of the family was summoned to receive one of the small boxes in which was a gift to celebrate the conclusion of Ramadan. Watching the women and their children receive these gifts, I was transported to the happier of my childhood Christmases, sparkling with snow, not with this alien sun, and scented sharply with pine instead of rose and sandalwood; nevertheless, there was on this exotic terrace the same feeling of a family in celebration of its faith, a faith that transcended for a while at least petty conflicts and jealousies. Susu, I decided, was a fortunate and protected child. Out of this reverie, I was surprised to hear Moudi call my name. I looked up at her and she was pointing to her father who was beckoning me. I went over to him and saw that he was holding out to me a small box identical to those he had presented to his family. Puzzled, I must have seemed very stupid, for I looked at Papa Mohammed without comprehending for a moment that he wanted me to accept his gift for myself. I was aware of a diminishing of the noise around me, as if everyone waited to see how I would accept Papa Mohammed's token of membership in his clan.

"Thank you, Your Royal Highness," I said, and I bowed my head. "I am honored."

When I looked in the box I found it contained a large medallion of heavy gold with the image of Papa Mohammed's brother, the late King Faisal, on one side and the skyline of the holy city of Medina on the other. Each member of the family had received the same gift except for Mama Sarah to whom Papa Mohammed had presented matching medallions, one in red gold the other in white, and little Susu who also received two emblems of his grandfather's affection. Despite the sorrow that later came between me and Papa

Mohammed's family, I still have the coin he gave me then and I will always keep it bright and untarnished as my respect was that day for the house of Abdul Aziz.

In the car going back to Mama Sarah's villa, Moudi could barely sit still, so full was she of important news.

"Guess what, Rosemarie? Can you suppose? We are going back to London! London! London!"

"Oh no, Princess! But why . . . ?"

"Why? Why? Susu's eyes, of course! My father agrees he must go there for treatment."

I looked at Susu who was sitting on my lap, chortling and wiggling his toes.

"His eyes? But his eyes are fine."

"Rosemarie! His eyes are not fine. No. Not fine. He cries but there are no tears."

"Princess Moudi, I'm sorry to give you the good news, but Susu's eyes have in fact begun to tear when he cries . . ."

As I had expected, Moudi ignored me.

"London! London!" she said. "London! *Ya aayuni! Ya aayuni!*"

I understood that what she had said was: "London, my eyes! My eyes!" and I knew too that for Arabs the eyes are as symbolic of great love as the heart is for us.

"Your eyes perhaps, Princess Moudi," I grumbled, confident she would not understand me. "But not Susu's!"

Oddly enough, that very evening I was to hear the same phrase in a different context. Susu was asleep and I was sitting on my own bed steeling myself to begin packing for our departure to Jeddah, for we were scheduled to stay there until Papa Mohammed summoned us to London. Suddenly, my door opened and Princess Mishaal walked in. She was very disappointed that Susu was tucked in for the night because as he grew older Mishaal took great joy in playing with him; sometimes, I admit, when I watched Susu and his aunt scurry after a ball in the corner of the nursery or laugh together at the antics of a wind-up toy, I felt I was in charge of not just one but a pair of royal children. With her playmate asleep, Mishaal sat next to me and chatted pleasantly in Arabic which I was too tired to understand much of. I had discovered that my comprehension of the language decreased as the day drew on, so in the morning I was nearly fluent but by evening I could only smile and listen politely, understanding every third word or so. Mishaal couldn't sit still for long; she jumped up, paced the floor, returned, sat down again, all the time laughing and talking. I knew she was telling me how much she liked London, how much she liked the end of Ramadan, how much she loved music and loved to dance. Then she leaned forward so close I could see the silvery flecks in her dark eyes.

"Look, Rolls-Royce," she said so seriously that for once her adaptation of my name didn't make me smile. I looked down and saw that she was holding in her slim hand an open locket containing the photograph of a young man.

"Ya aayuni! Ya habibi!" she whispered, and then snapped the locket closed, leaving me only with the swift impression of dark eyes set rather far apart and a handsome smile.

I thought about the little princess after she had gone. I knew from broad hints Moudi had dropped that Mishaal had been married for some time. Although she could not have been much more than nineteen, Islamic law allows girls to marry at thirteen; nevertheless, it was hard to imagine that "Mama Mishaal," who was unusually involved with her own children, would allow her darling, her daughter, to enter such an early union. Again there was the question I posed myself constantly about the women of the household: Did she have any choice? From observation, clues, and commonsense, I had come to understand that royal marriages in Saudi were usually by arrangement and for motives as likely to be political or economic as romantic by western standards. The perpetual divorcing and remarrying, whatever it did to the nervous systems of the partners involved, succeeded in keeping the money, the property and the power circulating, albeit only in a prescribed group of more or less related families. Somebody in power must have preferred to see Mishaal married, though living apart from her husband for the time being, to being divorced. Of course, there was the possibility too that Mishaal herself did not want a divorce, that she in fact was in love with her apparently faithless husband and hoped, as her Aunt Anud did, that someday he would return to

her. With all my heart I wanted that to be true but, although she
had not said so in words, I knew perfectly well that the photograph
Mishaal had shown me was not of her husband.

I wasn't sorry to get away from Taif or to be once again in Papa
Mohammed's beautiful garden, but this time our removal was the
most difficult we had ever made, for we needed to strip everything:
the stove, the beds, the stereo, every stick we had added to Mama
Sarah's minimal furnishing. We arrived in Jeddah not like a family
moving house but much more like an entire nation emigrating. The
moment I saw the towering chaos that confronted Susu and me
outside the guesthouse of Papa Mohammed's palace, I knew I must
either laugh or cry. In the event, I laughed then I struggled, I
sorted, I sweated, I raged, I shouted, and by nightfall it was all I
could do not to cry. Susu was finally asleep—it had been a matter
of finding the nuts and bolts for his dismantled cot which someone
had put inside the refrigerator—and I was up to my knees in his
clothes somehow mixed with all the household's bed linen, when a
servant came to interrupt me.

"Princess Moudi say . . . Susu's bear. You come get Susu's
bear."

"You tell Princess Moudi," I replied, keeping my voice under
control with great difficulty, "that at this moment I would not
come to get Susu's teddy bear if that teddy happened to be the last
teddy in the whole of the Arabian peninsula! You tell Princess
Moudi that I am not carrying one more object into this nursery
and nothing is welcome here, do you understand? Nothing, not
even a bear, unless it comes in on its own two feet! You tell Princess Moudi that next time she hires a nanny—which could be a lot
sooner than she thought—it had better be a camel or some other
beast of burden!" The servant understood nothing but my temper,
and she fled, leaving me on my hands and knees looking for Susu's
bath things—including the bath—under a mountain of cushions
and purple lampshades clearly belonging to Princess Jawahir. After
a few minutes, the door flew open. I looked up to see Moudi standing there with Fauza followed by some others.

"Lo and behold!" I said with unusual impertinence, "Mohammed has come to the mountain!"

"I told you to come get Susu's bear," Moudi said. "Why did you not come?"

I scrambled to my feet and enjoyed my six-inch advantage over her.

"Why didn't I come to get Susu's bear? I'll tell you why I didn't come. Princess; I didn't come because I was too busy, because I was too busy packing, unpacking, moving, loading, unloading, finding, losing, and doing a million other things I was not hired to do! That's why I didn't come, Your Majesty. I didn't come because a teddy bear was not uppermost in my mind. I didn't come because I was trying to find Susu's bed, and Susu's blankets, and Susu's food, and Susu's nappies, and it is only a miracle I did not have to find Susu! That is why I did not come . . ."

As Moudi watched my display her imperious expression melted gradually to astonishment, and her astonishment finally dissolved in laughter. Despite myself, I was tugged off my high horse and soon I was laughing too.

"What can I get for you, Rosemarie?" she said after a while. "What would you like? Anything, anything at all!"

"Oh, Princess Moudi," I said, holding my head in my hands. "How I would love a bottle of champagne!"

"I am sorry, Rosemarie, but that is one thing I cannot give you. You know there is no champagne in Saudi Arabia."

She closed the door gently behind her, and for half an hour or so I continued to seek and to find necessities in chaos. I was just about to go to bed at last when there was a light tap. I opened the door to find a bottle of vintage champagne on the threshold.

The next evening when I saw Moudi I thanked her for the champagne. She looked at me, round-eyed and with such a very sincere expression of sincerity I was tempted to be fooled by her.

"What champagne, Rosemarie?"

I had learned a considerable amount of Arabic, my servants had learned an insignificant amount of English, and language had nearly ceased to be a problem. When they have no common tongue people do communicate on levels more mysterious than that of language. Mistakes, however, do happen. I was with Moudi once on one of my expeditions for dress materials; she had returned from a foray into the cosmetics section of the open market and she called out to ask me if I had all I needed.

"Not quite, Princess Moudi," I shouted over the hullabaloo of the crowd around us. "I want five more zips!"

Suddenly all the shoppers were silent, staring at me, and Moudi turned on her heel to stride off down the street with me scurrying behind asking: "But what did I say? What did I say?"

The princess stopped.

"Rosemarie, don't ever use that word again! Certainly not in public!"

"What word?"

"That word!"

"Five?"

"No. The other word."

"More?"

"No. No. No. The other word."

"Zips?"

She gasped.

"Rosemarie! Don't say that word!"

"But what does it mean?"

Princess Moudi looked around, embarrassed, and finally she told me that Fauza would explain to me what the word meant when we returned to the palace. Fauza was delighted to give me a translation but she waited to do it till night when all the women were gathered for dinner, and she made a cabaret out of it, miming the man to whom the forbidden word belonged and leaving nobody in any doubt about exactly where the word belonged on the man. It was a very long time before the household staff took me seriously again.

That same shopping expedition resulted in another faux pas. I had bought a babygrow for Susu and that evening, when Moudi strolled into my room, I showed it to her.

"Look, Princess Moudi," I said. "Isn't this pretty?"

Moudi glanced at my purchase then did a double take and, moving faster than I had ever seen her move before, tore it out of my hands.

"No! No! No! Rosemarie, oh no!" she said, trying to rip the cloth apart with her hands.

"But what is it?"

"Look, look, look, Rosemarie!"

She held the garment up so I could see it.

"This is the Star of David! The star of Israel! You must not! You cannot!"

At least one Arab trader was as ignorant as I—or perhaps he was mischievous—because I had bought the babygrow in the souk. I scrapped it reluctantly but took my revenge later when I nearly broke Moudi's heart by telling her that Charlie Chaplin's mother, Paul Newman, and Kirk Douglas were all Jews and she would have to destroy her video cassettes of their performances. She was stricken. "But not Ryan O'Neal, Rosemarie," she said pitifully. "Not Ryan O'Neal!"

"No, Princess Moudi," I reassured her. "Ryan O'Neal is not Jewish. At least, I don't think he is . . ."

I liked Jeddah above all other Saudi cities but, oh, it was hot that October! And if I suffered I could not begin to imagine how the women in their long dresses with high necks and wrist-length sleeves must have felt in the waves of heat that pounded down on us, heavy with moisture from the Red Sea. Susu and I made our daily visits to members of the family who owned neighboring palaces, and to Mama Sarah who had returned from a pilgrimage to Medina and was staying with her son, Prince Fahd, the father of Mishaal. But despite the ubiquitous air conditioning we returned every afternoon like two wrung-out sponges: a big one and a little one.

Fashionable families of Jeddah spent weekends during hot weather at the place called by a name that had amused me so much months before: "The Creek." One day, Princess Moudi, who had been growing increasingly impatient for her father's summons to London, announced that all of us—including cook and stewards

—were going to spend a few restorative days at this resort where she had rented an entire hotel. Since "The Creek" was but a short drive from Papa Mohammed's guesthouse we did not need this time at least to pack the kitchen sink.

The hotel Princess Moudi had rented was dilapidated but so big even her numerous household could not fill it and our footsteps echoed in its halls accusingly, as if we were intruders on its silence rather than guests under its red-tiled roof. However, we did have a swimming pool refilled daily from "The Creek" which, it turned out, was an inlet of sea water and not the fresh mountain spring its name had evoked. Only Moudi and I wore swimsuits; all the others bathed in bras and long petticoats and bobbed around on the surface of the pool inside inflated inner tubes since Moudi and I were also the only ones who could swim. Moudi paddled back and forth, the women splashed and giggled from tire to tire and sang snatches of popular western love-songs, and while Susu napped I showed off with dives that took me underwater for nearly the length of the pool.

"Rosemarie! Rosemarie! Don't drown!" Moudi called out when I indulged in my aquatic display. "Susu needs you!"

Several times I gave Moudi instructions in diving, but the lessons always ended in royal belly-flops which she took stoically, coming back time and again for more until it hurt to watch her.

Although the antics of Moudi's household afloat had elements of fantasy and of comedy, I longed to strike out over an expanse of water uncluttered by mermaids in petticoats and inner tubes. Finally, I wandered off by myself one afternoon to take a look at "The Creek" and see if perhaps I could swim more freely there. "The Creek" was an inlet from the Red Sea—its parent body lay shimmering the breadth of the horizon—and it was surrounded by boulders sheltering pools of rank water and pebbles so sharp I could not tread on them without my sandals. Inching along a finger of land that extended far out into the water, I looked down and saw that the bottom of "The Creek" was paved with jagged rock and coral bristling with vicious black spines of sea urchins. Fish darted among the razor-sharp undersea formations, but their vivid colors seemed virulent and dangerous, like the feathers of poisoned darts. The air around me stank of sea life dying, dead, and drying in the sun. All in all, "The Creek" was one of the most malevolent bodies of water I had ever seen, and I was happy to leave it and return to the crowded pool.

When I was summoned to Moudi's quarters and asked to bring Susu along I knew that meant she had guests she wanted to impress with the beauty of her baby, and her prize European nanny. In her sitting room I found an assembly of western men, Americans I soon realized, about ten of them, comprising a group of architects and their assistants brought from Louisville, Kentucky, by Princess Moudi. How Princess Moudi found those architects in that remote city, I shall never know, for it was soon clear to me they had never worked in Saudi Arabia before. I gathered this from the curious glances they could not suppress at Princess Moudi, at me, at Susu, at the low cushions and chairs that furnished the room; also, thanks to my friend Gordon, I thought I recognized in their artificial subservient manner and in their eagerness to please even at the expense of honesty, what he had called "the greed of the luxury merchants."

"Rosemarie, we are talking about the new house I'm having built . . ."

"Oh yes, Princess Moudi?" I said calmly although it was the first I had heard of a new house.

"You must tell these men what you need for Susu and where you want your swimming pool."

"Our swimming pool? Oh yes, Princess . . ."

Although the meeting had its absurd side, I played along, and designed for Moudi and Susu and me a dream house with a swimming pool safe enough for the baby, yet deep enough for me.

"Well, yes, ma'am," said a bald man who appeared to be the senior partner of the firm and to whom all his colleagues deferred. "I don't foresee any problems . . ."

He didn't foresee any problems? It was then I knew for sure he had not worked in Saudi Arabia before, but I nodded my head.

"We ought to have this job finished by the time that cute little shaver is two years old . . ."

I coughed softly behind my hand.

"Now," he said to Moudi, "about the cold-storage house next to your kitchen . . ."

It was then I felt a wave of defensiveness about my adoptive family and their millions being strung along and stung by luxury merchants; after all, money meant little to Moudi but to the bald architect I knew it meant success, honor, and social class, so the princess, if she parted with her money thoughtlessly, was being degraded. I thought of him going home like a successful Don Juan to boast about his Arabian conquest.

"Princess Moudi, excuse me," I said, "but have you explained to these gentlemen about the power cuts we have all the time here? A cold-storage house wouldn't be worth a fig to us." I looked the bald man straight in his eyes.

"Even less than a fig," I said.

"Well then, ma'am," he said smoothly, "I guess we'll just have to add a house for your own generator . . ."

Although I knew I could never make a republican out of Papa Mohammed's grandson, I thought it was part of my duty to begin to expose him to varieties of life outside the palatial cocoon where we lived. To that end, one day I took Susu with me to the souk which I had come to know well since the day I lost my way among the stalls in streets that looped and wound like snarled thread. Susu had a glorious time; his little head turned from side to side, following a peacock blue shawl on one stall, a glittering mirror on another, here a mountain of pink and blue plastic buckets, there a spread of copper lamps glinting in the sun. By the time we returned to our driver and the Cadillac we were both tired out but very peaceful and happy.

On the way back to the palace, we were trapped in one of the worst traffic jams I had ever seen; a monster, even by Saudi standards. For the first twenty minutes or so Susu was merely fretful but when our air conditioning gave up the ghost, he began to scream in earnest. It felt as if the car had been lifted and placed in the center of a blazing oven, the upholstery seemed ready to dissolve, the glass of the windows wanted to melt. Poor Susu roared his misery and I tried, ineffectually, to help him. So close were our neighbors packed against us on either side, it was impossible to get out of the car and seek the shade of a stranger's house or even the shelter of a slim palm tree. Susu's face grew redder and redder, his cries were hoarse and even louder than the enraged horns hooting all around us. I wanted to send up my screams with Susu's as from within I felt the bubbling rise of real panic that exploded into terror when Susu suddenly grew quiet and lay back, fainting, in my arms.

"God, no!" I called out, pounding on the glass between us and the driver who was as helpless as I under the circumstances. "Rosemarie, take hold!" I told myself, struggling against my sickening fear. Susu stirred and sank abruptly into what I prayed was a normal sleep and not the deeper sleep of heat prostration. I listened to his breath as if my own life depended upon each exhalation and I found myself breathing with him, a little too rapidly, a little too shallow. With what stunning speed had our carefree afternoon become disaster!

"Please God, let him be all right. Please God, let me be the one, but not Susu. Please God, I will live my life without complaint; I will be less stubborn. I will be patient. I will be tolerant. Only please let Susu grow up into a tall, strong man . . ."

From someplace in my childhood rose the words of old prayers and I murmured them in German with my eyes on Susu's face as if it were an ikon.

When we finally arrived in front of the palace I was out of the car before it had stopped, holding Susu and shouting for Esher to bring me warm water. I sponged Susu down, gradually reducing his body temperature and I wet his lips with some of the tepid water: then I waited, and I prayed. At last, his eyelids fluttered, opened, and he looked up from my arms and smiled.

"Ya aayuni! Ya aayuni!" I said.

I held the baby close, and danced around the room as Mishaal liked to do.

"Thanks be to Allah!"

A few nights later I entered Moudi's room to chat with her about nothing very special, an easygoing innovation in our relationship

dating from the end of Ramadan. To my surprise I found a man
there, enrobed and in a dish-dasha, sitting on the floor and just fas-
tening the catch of a big suitcase. The image that rose was of a desert peddler come from the other side of "The Empty Quarter" to
show a beautiful and disdainful princess his pearls from the Persian
Gulf, his plundered lace, his coral, and polished quartz.

"Aha!" I said in a bantering tone. "I see the man has arrived
with all our riches!" Moudi looked up at me in surprise.

"How did you know that, Rosemarie?"

"It so happens, Princess Moudi," I said, still joking, "I have
X-ray vision and a supersensitive sense of smell!" She did not understand my words but my tone made her laugh.

"Now, Rosemarie, would you do something for me?" she said,
after the man had been dismissed, leaving his bag of wares behind
him. "Open that suitcase for me."

I undid the catch of the suitcase, lifted the lid, and gasped. Before me in neat stacks were tens of thousands of riyals! For the first
time, I saw how our money arrived and I also understood in a flash
of agitated surprise, what many of our suitcases must have contained as we moved from house to house, from country to country,
like gypsy millionaires. It is possibly a healthy attitude, though certainly one only the very, very rich can afford, that treats cash as an
object with no intrinsic value. It was thanks to this expensive and
extraordinary morality, plus the resultant Arab contempt for checks
and bankers, that our super-affluent household was often flat-broke
because Moudi had spent carelessly on jewelry or a new car, leaving not enough to pay for little extras like my salary until "the man
with the suitcase" came to call, sometimes bearing our money as if
it were so many pounds of grapes in plastic carrier bags from the
local supermarket.

"Okay. Fine. Good, Rosemarie," Moudi finally told me one day.
"Quick, get ready. Get ready. My father has telephoned. He says
we are to go quick, quick, to Europe!"

Her joy was so intense I felt as if I must be the only passenger on
a carousel who honestly did not want the brass ring; but I kept getting it anyway!

Our party was composed of Moudi and Susu, a servant I did not know called Safran, her six-year-old son, Hamada, our "watch-dog," who it so happened was also a doctor, and me. Susu and I were early at the airport. Moudi was late. We boarded our flight. Moudi dropped her veil. I sat, as usual, in the seat on the aisle. Susu sat, as usual, in the middle seat. I sighed and fastened my seatbelt with all the nonchalance I fancied a desert nomad brought each and every morning to the saddle of his old, familiar camel.

chapter 13

"So, you've become a commuter, have you?" Jennifer asked. "Has Saudi Airlines given you a season's ticket?" She tickled Susu under his chin; he chuckled and grabbed her finger. "What a grip he has! Have you been making this poor baby carry your suitcases?"

"I have to get him ready to carry suitcases as soon as possible. He certainly belongs to a family of nomads."

Susu and I were installed in a Mayfair service flat of our own; Princess Moudi had the flat next door and her servants had a flat along the corridor. Although there was a kitchen, a bathroom, and all the comforts—even our own television set and music center brought piece by piece from Saudi in the hold of our plane—the very effort by management to make our rooms homelike with vases, china ornaments, and scatter-rugs made them in a perverse way less cosy and more anonymous than a hotel room would have been. However, it was a quiet flat facing away from the street, and one window looked out on a courtyard-cum-garden where a large elm tree was touched with October rust against a chilly, gray sky.

The air outside had a cool dampness that Susu was unaccustomed to, and he looked around wide-eyed from under the hood of his jacket, as if he were a baby astronaut on an odd new planet. The shops were already trimmed for Christmas and I wondered what my little desert prince was making of the stuffed and painted Santas to be seen everywhere, looking not altogether unlike a nordic Papa Mohammed. The tang of festivity in the air of Christendom affected me and swept by an illogical but irresistible impulse I bought Christmas gifts and Christmas decorations to take back to

Saudi Arabia. Queuing with the Englishwomen who were laden
with their purchases, holding my own boxes of Christmas crackers,
a ball of tinsel, and a book of verse for Nedula, I relaxed into a
cosy contentment because I too had a family to make Christmas
for. Jennifer helped Susu and me into a taxi with my purchases
and waved us off into the chilly twilight where strings of colored
lights were looped like glowing boiled sweets. A few minutes later I
stood on the pavement in front of our block of flats with Susu in
his stroller and up to my knees in Harrods bags when I noticed a
group approaching us, waving and calling out. It was only when
one of the party rushed up to me, laughing and crying out "Rolls-
Royce! Rolls-Royce!" that I realized it was Mishaal and her family,
all of them smart and different from their Saudi-selves in European
street clothes.

Helped by my growing experience of instant-homemaking, I finally
looked around our flat one morning and felt comfortable in it. Simply by shifting a vase, rearranging the chairs, rolling up the scatter-
rugs, I had managed to imprint my personality on our surroundings. However, that same day when Susu and I returned from our
usual ramble the receptionist handed me my keys and notified me
we would all be moving in two hours. I raced upstairs and, sure
enough, everyone in our party including Princess Moudi herself
were busy packing! We were only moving to the Park Tower Hotel
adjoining Hyde Park but it might as well have been the other side
of the world: back went the stereo into packing cases, out came all
our valises, which already after only a few days in London had become too small.

I preferred being in a hotel, for the glamour and comfort of
hotel life never quite palled on me, nor did the magic of room service or the charm of strange, foreign languages assembled in a
corner of London where they belonged yet didn't quite belong. Jennifer and I celebrated the move by returning that night, with
Moudi's permission, to the Inter-Continental Hotel where we were
received like old friends.

It was there, later, in the discothèque that a remarkable thing
happened to me; at least at the time it seemed remarkable. Later, it
seemed simple, natural, and even inevitable. I met the chairman of

a large agricultural company from Leicester. He was in London for
a conference; he was a man of intelligence, humor, and that
cheerful self-assurance I had always admired. "And he's divorced
too!" my practical chum Jennifer pointed out to me.

The fact that for the first time, in "Farmer Jones," as I
laughingly called him, I had found a man of whom even my
mother would approve, did not dampen the pleasure I took in his
company. Jennifer became my generous and devoted babysitter,
doing her best to suppress her curiosity and greeting me on my return to the hotel when I had seen "Farmer Jones" with real joy in
my obvious happiness. As a reward for her service, I told Jennifer
that when I took my vacation from Moudi's household in the
spring she could, if she wished and if she was free, go to Saudi as
my replacement.

"Is that a reward?" she asked. "Or a punishment?"

"Rosemarie, why do you look so, so . . ." Moudi searched for a
word, "bright?"

To my annoyance, I blushed.

"Aha! Aha! Aha!" Moudi cried, her eyes luminous. Like the
other royal ladies of Saudi, Moudi placed all achievement and all
activity, all history itself, many notches under romance. And not
the romance of her own Bedouin ancestors' struggle with the shifting landmarks of earth's empty quarters, for Moudi and her female
relatives, romance was painted in Jawahir's favorite purple: it was
a Hollywood musical and when there were tears, they were supposed to be the kind that didn't smudge mascara. For the bored,
idle princesses—Moudi, Jawahir, Mishaal, even Anud waiting patiently for her faithless husband—romance was the only way out.
And since in real life there could never be a romance as consuming
as the one they all craved, in reality there was no way out for them.

"Aha!" Moudi said again. "Rosemarie is in love!"

"No, Princess Moudi," I said. "I'm not ready yet to fall in love
. . ." She looked so crestfallen, I smiled at her. "But I'm sure that
I'm ready to think about falling in love."

Papa Mohammed was installed with his male household in one of
the big houses of "The Boltons" that unexpected and super-

fashionable corner of Kensington known very well to a very few of
the richest people in the world. In this lushly feathered nest he had
created a corner of Saudi Arabia where his family—Mishaal and
her parents, Moudi, little Anud, Lulu, and any other of the clan in
London or passing through—stopped by for tea. With cheerfully
prejudiced eyes it seemed to me that of them all Susu was the patriarch's pet.

"If you ever cannot take Susu to see my father for tea," Moudi
told me, "be sure to call Safran to come and fetch the baby. Every
day at four o'clock my father sits and watches the door, you understand, Rosemarie? Waiting for Susu."

Susu and I made our daily visits and gladly. Often, the lad
Hamada would go with us, for it was he who had been chosen,
Moudi explained to me once, to grow up alongside Susu and, eventually, to become the favorite servant of his entourage as Fauza was
of Moudi's own. Hamada was even-tempered and bright, he managed to acquire a few words of English during our relatively brief
stay in London. He too had an eye condition, one which would en-
tail corrective surgery when he was old enough for it, and Papa
Mohammed paid for him to make the same round of leading
ophthalmic surgeons on which Susu had embarked.

Papa Mohammed's gatherings were very pleasant. Sometimes the
table was laid with a real English tea including cream cakes, scones,
and Dundee cake. Mishaal or Lulu would pour tea and coffee
while Papa Mohammed's favorite servant, Mohammed Ali, chased
Susu around and around the furniture, roaring and growling like a
playful lion.

More than any of his family, Papa Mohammed reminded me of
Mama Sarah, for he shared her rough pride and he too seemed a
conduit through which the traditions of his race passed into the
twentieth century. In history at least those two were well matched,
though perhaps not in piety or in temperament for Moudi had explained to me once that her parents' marriage had been arranged
in the old-fashioned way, which meant neither of them had any
right whatsoever to object to the proposal or demur from it. Passion, had it ever been there, no longer existed between Mama Sarah

and Papa Mohammed but there was a bond of courtesy and respect between them which I thought admirable and even enviable. Earlier, before we left for London, in Taif one day I had shown Princess Moudi a book my friend Gordon had given me in which there was a stunning photograph of one of the desert fortress-palaces, at peace and of a piece with its surrounding landscape of dark yellow sands.

"You see, Princess," I said, joking, "this is what I expected to find in Saudi Arabia. This is what I imagined your palace would look like."

Moudi had taken the book out of my hands and studied the photograph seriously, shaking her head.

"But, Rosemarie," she said, "that is exactly like the palace where we lived and where I grew up! Mama Sayida and I used to sleep on the roof in summer with a bowl of water to drink."

At the time, I had thought she exaggerated. It was only in London when I watched Papa Mohammed at the center of his family in their bright dresses with his white-clad staff behind him, I realized that he, like Mama Sarah, really did come from a stronghold in the ancient wilderness far from the morals and marvels of my western world; and despite all the western comforts of his life in Riyadh I felt that he could return to the stern ancestral places without regret.

After rain one crisp afternoon, Moudi and Mishaal went shopping on Bond Street with me and Susu in his stroller following behind them. The two princesses were giggling, carefree, cheerfully secure that nothing behind any of the glittering windows we passed was beyond their reach. Suddenly, they stopped short so quickly that we all nearly collided. A man had come out of a doorway. I had the impression of someone tall, rather portly and dark. He and Mishaal stared at each other for a shocked moment, then he hurried on into a car waiting at the curb. For the rest of that stroll Mishaal was unusually quiet and withdrawn, responding halfheartedly when Moudi attempted to distract her.

That evening, after Susu was safely asleep, I went to Moudi's

suite and without ceremony claimed one of her easy chairs. Moudi
was sitting on the matching sofa, looking through swatches of silk
for a dress she was going to have made.

"You know, Rosemarie, today we met Mishaal's husband, in
Bond Street."

"That man? The one who literally crossed our path?"

"Yes. Mishaal's husband. She did not know he was in London."
It was only then, when I heard that neither spouse had known the
other was in London, that I realized the depth of the rift in
Mishaal's marriage.

Could I have helped Mishaal? Could I have detoured her jet-age
conscience from its collision with medieval judgments? Even now,
no answer comes to me. Only in my mind's eye there is the image
of an unopened safe, part of the dowry from a desert bride, kept
without curiosity although nobody remembered its combination or
knew what it held; although nobody cared that it might have been
empty.

Sometimes Papa Mohammed's afternoon gatherings in London
were composed of men: the male members of his family, court
officials who happened to be in London, and more than once the
Saudi ambassador, who was called upon to act as interpreter when
Papa Mohammed had questions to pose about Susu's welfare. Also
there had been a "gift" for me, usually the equivalent of about
£300 from Papa Mohammed himself but through the agency of
Princess Moudi. I asked the ambassador if he would be so kind as
to thank Papa Mohammed on my behalf. While I made this
request I noticed Papa Mohammed watching me intently and it
dawned on me that he might just understand a great deal more
English than he had ever let on.

"Prince Mohammed has asked me to say that you belong to the
family," said His Excellency, my interpreter. He and the others
around us looked surprised.

Frequently it happened that when Susu and I arrived Papa
Mohammed was engrossed with the men in a card game and on
these occasions Susu played with Prince Sa'ad, Mishaal's brother,
or a friendly servant until the game was over, with me following

behind watching them and at the same time being afforded a good look around the premises. They were luxurious, to be sure, and yet they revealed some of the paranoia I often sensed around me in Riyadh. Was it possible my own imagination was sharpened by suspicion, or was it really a secret escape door under the staircase I saw, its outline half-hidden by wallpaper? The servant showed me with pride that the heavy front door had a complicated, unique locking device that would keep any intruder shut well out. Once, the servant dropped behind a sofa out of sight and the room was suddenly filled with the voice of a newscaster speaking Arabic which sounded so like Radio Riyadh I assumed Prince Mohammed arranged to have his local news transmitted by shortwave. Each of our rambles revealed something elegant or strange.

It was on just such an afternoon that Susu in the throes of his adventurous play slipped and hit his head on a smoked-glass table with that dull "thunk" familiar to anyone who has raised a toddler. I swept Susu into my arms, cuddled him, and distracted him with funny noises, before he could gather together his forces and begin to scream. A few minutes later we left and went straight back to the hotel where Moudi was waiting for us in the makeshift nursery.

"Is Susu all right?" she asked. "My mother just rang from Riyadh to tell me that my father had rung her from London to tell her that Susu hit his head on a glass table and he didn't even cry!"

"Do you know," I said, laughing, "how many English businessmen I have heard complaining in Saudi because it takes them hours—even days—to place a call to London!"

Not long after we had moved our household into the Park Tower Hotel, Papa Mohammed granted Princess Mishaal permission to remain in London after her family returned to Saudi on the condition that she stay with us, and soon she was installed next door to the suite I shared with Susu.

The combination of Mishaal's high spirits and "Farmer Jones's" regular visits to London seemed to trim ten or twelve years off my own mature sense of responsibility and I found myself giggling at Mishaal's antics, tapping time while she danced and even allowing Susu to stay up past his bedtime when his pretty cousin was in a playful mood, which was admittedly about five nights out of five. Perhaps it was because my own emotions were engaged for the first time since Stephen's death, giving me an extra awareness of amorous matters, but one evening as I was returning to the hotel I saw Mishaal alone getting into a taxi. I called her name and she looked up with glowing, happy eyes and I knew as surely as the pavement was under my feet and a drizzle was falling from the gray sky that Mishaal was going to see her beloved. Sure enough, a few nights later Mishaal came into the nursery to play with Susu.

"Susu! Susu!" she sang his name and held him against her cheek. "I will wait for you Susu. Susu. Susu. Will you be my husband?"

"Mishaal," I told her, "by the time he is old enough to marry, you will be a grandmother."

She stopped dancing and lay Susu down in his cot whereupon he whimpered to be picked up again.

"My love is in London," she said gravely. She then said something in Arabic, but I heard the word "Embassy" in English and guessed that her lover must be connected with an Arab Embassy. She sighed and stood for a moment in thought which, because she was usually so quick and merry, made her seem sad; then she laughed, took Susu into her arms and kissed him. I watched them, smiling, although it was well past his bedtime.

There are two basic reasons Arabian princesses come to London, and this trip was primarily for the second: this was not a shopping trip, it was a medical trip. Nevertheless, we took our treatment pretty much as we shopped: only the best would do and a lot more of it than we needed! Susu received a glowing bill of health generally and the concensus of ophthalmic opinion was that he did not need surgical intervention since his tear ducts had already begun to function and would soon be working at full strength. As for his general condition, one of London's most important pediatricians wrote Moudi a report that summed it up very well:

". . . there is no cause whatever for any anxiety . . . he (Saud Bin Abdul Majeed Bin Abdul Aziz) is well in advance of his calendar age . . . He is already walking . . . He already says a few syllables . . . While all this is very nice . . . I am concerned he may in fact be being overstimulated in order to perform his party tricks. If the mother wishes to have a larger child, it would be advisable for her to let him lead a somewhat more peaceful life . . . it is said that since May he has been travelling about and this . . . makes it difficult for any child to settle down to growing . . . If the child is overstimulated, lacks periods of peace and is constantly moving about, then the result will be a rather small child . . . It is no good then worrying about his size. Worry will only make matters worse . . . he is an excellent boy. He is short but his weight is exactly right for his age and height . . . Yours sincerely . . . P.S. I enclose an account."

This, except for the postscript, was precisely what I had told Princess Moudi in the beginning. I too was treated to a battery of tests and examinations which Moudi offered in precisely the same offhand way she offered shopping sprees at Harrods. Our journey, I suspected, would have been considered in some measure a failure had one of our party not needed treatment, so it was with satisfaction Princess Moudi announced she was booked into the Wellington Clinic for minor orthopedic surgery.

The Wellington Clinic is owned and operated by Americans who employ an English medical staff. Sixty per cent of the patients in the six-floor clinic are Arabs and most of them come from Saudi Arabia which explains why each room in addition to its large color television set can be furnished on request with a video cassette to show twenty-four-hour screenings of Arab films. Hardy Amies designed the uniforms for nurses who were apparently selected for their beauty as well as for their impeccable professionalism. In fact, it takes an X-ray eye to spot that under the drifts of flowers and potted plants, the high-pile carpet in decorator colors, and the gourmet menus with Arab alternatives, serious medicine is being practiced in what is much more the ambience of a luxury ocean liner than a surgery. Arabs are reluctant to sleep alone in a room or live alone among outsiders and King Khalid, who traveled inside Saudi with a normal retinue of eighteen hundred courtiers, when he became a patient at the Wellington booked neighboring suites for his entourage just as he would at a hotel. Moudi was satisfied with having Hamada's mother in attendance all day, but at night she released her servant to babysit with Susu. I suppose it might have been that only when she was traveling in the West did Princess Moudi feel safe enough to sleep alone in a room.

Susu and I came to visit his mother in the afternoons before tea with Papa Mohammed and after our own medical appointments. Except for the clinical paraphernalia at her bedside, Moudi could have been receiving us in the royal suite of a five-star hotel, although she was obviously in considerable discomfort. It was during one of these meetings that there was a tap at the door and in walked Mishaal whom I had not seen for several days. It was a moment or two before I actually recognized her; her face was black and blue, her cheeks were puffy, and a plaster covered the bridge of her nose. I gasped and even Susu stared at his cousin with his mouth open.

"You've had an accident! Mishaal, dear Mishaal, what happened to you? Why didn't someone tell me?"

Moudi laughed.

"No, Rosemarie. No accident. Mishaal has had her nose done."

Mishaal grinned at my expression and then winced in pain.

"But why? Her nose was perfect. It was a classical nose. It belonged to your face, Mishaal . . ."

Moudi cut me short.

"She wanted a European nose. Silly girl," she added, although I knew that Moudi too had considered plastic surgery and would probably have undertaken it in Paris had Papa Mohammed not summoned us back to Saudi too soon. Mishaal spoke quickly to Moudi, asking her what I had said and how I thought she looked. Now that the shock of her appearance was over, I considered her solemnly: her huge eyes, the cheekiness of her expression, indomitable, even with the odd protuberance where her nose belonged.

"Tell Princess Mishaal I think she looks like Mickey Mouse. And from now on whenever she calls me 'Rolls-Royce' I shall know precisely what to call her!"

Mishaal laughed with the rest of us although I could see she was in pain. Before Mishaal left the room while Moudi was speaking to someone on the phone, she touched a string of black worry beads she was wearing like a necklace.

"These are from my love," she whispered to me with touching shyness. On her bruised, bandaged face there was almost maternal tenderness and I knew she prized her inexpensive beads above all diamonds. "Mickey Mouse is growing up," I thought.

When Mishaal returned to the hotel after recuperating in the hospital, there was a swelling around her new nose noticeable only to those who had seen her before the surgery. She looked very pretty, but then she always had, and I missed her high-bridged profile, although she seemed quite pleased.

"*Mumkin an akun Inglizia, Americania, Alemania,*" she said solemnly, speaking to her reflection in the mirror over my dressing table, "*Mumkin an akun kul shai.*"

When her meaning got through to me, I felt a little displeased, puritanical even. She was saying that with her new nose she could be English, American, German . . . any nationality at all.

"Mishaal, Mishaal, we shouldn't try to be anything but what we are. We should be proud of what we are. You are a beautiful Arab girl and that's something to be proud of . . ." Mishaal didn't appear to hear my little sermon or to understand it; she went on gazing at her reflection not with vanity but with the calculating expression of a mature and objective critic.

One of the princess's suite of rooms in the hotel had been converted into what I called "The Music Room"; there, the hotel had installed our video set and our music center with its four speakers strategically placed to make inescapable the strains of Moudi's favorite popular love songs. While Moudi was in the hospital, Susu and I held little parties for just ourselves in the music room where we whirled around the floor cheek-to-cheek with only my feet touching the ground. When she left the hospital these parties continued and Moudi would sometimes stand at the door and watch us with a puzzled, amused look.

"How happy you two are!" she said once wistfully. "You're having a real party."

"Only a tea party, Princess Moudi. Only tea for two."

Moudi reached out her arms suddenly and I put Susu into them, but she held him too stiffly and soon he stretched his little arms toward me, whimpering. For just a moment I thought I surprised an expression of wounded feelings on Moudi's face, but immediately the hurt, if it had been there at all, became annoyance and she returned the baby to me with an impatient gesture. It seemed to me then inexpressibly sad that a royal mother who still searched for love, did not know when she held love in her arms.

The next morning I woke suddenly at five in the faint gray light of dawn to find Princess Moudi standing over my bed. She was in her nightgown and I assumed she was on her way to bed. It was clear by the stiffness of her posture and the glitter in her eye that she was in some kind of rage.

"Go to your room, Princess Moudi," I said calmly and with great firmness. "When I have fed Susu at six I'll come speak to you."

When he woke, I gave Susu his bottle, rubbed his back, and talked to him for a while, then lay him down again as he always took a nap after his first meal. Finally, I took a deep breath and rapped on Moudi's door. Instead of asking me into her room, she sailed past me into the nursery where she pounced on Susu, lifted him from his cot, and woke him.

"What are you up to, Princess Moudi?"

"I am his mother. I can do with my son whatever I want. Everything I do you always say is wrong!"

Susu began to scream. Moudi jiggled him frantically up and down a few times, then dropped him in his cot and sailed out as she had entered.

"Keep calm, Susu. Keep calm, darling," I said to the baby and to myself. "Don't be hasty, Susu. Stay calm. If Her Majesty supposes she can behave that way . . . ! Keep cool, Susu. Think. Who does she think she is . . . ? Now, now, stay calm."

Once again the explosion of Moudi's temper had caught us in London. It was my country, these were my people, and there was "Farmer Jones" to offer me the suggestion of a new life. I loved Susu with all my heart, but I was nobody's slave: not his, not his mother's.

That afternoon, while Susu napped, I knocked on Moudi's door.
"What do you want?" she asked shortly.
"To talk to you alone, Princess."
She motioned the servants to leave us.
"I've thought it over, Princess Moudi. If you're so unhappy about the way I take care of Saud then in fairness to yourself, and to your son, and to me, we must sever this relationship."
I spoke softly but my knees shook and a lump was welling in my throat. "The agency where you found me is just down the street. I would like you to ring them, please, and ask them for a new nanny. When she comes, I promise I'll stay on with Susu until she learns about him, about his ways . . ." My voice broke, but I cleared my throat and continued. "Then I'll leave."
Suddenly, Moudi looked tired. I could see under her chic new hairstyle and skillful make-up both the eager child she must have been once, and the embittered old woman she might one day become.
"Please, Rosemarie, don't . . ." This time it was her voice that became uncertain. "Yesterday I had some bad news from Saudi. Very bad. It was . . ." She hesitated and added, "bad."
"Moudi, why didn't you talk to me, tell me about it, let me know?" I asked her, all my anger, self-pity, determination, gone in a flood of compassion. "Look, Moudi," I said gently, "let's forget what happened between us. But let us make an agreement: if for any reason, either here or in Saudi, you want me to leave or if I feel that I must leave, then we will say it openly and calmly. Fair enough? Without bad feelings or anger. And in plenty of time for me to train a replacement because Susu must not be left without a good nanny."
As I was leaving, Moudi called after me. "You and Susu mean so much to each other!"
If only there had been envy in Moudi's voice for the love of Susu, her life might have been happier.

The time to leave London had rolled around again. Susu and I were paying our last visit to Papa Mohammed at "The Boltons" where we were received with the usual courtesy and affection. At the door as Susu and I were leaving, a servant slipped an envelope into my hand. The big door was literally closing behind us as I looked down and saw that I held one of the pink bank envelopes in which our money was often delivered, a mate to the hundreds of identical envelopes strewn casually around Moudi's suite. I riffled through it and was astonished to realize it contained fifty twenty-pound notes: £1,000! The door had been closed, making it clear that the donor of this princely gift expected nothing in exchange for it: not even thanks.

chapter 14

I strolled into economy class to stretch my legs. An American in the back of the plane had decided there was only one way he was going to get his allowance of alcohol into Saudi Arabia. Although Saudi Airlines served no liquor, they didn't object to him drinking his own and so that is precisely what the American had been doing pretty steadily since our departure from Heathrow. Because his seat was on the aisle, a stream of Arabs—men and women—in western dress had been passing him on their way to the toilets whence they emerged robed, veiled, and ready to resume life in their homeland. On outward trips, the transformation was reversed with robed Arabs entering the toilets after the halfway point to emerge in beautifully cut European dress. "Saudi Airlines welcomes you to Saudi Arabia" the American shouted out as a portly Arab, his dishdasha secured with a silken cord, returned to his seat for landing. The American stood up.

"Prepare for landing," he shouted, "in the country where kitchen towel, fan belt and bedsheet are the national costume!" A nervous titter greeted the American's sally, and his traveling companions did their best to prevent any further levity at the expense of their hosts.

I enveloped myself in the familiar Riyadh life as easily as Princess Moudi slipped into her cloaking abaya. Although the palace was by no means a cosy nest, there was no other place on earth then where I could have been received with so much joy by so many. In no time at all it was England that seemed a strange, alien country and the setting for a story someone had told me, less real than the scent of sandalwood with roses or the call to prayer that punctuated the day of Islam and made it comprehensible to Allah and his believers. Even the memory of "Farmer Jones" and the promise of seeing him again in a few months during my vacation was sweet yet fleeting too and as hard to hold as the snatch of a popular song heard in London. When I tried to imagine my own future it always included Susu and I took it for granted I would be near him, watching him grow at least until he was seven and joined the men, as was traditional, for his further education. I thought I was beginning to understand the pride of my Arab family and sometimes I caught a glimmer of their mysterious souls waiting like Mama Sarah's bony hands at rest, fierce as the scowl on Zuchia's face when she watched the blond infidel growing closer to Moudi and her son.

Only my stomach could betray my mind and my heart, and it was just a little while after our return that this prosaic organ fell prey once more to the national disease. This time, however, despite the urging of Moudi, Dr. Nabia, and even the royal physician, I flatly refused to enter the hospital. My servant, Esher, had been badly hurt in one of Ahmed-the-Killer's car crashes and she had gone home to Ethiopia to recuperate. In the meantime, I had been assigned a large, coarse woman from the sewing room who attended to Susu while I lay immobilized and feverish. Never had I seen Moudi in a rage as terrible as the one that took her when I told her that from my bed I had heard the new nursery servant shouting at Susu and slapping him. The anger of the royal mother fairly lifted the roof off that palace but to me it was music, and when the servant had been sent back to the sewing room in disgrace, I learned that the best cure for my complaint was simply to know Susu needed me. Susu, in fact, needed me badly, for he was not immune to the national disease either and suffered his own serious attack. In the long run, my illness did have one personal benefit, for I was granted permission to have food sent in from the Inter-Continental Hotel and later to take my meals in their dining room which afforded me another western oasis in that Arab world. Sometimes, when I left after dinner I would find Moudi who was forbidden to enter and eat in public, sitting in the car outside, eating takeaway hamburgers her chauffeur fetched for her and watching the foreign guests freely entering and leaving the hotel.

Like the first twinge of what promises to be a raging toothache or the first sneeze of a cold, I found myself in a strange mood as December drew on and a dull depression began to sneak through the cracks in my day: those moments when I wasn't busy with Susu, the half hour before I fell asleep, or those brief times my mind wandered from the work in hand. Christmas was coming with its burden of memories and with the curious realization that in another part of the world my people were commemorating an event that had taken place not very far from the strange land where I found myself envying their celebration. Fortunately, Gordon arrived not long before the holiday and took me on a round of informal dinner parties given by the cosmopolitan community in Riyadh, among them a rich, highly educated Arab who greeted us with worldly charm and fed us delicacies from French china while his wife—an educated professional woman—ate in the kitchen. We even had one dinner of goose and forbidden ham in an American household where the wife had somehow managed to find a real Christmas tree. I had gifts to wrap too and paper Santas to hang around the nursery looped with tinsel to dazzle poor little Susu who was just recovering from measles.

It was Christmas Eve. I stood out on the balcony in the cold, still night.

"Rosemarie," I told myself, "what more do you want?"

Christmas decorations? Over my head the stars gleamed just as they had over the births of kings. Shelter? I had been welcomed into an alien household and had been received there with marks of friendship. I was clothed, fed, and comfortable. Love? A baby was asleep in the nursery. Gifts? That morning Moudi had given me a necklace purportedly from Susu, that spelt my name in tiny diamond chips.

"What more can you ask, Rosemarie?"

"Princess Moudi," I said the next day, "I want to pray."

"Pray?" she said after a moment.

"Yes. It needn't be in a Christian church. I thought perhaps in a mosque. Your father's mosque?"

"My father's mosque?" I could see she was struggling and I had the unpleasant impression it was not to laugh. "Women don't pray in my father's mosque." she said finally.

"Where do women pray then?"

"Wherever the time to pray finds us. My mother often prays in the desert . . ."

A silvery sheen lay over the desert on Christmas day that reminded me oddly of snow and the clarity of icicles that used to hang from the eaves of my home in Germany. Ahmed Two stopped the car after we had driven for about an hour into the wasteland; grumbling, Fauza drew her abaya around her as a Hamburg matron snuggles into furs. I told Ahmed and Fauza to wait and I got out of the car which was parked at the edge of a large, man-made oasis. The air was gentle, already cool with approaching evening. The palms were planted in regular rows that formed straight lines or diagonal lines, depending upon which way I turned my head, putting me inside a square, a rectangle, or at the point of a triangle, depending upon how I chose to see myself in relation to them; beneath the lofty fronds silence was heavy yet made a sound of its own, the way silence does inside a seashell. Even the oasis invites a desert traveler to lose his way and I glanced frequently back at the car as I walked deeper into the strange orchard, until I became aware of a voice singing. Ahead of me was the heart of the palm grove and a canal of clear, sparkling water; beside the water, with his back to me, stood a man in a flowing white robe and it was he whose song I had heard. No doubt it was a workingman's song but it sounded elegant and effortless. I listened to him while the afternoon drew on and the colors of the desert ripened around me. A bird of prey circled overhead and gradually I was relieved of homesickness, of depression, and of nostalgia for past Christmases. There was no roof over the prayer I raised then to the merciful God of my own childhood and yet, not long afterward, I wondered

if He had heard me, or if a much more terrible deity was in attendance among those palm groves.

The December weather in Riyadh was unpredictable and could be
chilly, but there was always a patch of hot sunlight trapped around
the Al Yamama swimming pool which had again become my haven
and my escape. There I had encountered some old friends from the
European community whom I had not seen for months. Mrs.
Smythe, when she heard I had just returned from London, put to
me her passionate, searching questions about the weather, and her
husband offered me the usual choice of gin or whisky, then gave me
an Evian water, laughing as if neither of us had heard the old poolside joke before. So often did Mr. Smythe repeat his tippler's joke
in a teetotal country—"whisky, Rosemarie?" he'd ask for the fortieth time, and for the fortieth time bring me a Coke—I decided one
day to have a little fun of my own.

The bottle of champagne that had appeared on my threshold in
Jeddah was secreted among my possessions in such a way that it
had followed me like a talisman. It wasn't that I felt incapable of
polishing off the bottle by myself; on the contrary, there were many
days of high frustration in the nursery when I could have drunk a
lake of champagne and asked for more; the truth of the matter was,
I had never mastered the skill of opening a champagne bottle and
within the dry precincts of our palace there was nobody I dared ask
to do it for me. One day that December before I went to the pool I
put the bottle of champagne in a plastic carrier bag. I then seated
myself at the side of the pool and when I was sure nobody was
watching, I slipped the handle of the carrier bag over the arch of
my foot and lowered it into the water where the wine would dangle
until it was chilled. In due course, Mr. Smythe made his usual underwater crossing, surfacing near me, snorting and puffing.

"Mr. Smythe," I said, "I'd like something to drink."

"Certainly, Rosemarie, my pleasure." He hoisted himself out of
the pool and stood beside me; he hopped first on one foot, then on
the other, tilting his smooth, bald head to clear his ears of water.

"Now then," he said, "what will it be, my dear? A gin-and-it? A
scotch on the rocks, perhaps, the way the yanks like it?"

"I think today, Mr. Smythe, I am in the mood for nice, chilled champagne!"

"So be it, milady. Nice cool 'champers' all 'round!" he said. He turned toward the bar to get the "champagne," returning of course with three Cokes: one for me, one for himself, and one for his wife who had joined me at the poolside and was dangling her toes in the water too. Only when Mr. Smythe had handed the paper cups around did I draw the plastic bag up out of the pool. "Take this into the changing room, Mr. Smythe," I said, "and astonish us!"

"You don't mean . . ." he began in a voice that trembled with excitement.

Off Mr. Smythe went, faster than any walrus had been known to move on land, and in a few moments there was a gratifying "pop" from the area of the men's changing room. Flushed with sun, success, and the promise of bubbly, Mr. Smythe, holding the plastic bag before him with ceremonious care, rejoined us at the pool and soon he had filled our cups with purest vintage wine. As the cool champagne spread its warmth, I began to find the Smythes a really fine and upstanding couple, although I did notice that Mr. Smythe was tipping the plastic bag rather more often over his own cup than over either mine or his wife's, and soon he began attending to his speech with all the painstaking care of a gardener weeding among seedlings.

"Ex-cel-lent cham-pagne," he enunciated carefully.

"Trevor . . ." Mrs. Smythe said with that note of warning peculiar to a wife worried for her husband's sobriety.

"Trevor . . ."

In her concern was a glimmer of the reason the Smythes had left England and come to a country where there were no local pubs to lead Trevor through the stages of conviviality down into perdition! Realizing this, I felt great fondness for the Smythes and I admired their courage. Already, his eyes were faintly bloodshot and I hoped his laugh wasn't loud enough to attract attention. He passed the bag once more over his own cup then briefly over his wife's and mine.

"Going to tell you a story, Rosemarie," Mr. Smythe said after a few moments of happy, tipsy silence. "Damned funny thing. Happened while you were in good old England. Damned funny. Had a flood, you know. Streets running with water! First mud, then water. Went on for days. Blasted inconvenient. Then, one day, water's gone, just mud. First mud, then dust as usual. Asked this chap at work—teaches French—anyhow, asked him—'Gene, old chap, what's all this water about? Noah's ark all over again?' Long story short, he speaks the lingo pretty well, goes out and asks some questions. Comes back to tell me some workmen in the street, 'yobs' from the Yemen, chopping away with their pickax-thingibobs, don't you know, hit main water pipe. Whoosh! The old H_2O everywhere! Major flood. Powers that be round the villains up and slam them in jail. Big sin in these countries, you know Rosemarie, wasting the old H_2O!" He winked at me and made a pass over our cups with the plastic bag, then turned it upside down to all but wring it out over his own cup. "Major sin in any country wasting the old champers," Mr. Smythe said. "Where was I? So they slam these crinim . . . crilim . . ." He stopped, cleared his throat. "These villains, they slam these villains in the jug. Powers that be say 'Good-oh! Well done, lads. Now stop the leak and get rid of the water!' The order is passed down the ranks as usual, until it reaches chappie at the bottom and can go no lower. 'Stop the water, Abdul!' he is told. 'How do I stop the water?' Abdul says. 'The only men in Riyadh who can fix that pipe are the men who broke it, and the poor buggers are in jail!' "

Mrs. Smythe and I laughed as much at the telling as we did at the story; Mr. Smythe waited patiently.

"There's more," he said then. "They had to let the blighters out of jail to repair the pipe they had broken in the first place. 'But,' say the powers that be, 'there can be no crime without a punishment!' So, what do they do? As soon as the pipe is fixed, they thank the workmen, probably pay them something for their trouble, and put the poor sots right back in jail!" The laugh that emerged from under his mustache seemed to set the pool rippling around our feet.

Late one fair morning not long after Christmas, I clambered into the car as usual and made my way to the hotel. There, to my

surprise, I found the entire European community gathered and
muttering at the entrance to the pool, for all the world like a mob
of strikers at the factory gates. I pushed forward and found a notice
in English pinned to the door of the enclosure. We of the foreign
community were being informed that the swimming pool was
thereafter closed for mixed bathing. Men and women could swim
only on alternate days and, as a final insult to my way of thinking,
the men had been allotted four days out of each week while we
women were granted only three! "But does this mean I can't swim
with my own husband?" a woman next to me said. She was holding a little girl by the hand. "Does this mean my child can't swim
with her father? He's my husband. Do they really mean we can't
swim together?" Mrs. Smythe seemed the most distressed of us all;
she was wringing her hands and looked ready to cry.

"Oh dear! Oh dear! Oh dear! But this is dreadful. This makes
us like their own women! What shall I do? I have nothing else, no
place else to go." She turned to me. "These are *your* people. You
work for them, *live* with them. Why are they doing this to us?"
The venom in her voice appalled me; for a moment it seemed to
encompass me as well as the Saudis.

I could rant, rage, I could even quit if I had to, but there was
nothing Princess Moudi could do to help. It so happened that a
group of religious leaders had held a meeting at the Al Yamama
and one of them had looked down from the window of his room to
see the spectacle of men and women paddling in the same pool.

"Against the laws of religion, even my uncle Khalid the King
himself is helpless."

My search for an alternative swimming pool was to end only
after my return from holiday when I met a Swiss banker called M.
Raoul who had lived in Saudi for many, many years, spoke fluent
Arabic, and had penetrated unusually far for a foreigner into the
confidence of the royal family. I used to call M. Raoul our own
"Lawrence of Arabia," for he was one of those Europeans who
seems destined to accept an alien culture and to find its ways more
compatible than those of his own country. He had even developed
something of the look of an Arab with sun-dyed skin and a sharp,
hawkish profile; only his eyes reflected the blue-gray skies of his native land.

"Essentially, Rosemarie, you are a romantic," he told me once. "And essentially the Arab is not a romantic; he is a classicist who never gives theme precedence over structure. In other words, he has rules. And he obeys those rules in a manner you might think heartless. He even breaks his rules in a heartless way. I know you are coming to love these people, and I do love them; but someday you may find out what you really love is your own romantic image of them." Raoul leaned forward, his face a mirror of emotions I had seen on Arab faces: there was puzzlement, amusement, and a judgment devoid of either envy or sentimentality. "Be careful," he said. "This peninsula is unyielding, and it can be very dangerous."

But M. Raoul's warning lay in my future; meanwhile, the winter days slipped by unclouded by anything but the usual problems attendant on the land of *bukra, inshallah,* and *ma fi* ("tomorrow," "God willing," "out of stock"); once again, relatively small happenings stamped a day, a week, even a month when outside our compound more earthshaking things may have been happening.

One day I went out for a stroll with Susu and Nedula, and in the course of our play I picked up a piece of rope I happened to find on the ground and pretending it was a whip, I chased Nedula.

"Oh no," she cried. "You cannot beat me! It isn't Friday." I stopped a little breathless, and leaned against the trunk of a palm tree.

"Friday? What do you mean, Nedula?"

A guarded look came into her eyes, like a shutter half closed. "Friday is the punishment day in the big square. Friday is the day for beatings, and for . . ." Her right hand came down hard on the wrist of her left hand and made a cracking sound. I felt a lurch in the pit of my stomach.

"In the square? In public? Oh, my God! Have you seen this, Nedula? Or is it something they say to frighten silly little girls like you?"

"I'm not silly. I can read," she said. The shutter fell completely and I could not then or ever later make her speak of the public execution of sentences. I preferred to think it wasn't true and did my best to believe that until one day months later M. Raoul, his own eyes defensive and half shuttered, told me public floggings and amputations certainly did take place and Nedula could well have attended them.

"Wake up, Rosemarie," he said. "A race cannot live in purity according to the truth of Islam if wrongdoing is not swiftly punished and seen to be punished by men acting in truth's name."

"Their truth, M. Raoul," I said, "but not God's mercy."

He shook his head sadly, but the sadness was for my lack of understanding.

"Rosemarie," he said, "in Saudi Arabia the truth of Islam must prevail."

On my calendar the month of January was one of the most important in the year because it contained Susu's birthday. It was unusual enough for a Saudi to know his own birthday, and of our household Susu was the only one with it entered on his passport. It accorded well not only with tradition but also with royal vanity to leave birthdays unmarked. In Susu's case I convinced Moudi to make an exception. Before the big day came, I wondered if perhaps I had persuaded her too well, for it began to seem that Susu's first birthday would be a cross between a coronation and a state circus. Only with great difficulty did I dissuade Moudi from importing the most celebrated Arab singers and musicians and as it was my order at the Inter-Continental kitchen for a birthday cake kept increasing: first, it was to feed twenty, then forty, then fifty guests. The cake, when it arrived, was magnificent although admittedly it looked more like a wedding cake than a child's birthday cake, which I assumed the pastry chef had never before been asked to bake. I had gone into the souk the week before Susu's birthday and bought toys for each of the children invited: little cars, dolls, or modeling clay, depending upon age and aptitudes.

"A receipt!" cried the toy salesman, astonished. "A receipt! And you come from the house of Mohammed! Mohammed has two hundred million riyals and more. Does it matter if you take a little here? A little there?"

Nevertheless, I insisted upon my receipt and I got it. I had made a point of demanding receipts for every purchase I made on behalf of Princess Moudi, for I was repelled by the thieving I saw, petty on the part of the servants, but gross on the part of many European purveyors of luxury items, and I had promised myself never to become party to it, even if my honesty sometimes perplexed Princess Moudi herself.

The party was a great success. The corridors of the palace were full of balloons, the gifts were gaily wrapped, there was no end of refreshment, and the children, many of whom had never before seen a western-style birthday party, were delighted to be smeared with chocolate and coated in cake crumbs. Susu received many gifts, mostly chains of gold, medallions in precious metals, jewels, and cash. His grandfather sent Susu an envelope containing 50,000 riyals to match the sum he had given him at the end of Ramadan. Susu was not impressed. However, Prince Mohammed had also presented Susu with a toy ghost that talked, and that Susu so dearly loved he took it even into his bath with him. After the children's party, the women sent their offspring home with servants and repaired to Anud's house where a woman vocalist and five women musicians were already installed. Cars came and went, depositing new arrivals, taking others home, while the drivers sat outside the door drinking tea and hearing what they could of the entertainment. One large room was laid with a feast provided by Papa Mohammed: dishes on the carpet contained mutton cooked in different sauces, chicken, rice, familiar vegetables and exotic ones, cakes, sweets, puddings, fruits of every kind with juices, iced tea, and mineral waters. A servant holding an urn of hot water waited at the door so we could wash our hands when we had finished, a necessary grace since most of the women ate with their fingers, then we held our hands over the incense burner.

Then, it was back into the main salon for more music and traditional dancing, women alone, but with a fervor such as I had never seen on a western dance floor. At one point in the festivities, the noise level dropped suddenly; some of the women began to clap softly in time to the hypnotic rhythm of the music but all attention was on the center of the room where Mishaal danced alone. Her eyes were half shut, shining crescents under her full, heavy lids; she smiled but only to herself and she seemed unaware of her attentive audience. Her movements were sensuous but at the same time their form was so classical and pure they demanded to be seen with cold, critical judgment as well as with affection and surprise. In every way, Mishaal was an inspired dancer and the language of her movements was infinitely more sophisticated than anything I had ever heard her say. Dancing, Mishaal was no longer a lovable, giddy "Mickey Mouse"; she became a person of importance, interpreter for an ancient and lonely culture that had survived against all odds. I shall never forget the way Mishaal danced at Susu's birthday party and I try always to remember her like that: to remember her showing through her dance how well she understood her judges, for she herself was part of their tradition and design.

"Oh, oh, oh," Moudi moaned next day, looking for all the world as if she had a hangover although that was impossible since there had been no alcoholic beverages. "Oh, oh, oh, Rosemarie. You were smart to leave early. Mama Sarah came in at five this morning and found us all still dancing. That was bad enough. But Mishaal's brothers Prince Sa'ad and Abdullah were with us too, and Mama Sarah was so angry! She sent everybody home. It would be good to keep out of her way for today."

I didn't take the incident seriously, but Mama Sarah took it very seriously indeed and that same day the familiar guards on the palace gates were replaced by strangers.

Again the days passed a high point to resume their even pattern. Susu was beginning to imitate sounds and he was very nearly making words, or so it seemed to my loving ear.

"Sudani! Sudani!" I told him once, and pointed to the thin, black servant, doomed eternally to sweep the dust from corner to corner of our palace. "Sudani! Look, Susu, it is Sudani!" Sudani, still holding his broom, straightened up suddenly and spoke rapidly.

"What is he saying?" I asked Nedula who was with us.

"He says he comes from the Sudan, but his name is Ayatilla. He says he does not like it that you call him 'Sudani! Sudani!' for that is not his name, it is his homeland. He says you would not like it if he called you 'Germany! Germany!' "

The servant stood straight, tall, reminiscent of warrior princes conquered and brought into slavery. I apologized sincerely in Arabic and thereafter I always called him Ayatilla. It so happened that one of the first identifiable sounds Susu made were his cries of " 'Teeya! 'Teeya!" whenever he caught sight of the servant with his broom.

I met Jennifer at the airport when she came to relieve me for my month's holiday. From the receiving side of the airport window, I saw the flash of her red hair and for a moment I gawped at her cotton dress, her cheerful costume jewelry, just as the Arabs once had gawped at me.

"It has been a year! I've been here a whole year!" I thought, but the words had no real significance. Arabia turns a year into both a century and a minute. On Jennifer's face I saw a mirror of myself twelve months earlier: a little scared, stubborn, surprised both by the strangeness of the crowd and by the strangeness of herself within it.

"At least you had me to meet you," I told Jennifer later. "Try doing it alone!"

I settled her in and introduced her to the servants, including a new one called Amnah, who spoke tolerable English. My own bags were packed and since I was leaving early I went to say good-bye to Moudi.

"Rosemarie, which one do you think is the nicest?" She gestured to two dresses draped over her bed; both were heavily embroidered in gold threads with the Saudi seal; one was dark brown silk and the other was black.

"You know you don't look your best in black, Princess," I said. "Take the brown one. It's magnificent."

She took up the dress and handed it to me.

"It's for you," she said. "A gift from Susu. He wants everyone in London to know that you come from Saudi Arabia."

There couldn't be much doubt among the many Arabs staying at London's Inter-Continental Hotel, where I spent most of my holiday, that I came from Saudi Arabia. "Farmer Jones" was down from Leicester, so the month passed very happily. We met every evening for dinner and sometimes, when a meeting was going to keep him late, I waited for him in the discothèque, where I was so cosseted and cared for by Aydin and Tony, his assistant, that I felt as if I was in my own living room.

My holiday was happy, glorious, and more than that. Never since my employment in Saudi had I been given so many reasons to stay in Europe. First, the memory of Stephen no longer gave me pain; it had become a positive part of my life, and a memory of love, not of loss, of joy, not of grief. Given this new, healthy attitude, my relationship with "Farmer Jones" had been able to grow in depth and importance so that at times it seemed to deserve all my devotion. Then too, I had saved a lot of my salary; I had money in the bank. And finally, European Ferries, where I had once been so happy, had offered me my old job back again. The balance tipped back and forth at various times and even in the course of a day: on one side was London, "Farmer Jones," my old job back again. On the other was Riyadh, the friendship of Moudi and her family, the lure of Jeddah's gardens, and, of course, a weight to tip all balance: love of Susu. In the end, that time as it had been the times before, I had to go back to my little prince. When I left Heathrow that day in early spring, I didn't know how near to the end my sojourn in Saudi was drawing. I was thinking about Susu, about Mama Sarah, about Moudi. I thought about the old servant, Mama Sayida, who had boasted once to Esher about what a good slave she had been and I vowed to be more attentive to the old woman and visit her more often with Susu, for it was she, I had learned, who had raised Moudi from infancy and therefore the former slave was in a sense Susu's grandmother too. Jawahir was going to be married soon and there would be a party with feasting and music. I looked forward to it, and planned what I was going to wear. Mishaal would dance again. I hoped it wouldn't rain. As the plane circled Riyadh and I looked down to see the amber lights of the familiar city there was not a thought in my mind that could not have lived comfortably in the mind of an Arab woman, homeward bound.

"It's been hell. I hate it here," Jennifer said. She was thinner and, despite a suntan, her face was drawn. "How do you stand it? It's so

. . . so . . ." She looked around as if to find the word someplace in the nursery. "So claustrophobic. And so, I don't know . . . can't you feel how strange it is? I know they were all talking about me. And things don't work properly. Rosemarie! That washing machine! And everytime I went out in the car with your lunatic driver, I just sat there and prayed. Who's that creepy fat Zuchia? And your princesses! Half the time they're wearing Paris nightgowns and half the time they eat with their fingers. Gross! The food is disgusting. And . . ." She stopped, looking embarrassed, and then she confessed: "I really don't like the *feel* of the place."

Moudi had offered to let Jennifer stay on for a few weeks, fully paid and with no work to do, so she could attend Jawahir's wedding.

"No, Rosemarie, I'm sorry. Please try to understand. It's nice of her, I guess, and I suppose I'm grateful, but I just cannot do it. I cannot stand another minute here. I want to walk alone in a street, drive a car, order a gin-and-tonic . . . I'm sorry Rosemarie . . ."

She looked around the room again, then pulled hard at her hair.

"I'm going crazy in this place!" she said.

It was several days after Jennifer left that I met M. Raoul, a member of the foreign community so much in the confidence of the royal family that our encounter actually took place inside the precincts of Mama Sarah's palace where he had come by personal request of Prince Mohammed to replenish our stock of baby food, as he had recently returned from Europe. M. Raoul had his own swimming pool in an enclosed yard behind his bungalow and Moudi was delighted to give me permission to use it, she was even relieved to have my constant complaints about swimming stilled.

"Well then, Rosemarie, how goes it?" M. Raoul said, reaching over to refill my glass with lemonade. Although the foreign community was known to drink clandestine alcohol, M. Raoul never did; nor did he smoke, and I had a hunch he was a convert to the Moslem faith, although he never said so directly.

"Today has been pretty good," I said, and immediately launched into a recounting of the mass of details that composed my palace day, only slowing to a halt when I had noticed his expression.

"Rosemarie, beware of going native!" he said.

"You're a fine one to talk," I told him.

"But I'm a man. There are some hard facts about Arab life and one of them is that it really is a man's world out here. The women must occupy themselves with trifles. It can actually be dangerous for an Arab woman to be too bold or forthright; but you're a western woman and you mustn't get bogged down here. Keep well away from any plots or intrigues going on behind your palace walls. Remember, you're the Westerner and you're the *only* Westerner in the household, so if anything bad happens, anything at all, you will be first in line for blame. I know, I know, it isn't logical, but don't apply your western logic here. Just promise me you'll never forget that as a foreigner you are vulnerable, and that a foreigner is never, never altogether trusted by the Arab." A shadow crossed his face. "We can enter their businesses, their homes, on sufferance, even their faith after a long, long time; but we cannot ever enter their minds."

"But what could happen in the palace? What intrigues do you mean? What bad thing could happen?"

He didn't answer; instead he asked another question.

"How do you get on with Prince Mohammed?"

I told him how much I admired the patriarch who was so gentle and loving with his grandson.

"Do you know what your gentle grandfather is called in some quarters?" M. Raoul asked me. "He is called 'Mohammed of the Two Evils.' Yes. Does that surprise you? He is the oldest brother and should by rights be King, but he was two times passed over for the kingship."

"Why?" I asked.

M. Raoul shrugged and reflection of the Arab shutter dropped behind his pale eyes.

"Prince Mohammed can be . . . he can be erratic, let us say. Choleric. He is a man of some temper. Be thankful you haven't seen it!" We sat quietly, absorbing the rays of the spring sun; whatever his attraction to the ways of the Arabs, M. Raoul still had a Westerner's taste for basking and swimming.

What he omitted to tell me (or perhaps did not know himself) was the legend of how Prince Mohammed came by his strange title. I learned it later myself from a Lebanese banker who had been resident in Saudi for eighteen years. He and his wife invited me to join them at the famous Inter-Continental Hotel barbecue, held every Wednesday in their lovely gardens. It was a delightfully balmy summer evening, the air filled with the scent of flowers and the aroma of barbecued food. My host started to tell me this story which is known to few people—and which few believe. "You may have heard, Rosemarie," he said smiling, "that your Papa Mohammed as you call him has been named Mohammed Abu Shaarain—Mohammed of the Two Evils?"

I nodded and said I had often wondered why.

"Well, he received the name many years ago when he was still a young man. The story goes that one afternoon his father, the late King Abdul Aziz was taking coffee with his other son, Faisal, the King who was later killed. While they were together Prince Mohammed suddenly came to them and told his father: 'You have been King for long enough. I want to be King now!' Mohammed's elder brother, Faisal, jumped up and withdrew his sword to protect their father, but King Abdul Aziz, an old and war-wise warrior, made Faisal sit down. He said to Mohammed: 'Very well, why don't you go out to the public and announce that you are King now?' Mohammed immediately left the room to do so but no sooner had he left than he was brought back—in the company of his father's guards who had him under arrest.

"The King slapped him twice around the face—slap—slap—once right, once left saying 'This, my son, is for the time you have been King. I hope you have learned a lesson.' The guards led him away and he was released.

"So you see, Rosemarie, it was from this time that the people, and perhaps even some of his family too, began to call him 'Mohammed of the Two Evils' because one evil spirit would not have dared to make Mohammed act as he did. A person would have to be possessed by two Evil Ones to try to dethrone his own father, especially so powerful a one. Mohammed may be old and wise now, but his nickname has never been forgotten and it has followed him all his life. Now and again you will hear it. They say Arabs never forget nor forgive."

A question from M. Raoul surprised me.

"Do you know Princess Mishaal?" he asked suddenly.

"Yes. Of course. Mishaal is happy and young. All sunshine. She dances . . ."

"Rosemarie, listen to me," M. Raoul said. He raised himself from his deck chair in one motion that was reptilian and a little repulsive. "Listen well to me," he said, "keep away from Mishaal." He lowered his voice, although nobody was near to hear us. "Do you listen to me? Stay away from that girl. There is trouble gathering around her and if you are anywhere near, you'll be caught in it too." So intense was his tone, and his eyes, narrowed in the sun, had become so piercing, I too looked around to see if we were being spied upon, and I felt against all will and reason drawn into a dangerous conspiracy.

"What has she done?" I whispered.

He sat back, his eyelids lowered like a lizard's.

"There's no reason you need to know anything. Just keep out of Mishaal's path. I'm afraid it's a steep path and it is going down."

He would not say another word. I wondered if perhaps too long a sojourn in Saudi had driven him mad.

Jawahir's wedding began long before the event itself with the activity of the royal dressmakers: Siam, the Lebanese, and Fatimah, the Egyptian. For weeks before the big day their machines had been humming late into the night while their assistants, pre-empted from the staff for the occasion, scurried back and forth with yards of colorful fabric that Nedula told me was to make the uniform dress for all the servants of the Abdul Aziz clan.

"It's very dear," Nedula said, clearly impressed. She held up a swatch of the stuff she had salvaged from the sweepings; it was of a black background patterned in lozenges of various bright colors.

"Sixty riyals a meter!" Nedula said and, since at the time such a sum was worth about £10 and there were countless servants to be clothed, I shared her astonishment.

Not far behind the seamstresses came the electricians to install a special generator on our roof, meant to cope with the extra demand made by hundreds and hundreds of colored lights that were already festooning the palace and its surrounding trees. Before the generator actually functioned correctly innumerable "test runs" were made, each of them unsuccessful and resulting in a blackout of lights, air conditioning, and even our fresh-water pumps. Meanwhile, lorryloads of sand were being delivered so gardens, grass, and struggling shrubbery could be flattened to make the ground even underfoot. Then a gigantic marquee, several times the size of a football pitch, was raised and ornamented with lights.

On most normal days a small plane flew overhead and sprayed the palace grounds with insecticide, but for this special occasion the exterminators arrived, weird and outlandish in their masks with tanks on their backs as if containing oxygen in a hostile atmosphere. For a day after they left, the grounds, the palace rooms, the air itself, was full of dead and dying insects; so many diminutive deaths took place it seemed to me they must by sheer number count in heaven as equal to one human death at least, and I found the episode depressing. When the corpses had been swept up and burned, carpets were laid everywhere: under the marquee, over the sand which lay in turn over the garden, along every drive and footpath. Hundreds, perhaps even thousands, of garden chairs in red and blue stripes edged the carpet.

At last, the palace was full of real flowers instead of our usual faded pink plastic daisies; we had lilies, carnations, gladioli, camellias, and every sort of waxy blossom, so perfect that many of them looked remarkably like plastic, against boughs of leaves sprayed gold. The biggest room was set for what I assumed would be the family dinner, but Jawahir's sitting room had a table set for only two: the bridal couple. Nedula, in her unabashed way, told me that in the old days it had been customary for the entire family to crowd around the nuptial bed and satisfy themselves that the union was consummated; that practice had been given up, however, at least in the big cities, so Jawahir and her new husband would have privacy after the ceremony.

Nedula, Susu, and I tiptoed in for a look at the bridal chamber

and I was surprised to see that there Jawahir's taste for purple
lapsed. The bed was vast and its headrest was bright red leather
studded with brass; there was a dressing table to match. In one
corner of the enormous room was a stereo set already playing a pop
tune equipped with a board of brightly colored lights that flashed
on and off in time to the music. As modern and expensive as the
room was, it had a barbaric quality underlined by lilies arranged on
towering pedestals.

With Moudi's approval, Susu was double-locked into the nursery
where I could check on him at regular intervals, and he would be
safe from hordes of kissing cousins. Moudi looked magnificent and
I thought she was the most beautiful of all the women there; her
hair had been set in a mass of curls, she wore a rich brown dress
sprinkled with diamante and around her neck was a string of perfect diamonds, deceptively simple and pure. Moudi received my
compliments with so much appetite and hunger for them, I felt
very tender toward her. Nedula had disappeared, but Moudi told
me to stay close to Dr. Nabia, who would explain to me what was
happening and identify the guests. The doctor and I posted ourselves in a convenient corner, half hidden behind a massive flower
arrangement, and we watched the crowds of women stepping out of
their chauffeur-driven cars to climb the grand front staircase; each
guest was enveloped in her own specially made perfume and soon
their scents like their voices blended into a kind of roar around us.
"The king's sister," Dr. Nabia said. "That one . . . emeralds . . .
see? Five daughters, poor thing . . . and the one behind . . . isn't
married yet . . . Goodness, Rosemarie! Look at her, the one in orange chiffon, how did they ever get her hair to stay that way! Now
that one, that one, the one with rubies, see? She is from the Faisal
family . . ."

The vast rooms and the compound began to fill with lace,
chiffon, satin, sequins, almost all cut and draped in Paris theoret-
ically for the pleasure of men, but now to be seen only by women;
a bright mass of silk lay around us, unrelieved by tuxedoes or uniforms, a dizzying swirl pricked here and there with the flash of sapphires.

"We still wear our jewels as the Bedouin tribeswomen do . . ."

Dr. Nabia said, shouting into my ear yet still hard to hear over the increasing noise. "Notice, Rosemarie? Five, six necklaces at a time . . . all the wealth . . . the dowry. You see? Diamonds instead of silver . . . not coins but pearls . . . same idea . . ." Her hand touched the single strand of pearls that she wore.

Until past midnight the guests milled and talked while an all-women band, flown in specially from the Lebanon, played constantly to accompany a celebrated vocalist whose voice sparkled now and then through the surrounding hubbub. Out of the rich blur, I noticed a gemstone of particular brilliance or a dress more sumptuous than the rest. Princess Anud, usually so self-effacing, wore a virtual cascade of platinum and rubies; behind her stood a servant with a small casket ready to receive the jewels should they become too heavy for Anud to bear. Like pets of a medieval court, the children moved knee-high among us; the little girls were in organdy, light as tinted puffs of smoke, the little boys—the only males present—were dressed in velvet evening suits and ruffled shirts.

The marriage took place in the room where Susu and I had always been received by Papa Mohammed. At one moment the crowd seemed to increase, grow silent, then part for the bride and groom. Jawahir was in a western-style dress of heavy cream satin, her antique lace veil was lifted to show her glowing face to the assembled women; her groom wore a thobe of white silk, over that a sheer black abaya embroidered in gold and, above it all, an expression of agonized embarrassment as he passed under the gaze of his kins-women-in-law and their friends. As Jawahir and her husband passed across the room toward the large marquee, from the ranks of women in their resplendent western finery and their fabulous jewels, there arose that sound it is easy to imagine was made by the very first human voice to be raised across the hostile desert: a high-pitched ululation that is one of the strangest and loneliest expressions of celebration anywhere on earth and is heard only among the Arab women. Dr. Nabia and I followed the couple, pushing through the crowd, and we watched them seat themselves on chairs that had been elevated upon a dais and garlanded with jasmine, white roses, and carnations.

More than one banquet was laid, so along with perfume and sandalwood the air was thick with the smell of savory dishes, sweets, and freshly milled coffee. It was growing late and Susu, whose appetite did not respect special occasions, would be awake and wanting breakfast at six, so I said good night to Dr. Nabia and started back toward the nursery. On the way, I literally collided with Mishaal. She wore opals and because of my conversation with M. Raoul I remembered that in western folklore it was a stone purported to bring bad luck at a wedding. The dull glow of Mishaal's necklace and the iridescent blue silk she wore, gave her a shimmering aura but the arms she threw around my neck were solid and surprisingly strong.

"Rolls-Royce! Rolly-Royce! Happy! Happy!" Mishaal stood back, her face was suffused with diabolical wildness that reminded me of hunters and gamblers.

"Mishaal . . ." I began.

I don't know what I intended to say—a greeting? a warning?— for behind Mishaal, swathed in black and stamped with lozenges of bright color I saw the wide face of Zuchia. She was watching us and in her ugly eyes there was keen satisfaction.

I slept badly and when I woke before six the light around me was milky and thick. From my window overlooking the city there was nothing to see: no city, no color, no sun, no sky. I had awakened to find not my toothbrush, breakfast, another day; I had awakened to find another dream. A fog, the first I had seen in Saudi, had drifted in over Riyadh during Jawahir's wedding night and quilted us in clouds. The usual early morning sounds were muffled and if dawn birds were flying, I couldn't see them. I remembered Mishaal's opals and her flamelike dance; the image grew muzzy in the fog, retreating yet reaching out to me. I shivered and wondered if I was catching cold.

chapter 15

As a child I had been afraid of lightning, hiding my head under
the pillow at the first peal of thunder; but in Riyadh I had no fear
of the storm, precisely because it was bigger than life. The same
calm overtakes sailors during hurricanes at sea I've been told. The
last thunderstorm that Spring was late, but violent, as titanic forces
seemed to grab the sky on either side of the horizon and pull so six
or seven rents blazed simultaneously in the canopy over Riyadh. From
my window I watched the blackness of the stormy night illuminated suddenly, as if a camera had caught the city in its flash. One
great peal of thunder woke Susu, who cried for a little while, then
fell asleep in my arms, with his face turned to the hollow of my
throat, as I stood waiting until the storm ended as suddenly as it
had begun.

Summer had begun and we should already have left for Taif.
Mama Sarah was packed and eager to be off because, she explained
to me in pantomime, she mistrusted air conditioning and she had
hoped to be away before its insidious buzz became a necessary condition to survival in Riyadh. Saudi Arabia, however, was a mon-
archy in the emotional sense, and as long as King Khalid remained
in the capital, viziers like Papa Mohammed were expected to stay
as well, and their families with them. The King had just come back
from London where he had undergone hip surgery, so his recovery
as well as his return were cause for immense public rejoicing which
appeared to result from the genuine respect of his subjects as much
as from their prudent politics.

Admittedly, the people rejoiced too in the very fact of rejoicing; for the peasantry of Saudi there were few holidays from a lifetime of work. Riyadh was dressed overall, and for miles around the city carpets were strewn on the desert and tents pitched over them for the folk who came to celebrate. Day and night the air was filled with music and a drumbeat that Susu confused with his own pulse, so he skipped in time to it. Once, on my way out to visit M. Raoul, our big Cadillac was blocked by a line of men dressed in white and armed with swords that flashed, circling in the moonlight, tamed but dangerous as the King's falcons, sharp enough to split a hair. The men danced forward, backward, turning, dipping, their swords always swinging within millimeters of murder, while drums were beating for them.

Inside our palace too there was fierce emotion. When the King came safely home from London, Susu and I joined Moudi with the others to sit on the floor in front of her big television and witness the monarch's arrival at the airport. The officials in their cream thobes milled on the field until the gangway was lowered; then a group arranged themselves into a receiving line, at the head of it Papa Mohammed. It was the King who bowed his head and kissed the hand of his older brother. I turned to smile at Moudi and saw her eyes were full of tears; the other women were silent, awestruck by the occasion and by the might of Allah that had spared the ruler's life.

Moudi was not unduly unhappy about our protracted stay in Riyadh because she hoped Papa Mohammed would be persuaded to offer her another summer trip to Europe. I did not want to return to Europe so soon, but no more did I want to go back to the boredom and mosquitoes of the previous summer, so this year I joined the chorus of moans and groans whenever Taif was mentioned. Only Mishaal seemed unperturbed at the prospect of spending the summer in the detested resort; in fact, she seemed pleased enough to be going there, and she smiled sagely to herself whenever Moudi and I complained.

"Isn't it funny, Moudi," I said one evening when the princess and I were alone, "how Mishaal doesn't seem to mind going to

Taif this year. She hated the thought of the place last year." Moudi shrugged and continued to apply her make-up although we were going no further than the drawing room to join the women for the usual videotapes.

"She has to think about many things," Moudi said. She rubbed green color into her upper lid with the end of a finger. "You know what happened today? Mishaal's husband went to the King to ask permission to take a second wife." Moudi had begun to outline her mouth with a thin brush and conversation ceased until she had finished. "Well, anyway, my uncle said 'no.' He said Mishaal's husband could not take a second wife unless he first gave Mishaal the divorce. My uncle understands it's hard for a woman when her husband takes a second wife."

Applying powder with a camel-hair brush took concentration; then Moudi leaned close to the glass and fluttered her lashes at her reflection. "But Mishaal's husband said 'no'; he said, 'no divorce.'"

"But why, Moudi? They don't live together, they don't seem to love each other. Why not agree to a divorce?"

Moudi turned from the mirror and shook her head at me as if I failed to see what to everyone else was obvious.

"Mishaal is from a very great family. My family. For Mishaal's husband it is a good, good match. Maybe it is true that he doesn't love his wife"—Moudi rose from her dressing table, smoothed her skirt, and cast herself a last glance—"but he might love the marriage."

Prince Mohammed had come for a visit to our palace. Mishaal was waiting with me and Susu for Moudi, who was bound to be late for this, as she was for all audiences worthy of the dramatic entrance. Finally Mishaal, Susu, and I went on ahead. Papa Mohammed received Susu with a big hug at the door to the reception room and carried him in his arms to the waiting chair while the rest of the household followed. Before seating himself, Prince Mohammed turned, chucked Mishaal under her chin, and said something that made her giggle. Only after each member of the family had been received and embraced did Moudi appear at the door in a

magnificent couture creation to sweep into her father's arms as in
the last reel of an old movie. The atmosphere was pleasant and
relaxed; Papa Mohammed even spoke a few words of greeting to
me in tentative, accented English, much to the admiration of his
family. In due course, the patriarch rose to leave but just as he
reached the door Mama Sarah in her enveloping black stepped forward and spoke to him softly. I was standing behind them with
Susu, and I saw Papa Mohammed's spine stiffen.

"Where is she?" I heard him ask.

The door was opened by a servant and there, sitting on the
threshold, was a princess of the family whom I had seen from time
to time at Moudi's dinner table. Her eyes were downcast, streaming
tears, one arm was in a sling and there was plaster over her nose;
she had a black eye too, a beauty, turning yellow around the edges.
When Papa Mohammed bent down to talk to her a servant nearby
reached into a plastic bag and pulled out a bloodstained nightgown, holding it up for everyone to see. I understood enough
Arabic to know the princess was telling the patriarch, between sobs,
how her husband had come home late one night, dragged her out
of bed, and beaten her. She was making application to Papa
Mohammed for justice. I had never seen such a transformation as
came over the old man then; he turned pale with anger and his
eyes were like the lightning over Riyadh. I was standing close
enough to see his hands tremble as if he needed superhuman control to prevent them from seeking out the bully and throttling him.
His rage was palpable; I thought I could smell its smoke. The
women all drew back as if to save themselves from imminent explosion; even Susu threw his arms around my neck. With a sharp
oath or exclamation Papa Mohammed whirled around and strode
out of the palace toward his waiting car; the servants scattered in
front of him. That was the first time I had seen the rage of Prince
Mohammed, and like all the other witnesses I hoped I would not
ever see it again.

It was not long after Prince Mohammed's visit that Susu and I
heard Moudi screaming in a rage of her own; she seemed to be
dashing back and forth in the corridor outside the door of Jawahir's apartment where Susu and I had lived since the wedding.

Suddenly she burst through the door of the purple drawing room and stormed around us. Mishaal's handsome brother, Sa'ad, stood in the doorway looking alarmed.

"How should I know?" Moudi was shouting. "How should I know where Mishaal is? Why does this boy always ask me where his sister is? Is it my job, Rosemarie, to care for Mishaal? Is it?" She stopped in front of me and beat her chest with clenched fists. "Haven't I got enough to do? I have Susu to take care of, haven't I? How am I supposed to know where Mishaal is every minute? It's not my job!"

Moudi's anger was disproportionate to the cause and seemed to hold an admixture of jealousy perhaps, or fear. Suddenly she lifted both fists toward the ceiling, put her head back, and shouted as if she dared the King himself to hear her. "I'm going crazy in this place!"

As the heat increased, melting energy and restraint, I think Moudi would have been willing to go anywhere out of Riyadh, even to Taif, but Susu, having passed his first birthday, was still awaiting his traditional audience with King Khalid. At last, the summons came, and dressed in our finery we drove off to the King's palace. His Majesty was not yet ready to receive us so we were asked to wait in an antechamber where there was another little boy about Susu's age; he too was with a European nanny who was doing her best to keep the tot's playsuit clean while he investigated the dusty side of all the cushions and chairs. We two Europeans sized each other up, then cast critical looks upon each other's charges, before we finally entered into conversation. She was a lanky Australian named Jill; she lived in the King's palace where there were six other nannies, she told me, all caring for various of the royal family's numerous offspring. When I suggested we meet one evening for a meal at the Inter-Continental, she was astonished.

"Are you allowed to go out for meals?"

"You bet I am!"

She shook her head. "I don't think we could do that. As a matter of fact, I know we couldn't. We're never allowed outside."

I learned that Jill and her colleagues were virtual prisoners in their luxurious quarters; they had not been to a pool outside or to dinner in a Riyadh hotel. If they were not terribly unhappy it was because at least they were well treated. They had heard tales, Jill told me, of nannies in Saudi assigned filthy living quarters, cheated of their wages. No better off than slaves. I also learned from Jill that it was possible to be issued with a multiple exit visa—although none of the nannies had one—which avoided the tedious business of applying for each departure. As we stepped out into the big hall to meet the King, I resolved to get myself one of those precious visas as soon as I could.

Jill introduced Susu and me in fluent Arabic, and the King greeted us with great favor although he walked with a stick and was still too weak from his ordeal to hold Susu in his arms or do more than tickle him and give him a kiss.

The first week of July had come and with it an oppressive heat that crouched over Riyadh, stifling us and making us angry. Yet again I had quarreled with Moudi; this time because I wanted a multiple exit visa. She had finally agreed and taken my passport, which had not yet been returned to me despite several applications. The air conditioning had broken down twice on the previous day, Moudi was sulky, and I needed some time off. With Moudi's half-hearted permission, I left in the morning to spend an entire day of freedom beside M. Raoul's pool, honestly pleased that my host himself was working that day in Riyadh so I would have just his servants in attendance.

Memory plays games, making me unable to differentiate now between my actions and reactions then, or to be sure what came before the tragic event and what came after it. However, as I remember that day, it did not yield anticipated pleasure. Was it the thought of Susu that kept me from relaxing? Was it the extreme heat? Was it a genuine premonition that blighted those free hours and made me restless to be on my homeward trip?

In retrospect, it seems to me the palace gates themselves were open and untended. I'm sure the courtyard was deserted, no servants milling around the cookhouse or scratching at the flower bed.

Our fountain, always dusty and dry, seemed suddenly menacing with nobody perched on its surrounding wall or surreptitiously dropping rubbish into the basin. Heart pounding, I raced upstairs past Mama Sarah's apartment which I knew, without pausing, was empty.

"Susu! Susu!"

The door to Jawahir's apartment, now ours, was ajar; it opened farther, then more, and Susu toddled toward me, his arms outstretched.

"Susu! Thank God! But where is everyone? What's happened?"

In the purple sitting room where more than a year before I had entered as a stranger, the chairs were all empty and the stereo for once dead quiet. Only Esher sat in the middle of the carpet, next to her a servant I didn't know.

"Esher, tell me, what's wrong? What's happened?"

"Everybody go Jeddah," she said.

I held Susu very tight. I knew I must listen, but I did not want to hear what Esher was about to say.

"Mishaal has drowned."

The familiar shock of loss plummeted through the center of my being.

The palace was empty and so quiet I thought of those Egyptian tombs where pharaohs were buried with a retinue of dead servants. I had only grim thoughts, but I tried to keep Susu from sensing them as I fed him, played with him, and finally laid him down to sleep. Then I sat in the still, darkening room for a long time, numb, unthinking, but feeling on the far edge of my mind that something was wrong; more wrong even than Mishaal's drowning. It was midnight before I fell asleep at last, to be awakened almost immediately by the ringing of the telephone near my bed.

"Rosemarie? Rosemarie? Are you there?" Moudi's voice was shrill and agitated. "Rosemarie, something bad, bad has happened. Mishaal has drowned!"

"Yes, yes, Moudi. Where?" I asked, fuddled with sleep.

"In 'The Creek,' Rosemarie. We found all her clothes there. She must have gone to swim at night—it was so hot, bad hot—and then . . . oh Rosemarie! Everyone is looking but we have found nothing yet."

Chilled by the memory of that awful place, "The Creek," I put the receiver back in its cradle and returned to my bed, but not to sleep. Behind my stinging eyelids I saw the spines of sea urchins and the ledges of sharp coral where a body could be lodged until claimed entirely by the hostile element where it was trapped.

"No!" I said to the dark room. I sat up and switched on the light. "No!" I said again.

Moudi swam badly, but the other princesses, so far as I had noticed, did not swim at all. A midnight plunge into the sea was simply not the sport of an Arabian princess whose concern for her coiffure, if not for her life, would outweigh spontaneity. And even if she had by some remote chance gone to bathe by moonlight, Mishaal would not—could not—have chosen a place that discouraged even a strong swimmer like me. The possibility that Mishaal might have killed herself, I dismissed immediately; although the young princess had become more serious and introspective, she was as far from being the suicidal type as she was from mastering Einstein's theories of relativity. I jumped out of bed and began to pace the floor, full of a curious wildness.

"She's alive! I'm sure she's alive!" I said aloud, and twice I had my hand on the phone to call Moudi in Jeddah; but dawn was already coming and Moudi would no doubt just be going to bed.

"Listen, Moudi, listen to me," I said when the princess rang me later that morning. "Mishaal is not dead. I'm sure of it. I cannot believe Mishaal would go into 'The Creek' to swim; not in a million years. She must have run away. Moudi! Oh, Moudi, I'm sure Mishaal is alive!"

Moudi made a sound, perhaps a word of disagreement, then I heard her speak in Arabic to someone at her side.

"I've just told my brother what you said, Rosemarie." She lowered her voice; it became muzzy, as if she were pressing the receiver against her mouth. "Listen, don't say anything like that. Please, Rosemarie. If Mishaal has done what you said, she will be killed."

The day continued, relentlessly normal. Susu and I played, ate, played again, and then in the early afternoon I took him to the hospital for the last of a series of immunizations. I was performing normally but my mind was in tumult. As often as I assured myself I must have misunderstood Moudi's words, so often did those words return filling me with helplessness and dread. I had tried all afternoon to ring Moudi in Jeddah, but the line had been constantly engaged, and that too began to seem ominous.

Jiggling Susu's stroller to keep him entertained, I sat in the waiting room of the modern hospital, but my emotions were engaged miles away in Jeddah. With us, seated nearby, was a distant member of the royal family whom I had met briefly in the past. She rocked back and forth with her eyes closed, and even when her servant pointed to us and whispered our names, she could not be shaken from her illness and pain. The servant, however, did not take her eyes off Susu and me, watching us with greedy curiosity. Finally, she leaned near to us as she could and hissed through her teeth until I looked into her hungry, stupid eyes.

"Mishaal has been found," she whispered in Arabic. "Mishaal has been found," she repeated, a little louder. Then she drew her abaya close around her face, and sat perfectly still with only her glittering eyes moving.

All logic told me I should rejoice that Mishaal had been found, but the chill of the preceding day would not be relieved, nor my impression that the words "Mishaal has been found" were uttered with unwholesome appetite. We returned to the palace, still empty of virtually everyone but Esher who stood waiting for us at the door to our apartment.

"Esher, is it true? Has Mishaal been found?"

Esher nodded. "Yes," she said. "Mishaal lives." Her eyes were wide and solemn.

"Thanks be to Allah!" I cried, but Esher jumped at my words, as if I had slapped her, and in her face I read a message I was not yet willing to accept.

When the telephone rang again, Susu had just settled down to sleep and I had been sitting, staring into space, trying by force of will—by sheer stubbornness—to make a lie of what already deep in my heart I knew was not a lie.

"Moudi?" I said, speaking softly because Susu slept nearby. "I tried to get you all day, your line was engaged. I hear Mishaal has been found?"

"Yes," Moudi said shortly.

"Al Hamdulillah! Thanks be to Allah!" I said, and even to my own ears the words held a note of question. Moudi was quiet for so long I thought she had gone; then she asked me how Susu was and how the weather was in Riyadh. A conspirator in my own ignorance, I said Susu was fine and the weather was intolerably hot.

It was the worst headache I had ever had; no aspirin eased it and in the torpid air there was no breeze to cool my forehead. Susu sensed I wasn't well, and he made small complaint when I asked Esher to take him for an hour in the afternoon so I could close my eyes against the light. The throbbing pain was so bad it swallowed my ability to think coherently and I was grateful to it for that. When the telephone rang again it took an enormous effort to remove my arm from across my eyes, to find the apparatus, and then to speak into it intelligibly. A long moment passed before I realized the sound I heard was Moudi, sobbing.

"Moudi? Moudi? Is that you? What is it?" Breathless with foreboding, I sat up; the ax slipped immediately to the base of my skull and pounded there. "What is it, Moudi? Tell me? For God's sake, Moudi, tell me what it is!"

"Oh Rosemarie, Rosemarie," she said, her voice ragged from crying. "It was a dream. I had a bad, bad dream. Oh, Rosemarie, I had so bad a dream."

Dropping my forehead into my hand, I summoned courage to hear what I already knew. "What did you dream, Princess Moudi?"

"Rosemarie, it was so bad. It was so bad a dream . . ." Sobbing still, she hung up suddenly as if she could not speak anymore.

During the next day, if I had allowed myself to stop working or concentrating on Susu, I would have been engulfed by despair. But I stayed busy, I functioned despite the headache that continued to pound at me, and even during the sleepless night I did not let myself know. It was on the afternoon of the second day following her nightmare that Moudi telephoned again. She was too cheerful and strained as she chattered about Susu and about the shops in Jeddah. Finally she paused, and I had to ask the question: "How is Mishaal?" There was the silence of a moment; I held my breath. Moudi's voice, when it came, was shrill and edgy.

"What do you mean by that? Mishaal is dead."

My hand froze on the telephone.

"Don't you know what happened, Rosemarie?" Her voice became lower and slightly singsong, as if she spoke from memory. "Mishaal should have known what would happen. She brought disgrace upon our family. Shamed us. She should have known it would disgrace us, shame us, when she tried to run away with her boy friend. She should have known we would have to kill her." There was a prickling on the backs of my hands, the room spun once; I had to lean on the table.

"You don't mean that, Moudi," I said softly.

"Yes. Yes, I do. My father said we do it to the poor people, we do it to the ordinary people, and so we must in justice do it to our own family too. My uncle, the King, he cried, and he went to my father, and he asked him not to do it; but my father said in justice it had to be done. And now my father is so angry nobody dares talk to him."

Dusk was coming; I watched the square of sky outside my window grow dark.

"How was it done?" I asked.

"They covered her eyes," Moudi said. "They tied her arms to her body. They put her in the street. They hurt her until she died."

"God have mercy," I whispered, although I knew it was too late for mercy.

"They cut his head off," Moudi went on. "He knew she was married. They did it in the big square." There was one more question that I had to ask against all horror of horror.

"Did you see it?" The soft click between us as the connection was broken echoed like the slamming of a door.

Outside from my balcony the birds could be seen to loop and circle as they had done every dusk of Mishaal's short life and every dusk before; as they would continue to do for every dusk to come. My headache had vanished but so had the acceptance of loss that had finally come to me after Stephen's death; I struggled to regain that healing surrender, there, under the sky where I had first found it, but it eluded me. Almost to the point of making myself sick with fear, I could only imagine how frightened Mishaal must have been when once she realized the sentence was not an idle threat; when she knew for sure that her countrymen would be armed to hurl at her their quarrels, their bitterness, their poverty and envy, to bury her alive under the mass of their own frustrations. I closed my eyes to the bright Arabian sunset and I wept, knowing that for me too the adventure was over.

"It wasn't the first time, Rosemarie," M. Raoul said, his voice sounding effeminate and a little sly over the phone. "She tried it last year. Remember when she had her hair cut short? She tried then to run away disguised as a boy. They caught her at the airport. She almost got through customs, but a couple of soldiers spotted her. One of them said she was too pretty to be a boy and they took a ten-riyal bet on it. To settle it, one of them contrived to walk in front of her and bump into her. And that's how they found out. They arrested her and she was taken home. But she escaped any serious punishment because she was on her own. This time she had her lover with her, so it couldn't be ignored. Rosemarie, are you there? Listen, let me say to you just once that it isn't good to talk too much on the telephone. You understand me? Also, I suggest you stay put inside the palace. As long as you're there, you're the family's responsibility. As for me, I'm going to lock up the house in Riyadh for a while. I'm going on a business trip to Kuwait."

His laugh was short and rather unpleasant. "Until the hot season is over," he said. "Remember what I told you, Rosemarie, when there's trouble it is not a good thing to be an infidel among the Arabs."

As close as I could reckon, that Monday was the third day after Mishaal had been executed in the public square of Jeddah.

"Do not criticize, Rosemarie, accept. Just accept if you want to stay sane." Those were the words Peggy had spoken to me at our last meeting so very long ago; and I had then asserted my stubbornness and told her that if something was wrong, I would never accept it. All that night I lay awake pitting logic against emotion. Logic told me that, after all, it was their way and their justice, that Mishaal had known the risk she ran trying to escape the fate of a Saudi woman. Political asylum could not be offered anywhere to victims of so prevalent a tyranny as that of Arab men over their chattels. Perhaps Mishaal had even understood it would no more be possible for her to escape capture and punishment than to escape the centuries of subsistence on the desert that had created the code that killed her. But emotion repeated to me then that Mishaal was no suicide, nor one to throw her life into a gesture; and I knew perfectly well she had expected to escape with her beloved to that fairy-tale land that is the prize of true love as depicted by the films she watched night after night on Moudi's video machine. Sometimes, I felt I almost understood why Papa Mohammed had taken his dreadful course, for indeed not to have done so would have been to betray the responsibility passed down to him through centuries of patriarchal authority. Sometimes, in the course of that long, long night I even suspected another motive to Mishaal's execution; if Papa Mohammed had not made an example of her, perhaps he feared that other daughters of the family would try the same thing. Perhaps Mishaal was an example. Sometimes I persuaded myself she must be alive, hidden in a desert fortress, while some innocent slave had been killed in her place. But then I heard Moudi saying "they hurt her until she died," and echoes of terror and pain made me sit bolt upright, sweating. It was not my way, however, to make a decision based on fear or emotion, so I tore away from the image of Mishaal in pain, and I tried again and again to understand and to accept not just her death, but the context of her death. Unless I could do that, I was not sure I could remain in Saudi Arabia, and even the thought of Susu's rosebud mouth did not then quite tip the balance.

Morning came at last, an endless distance from the previous dusk, and with it the impression that I was close to a decision of some kind. Still the palace was empty of all but me, Susu, and a skeleton staff. Moudi, whom I was never to see again, rang in the afternoon from Taif and asked me to arrange for Susu and the remaining servants to join her the following day.

"Rosemarie, you'll come out later. Do you mind? There are reports from the hospital, very important, about Susu. I want you to wait for them and then join us. Do you understand?"

Had my decision been made? Had it made me? What was I going to say when I began to speak.

"Wait, Rosemarie. Please wait," Moudi interrupted me. "Be patient with us. Wait. Please, Rosemarie, wait."

Even my fingers were numb as I folded Susu's clothes and put his favorite toys near the top of the case where they would be easily found. Then I sat watching him as he slept, loving him with an intensity that made every cliché about love seem wise: meltingly, with all my heart and soul, eternally, and so very much I would have died for him.

"There are worse things than dying for love, Susu," I whispered to my prince. The next morning was going to be the dawn of my own execution; for on the next morning I would let Susu go without me, let him go, knowing—for I did know at last—that I would never see him again. So much I had accepted, but then the worst thought of all came to me: Susu hadn't yet the talent of memory and I would not live on in his future. Would anyone even tell him that once he'd had a stubborn German nanny called Rosemarie? At that moment, I would have forgotten conscience, kings, and princesses, to stay with Susu; but there was one thing I could not forget: yet again it was Susu himself who made up my mind.

Susu's people and my own were separated by centuries; the achievements of his forefathers were alien to me, and so were the laws, the philosophy, the very emotions, that had evolved to guard those achievements. Susu's people were beyond my reach in time; I could not join them as M. Raoul tried to do by learning their language or imitating their faith; no more could I expect them to join my people. Hadn't I seen the excesses and vulgar extravagances these proud tribesmen gave way to in the cities of the West? Our ways did them no good at all and their great kings had been correct to question the telegraph, the telephone, the radio, as devil's gifts. Zuchia had been correct to watch me with suspicion. Had Moudi been helped to happiness by any of the frivolities she imported from my world? Had Mishaal? Change would come to the Arabian peninsula and the centuries between Susu and me would be devoured by time, but not yet, not too fast.

"Can you—can anyone—promise our brakes will hold?" Dr. Nabia had put that question to me many months before, and I finally knew the answer. As I had kept Susu from the kisses and prodding fingers of his kinspeople because that was not the modern, European, hygienic way to raise a baby, even so, by wise measures and well-meaning innovations I might have diverted him from the full experience of his own destiny, and my love for him, seeking only to do him good, could have brought him into danger.

Nevertheless, leaving Susu was going to be the hardest separation I had ever endured, precisely because I was undertaking it by my own choice. There was no hesitation, the decision had been made during my sleepless nights, but certainty could not stop me pacing the floor, trying unsuccessfully to outrun misery. When the telephone rang in the silent palace, it made me jump. For some time there was silence on the other end of the line broken only by small noises that let me know someone was there; and immediately I was reminded of those earlier anonymous and silent phone calls I had received. I said nothing; I waited.

"Are you a Moslem?" asked a man's voice after a time.

"No. I'm not a Moslem. I'm a Christian."

"Then I wonder what you will do when you die in this country?" my caller said in good, accented English.

"Who is this? What are you talking about?"

"Don't you know what Prince Mohammed plans to do to you?"

After the sorrow and pain I had been feeling, I welcomed anger. "Now you just listen to me," I said, "all my emotions are occupied at the moment. I cannot be frightened right now and you're just

wasting your time. May I remind you that it was your own Prophet
who said each of us was entitled to worship as he pleased!" I
slammed the phone down. The instrument, like all the others in the
palace, was on a cord two hundred meters long. I used to watch
the servants in the morning walking back and forth among the
rooms, unweaving the flex that the princesses had knotted the night
before in their peregrinations with the phones under their arms.
Thanks to the long cord I was able to take the apparatus into the
kitchen, where I locked it in a cupboard; a satisfying gesture that
reminded me for a moment at least of who I was.

At the airport, Susu clung to my neck. Esher had to pry his fingers
away.

"Susu, ya habibi, my baby, I'll be with you soon. I'll see you
soon," I said, lying out of love. I felt his fingers loosen, and then
the weight of his sturdy little body was torn once and for all from
my arms. There was a moment when, like Mishaal, I would have
seized my love and fled away, anywhere, whatever the risks. But I
turned and ran into the airport building, with my hands over my
ears to shut out Susu's cries. Even loving Susu, I envied him at that
parting because he would forget it, while I would carry it with me
always.

When I returned to the palace, I unlocked the cupboard, removed
the telephone, and rang Taif to tell Moudi, Susu was safely on his
way. As I spoke, I wept, and she, on her end of the line, was weep-
ing too.

"Susu loves you," Moudi said. She hesitated. "I am your friend.
I am always your friend. Esher telephoned me last night and told
me about why you locked the purple phone in the cupboard.
Please, Rosemarie, don't think too bad of us. There are those jealous of the love we bear you."

Neither of us was capable of speech for a moment.

"You know I have to go away now, Moudi. I have to go
home . . ."

"Yes, I know. Papa Mohammed, he said so too. I begged and
begged, but he said it was best for you if you go now. There are

some who think bad things . . . you understand? He says you have
been good, loving to Susu. He is grateful. But he says too that
you must go now. Take anything you want, please. Take the stereo,
take the sewing machine, take anything. I will send you enough
money."

I reached for a tissue and tried to dry my eyes, but I couldn't
stop the tears flowing. Moudi was crying openly.

"Please don't cry, Moudi. Don't cry. You know what we say in
the West? We say 'you cannot fire me because' "—I was laughing
and crying at the same time, shredding one Kleenex, reaching for
another—"because I have already quit . . ."

Moudi made a sound between a sob and a giggle. "To the end,"
she said, choking, sniffling, and speaking with difficulty, "to the end
you are our Rosemarie. You are so"—I heard the undignified use
of a Kleenex on her end of the connection—"you are so . . . oh,
you always have to win!"

For the next three days while waiting for Papa Mohammed to arrange my departure, I stayed within the walls of the palace as M.
Raoul and my own judgment advised. The anonymous caller per-
severed in his attempt to scare me although his tone was becoming
progressively more wistful than menacing. I was completely alone.
Once, there was a racket in the hall and I ran out to look over the
balustrade. A small bird had somehow found its way into the palace, and now it could not get out. It was fluttering up and down
the hall, flying against shutters and doors in a desperate attempt to
escape. In retrospect, I cannot help but think of Mishaal. Then, I
simply went and opened a shutter and watched the bird fly to the
open air.

The air conditioning had been turned off so the corridors were
packed with hot, thick air; here and there a trace of sandalwood
made me stop and turn my head as if my name had been called by
a friend. Wandering from room to room, I felt in a place where
tragedy had surprised people in the even course of their lives: it
might have been the fairy-tale palace of a princess after the spell
had been cast to bring her down. Sudani's broom leaned against the
wall as he always left it; next to it, rarely used yet mysteriously bro-

ken, was the Hoover I had been able to make none of the servants understand. In Moudi's sitting room there was the big television where we had watched the arrival of the King, its screen was waiting for a picture and above it the incense burner, still holding ash, was cold. Dust was on the big table where I had sometimes dined with Moudi and Jawahir and Mishaal. The brown leaves of the beech tree in the mural though inappropriate to Mrs. Smythe's moist England suited the heat and loss that stifled me.

In Susu's nursery I remembered him, and I remembered Mishaal as I was going to try always to remember her: not frightened, breaking, pleading for hope. I would remember Mishaal young, laughing with Susu, dancing, a little silly, impetuous, yet much more daring than we had ever known; I would try to remember her so, as Juliet in an Arabian tragedy.

I lifted Susu's pillow and held it in my arms; it smelled of sandalwood, milk, and innocence. Caught between the cushion and its case was a small, hard object which, when I drew it out, I found to be an amulet of gold that Mama Sarah had given Susu and that he always wore. The chain must have parted in his sleep.

Only when the plane had actually lifted off the runway did I believe in my departure, only when Saudi Arabia lay below me, a fierce, inhospitable landscape that from the vantage point of birds, of stars, of airborne travelers, might easily have been judged devoid of human life.

"Take anything," Moudi had said.

In the palm of my hand lay Susu's bit of gold with its Koranic inscription, proof of faith and life in his wild, desert country where I had come as a lost pilgrim and where I had been healed of my wounds. That healing was what I took away with me. What had I left behind? Susu knew. Even after he had forgotten me—Rosemarie—he would still benefit from the enrichment of my gift: I had given him my heart, it was with the little prince in his country and there it would stay forever.

بسم الله الرحمن الرحيم

Kingdom of Saudi Arabia
Moudi Bint Mohammed Bin Abdul Aziz
Al-Saud

المملكة العربية السعودية

موضي بنت محمد بن عبد العزيز آل سعود

أنا موضي بنت محمد بن عبد العزيز انني سأذكر روز مريب بكل خير ﻷنني
انني لم اجد منها سوى كل فعل جيد لن انساها ابداً ولكن
لظروف عائلتي خاصه اضطررت بأن استغني عن خدمتها وانا
انا آسف كل الاسف على هذا .. لقد ربت ولدي سعود بن عبد الحميد
بن سعود بن عبد العزيز لمدة سنه وسبعه شهور وبالرغم من
قربه منها انها احسن تربيه فضلاً وبا أسفي على ولدي بعد
ذهابها ولكن كل ظروف عائلتي وما ضري وفطري .. وأتمنى
لها كل خير وارجو من كل من يتعامل معها ان يثق بها ويحترمها
وارجو منها ان تسامحني لأنني لظروفي العائليه قطعت هذا
وأتمنى لها كل توفيق

IN THE NAME OF GOD THE COMPASSIONATE
THE MERCIFUL
KINGDOM OF SAUDI ARABIA
MOUDI BINT MOHAMMED BIN ABDUL AZIZ AL-SAUD

I, Moudi Bint Mohammed Bin Abdul Aziz, have the highest regard and memory for Rose Mary. Her work was excellent and I shall never forget her: but for private family reasons I had to let her go, and I deeply regret having done so.

She brought up my son, Saud Bin Abdul Majeed Bin Saud Bin Abdul Aziz, for one year and seven months, and she did a magnificent job indeed. I deeply regret that my son will have to do without her, but family matters had to intervene.

I wish her all the best, and I wish that whoever may deal with her will trust and respect her for she is truly a great human being.

I beg her to forgive me. I had to let her go only because of private family reasons. I wish her all the best.

(signed)
Moudi

(official seal)
Princess Moudi Bint Prince Mohammed
Bin Abdul Aziz Bin Abdul Rahman Al-Faisal
Al-Saud

index